Louis Bromfield

THE
GREEN BAY
TREE

Grosset & Dunlap, *Publishers*

NEW YORK

TO

MY MOTHER,

WHO MUST HAVE KNOWN
AT SOME TIME IN HER LIFE
HATTIE TOLLIVER

"Life is hard for our children. It isn't as simple as it was for us. Their grandfathers were pioneers and the same blood runs in their veins, only they haven't a frontier any longer. They stand . . . these children of ours . . . with their backs toward this rough-hewn middle west and their faces set toward Europe and the East and they belong to neither. They are lost somewhere between."

"Every one of us is different from the others. There are no two in the least alike and no one ever really knows any one else. There is always a part which remains secret and hidden, concealed in the deepest part of the soul. No husband ever knows his wife and no wife ever really knows her husband. There is always something just beyond that remains aloof and untouched, mysterious and undiscoverable, because we ourselves do not know just what it is. Sometimes it is shameful. Sometimes it is too fine, too precious, ever to reveal. It is quite beyond revelation even if we chose to reveal it."

THE GREEN BAY TREE

I

IF you can picture a little park, bright for the moment with the flush of early summer flowers and peopled with men and women in the costumes of the late nineties—If you can picture such a park set down in the midst of an inferno of fire, steel and smoke, there is no need to describe Cypress Hill on the afternoon of the garden party for the Governor. It was a large garden, indeed quite worthy of the name "park," withdrawn and shut in by high walls of arbor vitæ clipped at intervals into small niches which sheltered bits of white statuary, some genuine, some of them copies. The Venus of Cydnos was there (in copy to be sure), and of course the Apollo Belvedere, a favorite ornament of formal gardens, as well as the Samothrace Victory dashing forward, it seemed, to soar high above the cloud of smoke from the neighboring blast furnaces.

Here and there the hedge displayed signs of death. There were patches where the green had become withered, and other patches where there was no green at all but simply a tangled wall of hard, dead twigs. Where death had touched the barrier it was possible to see beyond the borders of the garden into regions filled with roaring furnaces, steel sheds, and a tangle of glittering railway tracks cluttered by a confusion of semaphores and signal lights which the magic of night transformed into festoons of glowing jewels—emeralds, rubies, cabuchons, opals, glowing in the thick darkness. But it was not yet dark and no one at the garden party peered through the dying gaps in the hedge because by daylight there lay beyond the borders of the garden only ugliness of the most appalling nature.

The little park sloped away on all sides from a great brick house, conceived in the most bizarre union of Georgian and Gothic styles. It was large and square and faced with white stone, but beyond this the Georgian style played no part. The roof carried a half-dozen high pitched gables; the windows were tall and pointed in the manner of a church rectory, and the chimneys, built of white stone, were carved in the most ornate Gothic fashion. Over all clambered a mass of vines,—wood-bine, virginia creeper and wistaria—which somehow bound the grotesque combination of styles into one harmonious whole, characterized by a surprising look of age, considering the fact that the house stood in the midst of a community which less than a century before had been a complete and trackless wilderness.

The vines, like the hedge, had been more green and exotic at some earlier day. In places there were now no leaves at all, and elsewhere, though the season was early summer, the leaves appeared sickly and wretched, surrounded by dead bare tendrils pressing desperately against the faded bricks.

On the whole, however, the garden was at its best. Along the gravel walks leading to the arbor, irises raised crowns of mauve, royal purple and yellow. Peonies in the process of bursting from tight green buds into great pom-poms of pink and white tumbled across the flagged walk. At the feet of the flying Eros (made of cast iron and painted white), who carried a ring in one hand and thus served for a hitching post, ground pinks and white violets, brought from England by Julia Shane's grandmother, peeped from among the blades of new grass. But the greatest splendor had its being in the wistaria. High up among the branches of the dead oak that towered gauntly above the horse block, its cascades of mauve and white and purple poured like water escaping from a broken dam. From the black iron portico tumbled more torrents of blossoms. They appeared even high up among the tips of the pointed cypresses which gave the house its name. To be sure these were not true cypresses at all, for true cypresses could not have survived the harsh northern winter. In reality they were cedars; but their tall, green-black spires, swaying in melancholy fashion at the least breath of air, resembled cypresses as one brother resembles another. John Shane, perhaps because the name roused memories of some secret world of his own, always called them cypresses and such, to all purposes, they had become. None knew why he called the house Cypress Hill or why he loved cypresses so much that he called cedars by that name when nature cheated him out of his heart's desire. The Town set it down simply as another of his eccentricities. One more craziness no longer disturbed the Town. And John Shane had been dead now for more than ten years, so perhaps the matter was one of no importance whatever.

Under the wistarias on the wrought iron piazza his widow, Julia Shane, leaning on her stick of ebony filigreed in silver, surveyed the bright garden and the guests who moved about among the old trees, the men clad in sober black, the ladies in sprigged muslins or bright colored linens. She was a tall thin woman with a nose slightly hooked, which gave her the fleeting look of an eagle, courageous, bold, even a little pitiless and unrelenting. An air of dignity and distinction compensated the deficiencies of beauty; she was certainly not a beautiful woman and her fine skin was already crisscrossed by a million tiny lines no more substantial than cobweb. Like the women of the generation preceding hers, she made no attempt at preserving the illusion of youth. Although she could not have been long past middle age, she dressed as an old woman. She wore a gown of black and mauve of the most expensive materials, —a sign of mourning which she kept up for a husband dead ten years, a husband whose passing could have given her no cause for regret, whose memory could not possibly bring to her ivory cheeks the faintest flush of pleasure. But the black and mauve gave her great dignity and a certain melancholy beauty. On her thin fingers she wore rings set with amethysts and diamonds and about her neck hung a chain of amethysts caught in a setting of old Spanish silver. The chain reached twice about her thin throat and hung to the knees.

She had been standing on the piazza, a little withdrawn from her guests, all the afternoon because she knew that the mauve of her gown and the dull lavender sparkle of the amethysts blended superbly with the tumbling blossoms of the wistaria,

She had not been, after all, the wife of John Shane for nothing. People said that he had taught his wife to make the best of herself because he could bear to have about him only those things which were in excellent taste. People also said that his wife was lame, not because she had fallen by accident down the long polished stairway, but because she had been thrown from the top to the bottom by her husband in an insane fit of rage.

From her point of vantage, her bright blue eyes swept the garden, identifying the guests—those whom she desired to have there, those to whose presence she was completely indifferent, and those whom political necessity had forced upon her. About most of them centered scornful, bitter, little thoughts that chased themselves round and round her tired brain.

Over against the hedge on the far side of the little pavilion stood a group which, it appeared, interested her more than any other, for she watched it with a faint smile that carried the merest trace of mockery. She discerned the black of the bombazine worn by Hattie Tolliver, her blood niece, and the sprigged muslin of Hattie's daughter, Ellen, who stood by resentfully with an air of the most profound scorn while her mother talked to Judge Weissman. The mother talked voluably, exerting all her power to charm the Judge, a fat perspiring Oriental and the son of an immigrant Viennese Jew. And the efforts of Hattie Tolliver, so solid, so respectable, so downright, were completely transparent, for the woman possessed no trace of subtlety, not the faintest power of dissimulation. She sought to win favor with the Jew because he was the one power in the county politics. He ruled his party with an undisputed sway, and Hattie Tolliver's husband was a candidate for office. Perhaps from the pinnacle of her worldliness Julia Shane detected a quality naive and almost comic in the vulgar intrigue progressing so blatantly on the opposite side of the pavilion.

There was also a quality indescribably comic in the fierce attitude of the daughter, in her aloofness from the politician and the intensity of her glowering expression. She was an obnoxious child of sixteen, wilful, spoiled, savage, but beyond the possibility of denial, she played the piano superbly, in a truly extraordinary fashion.

Presently Julia Shane, behind the shelter of the wistaria, sniffed suddenly as though the wind had carried to her among the delicate odors of the flowers the offensive smell of the fat perspiring Jew. He was there by political necessity, because the Governor desired his presence. Clearly she looked upon him as an intruder who defiled the little park.

Farther off at the side of the empty kennels, all buried beneath a tangle of vines, another group had gathered about a table where pink ices and pink and white cakes were being served. About the great silver punch bowl hung a dozen men, drinking, drinking, drinking, as though the little park were a corner saloon and the little table the accustomed free lunch. For a moment Julia Shane's gaze fastened upon the men and her thin nostrils quivered. Her lips formed themselves to utter a word which she spoke quite loudly so that three women, perfect strangers to her who stood just beneath the piazza, overheard it and spread the story that Julia Shane had taken to talking to herself. "Pigs!" she said.

II

IN other parts of the garden the bright parasols of the gossiping women raised themselves in little clumps like mushrooms appearing unexpectedly through the green of a wide lawn. The Governor was nowhere to be seen, nor Lily nor Irene, Julia Shane's two daughters.

The guests began to depart. A victoria with a driver on the box came round the corner of the old house. A fat dowager, dressed in purple and wearing a gold chain, bowed, and the diminutive young man beside her, in a very tight coat and a derby hat, smiled politely—very politely—Mrs. Julis Harrison and her son Willie, of the great family which owned the Mills.

Julia Shane bowed slightly and leaned more heavily upon her ebony stick. A second vehicle appeared, this time a high buggy which bore the county auditor and his wife . . . common people who never before had entered the wrought iron gates of Cypress Hill. The fat and blowsy wife bowed in an exaggerated fashion, never stopping the while to fan her red face vigorously until she discovered that her elaborate bows were expended upon the back of Julia Shane, who had become suddenly absorbed in the rings that glittered on her bony fingers. The smile froze on the fat lady's face and her heavy lips pursed themselves to utter with a savage intensity of feeling the word "Snob!" Indeed, her indignation so mounted under the protests of her tipsy husband, that a moment later she altered the epithet to another more vulgar and more powerful phrase. "Old Slut!" she said aloud. The two carriages made their way down the long avenue between the rows of dying Norway spruce to the gate where Hennery, the black servant, stood on guard.

Outside, with faces pressed against the bars, stood a score of aliens from the hovels of the mill workers in the neighboring Flats. The little group included a dozen women wearing shawls and a multitude of petticoats, three or four children and as many half-grown boys still a year or two too young to be of any use to the Harrison Mills. They pushed and pressed against the handsome gates, striving for a glimpse at the spectacle of the bright garden animated by the figures of the men and women who ruled the Town, the Flats, the very lives and destinies of the little throng of aliens. A baby squalled in the heat and one of the boys, a tall powerful fellow with a shock of yellow hair, spat through the bars.

At the approach of the carriage the black Hennery sprang up and with the gesture of one opening the gates of Buckingham Palace, shouted to the crowd outside, "Look out, you all! There's carriages a-coming!"

Then with a great clanging and shooting of bolts he swung open the gates and Mrs. Julis Harrison and her son William swept through. The hoofs of the dancing horses beat a tattoo on the cobblestones. The mother saw nothing, but the narrow eyes of her son appraised the group of boys and even the babies as potential workers in the Mills. These Dago children grew rapidly, but not fast enough to keep pace with the needs of the growing furnaces; and so many of them died before they reached manhood.

As the carriage swung into narrow Halsted Street, Mrs. Harrison, leaning forward so that the gold chain swayed like a pendulum from her mountainous bosom, surveyed the wretched houses, the yards bereft of all green, and the shabby railway station that stood a hundred yards from the very gates of Shane's Castle.

"You'd think Julia Shane would move out of this filthy district," she said. "Sentiment is all right, but there's such a thing as running it into the ground. The smoke and soot is even killing the flowers. They're not half so fine as last year."

Her son William shrugged his narrow, sloping shoulders.

"The ground is worth its weight in gold," he said. "Three railroads—the only site left. She could get her own price."

In the corner saloon a mechanical piano set up a tinny uproar and shattered fragments of The Blue Danube drifted out upon the hot air through the swinging doors into the street, throttling for the moment any further conversation.

The county auditor and his wife drove uncertainly through the gates, for the county auditor had drunk too much and failed to understand that horses driven with crossed reins do not respond according to any preconceived plan. His wife, her face red as a ripe tomato, took them from him and swore.

"She needn't think she's so damned swell," she said. "What's she got to make her so proud? I should think she'd blush at what has happened in that rotten old house. Why, she's got nothing but Hunkies and Dagos for neighbors!"

She cut the horses across the back, dashed forward, and passed the victoria of Mrs. Harrison and her son William at a triumphant gallop.

With a loud, officious bang, Hennery closed the wrought iron gates and the wise, old faces of the alien women pressed once more against the bars. One of the throng—the big boy with the shock of yellow hair, a Ukrainian named Stepan Krylenko—shouted something in Russian as the gates banged together. It was a tongue foreign to Hennery but from the look in the fierce blue eye of the young fellow, the negro understood that what he said was not friendly. The women admonished the boy and fell to whispering in awe among themselves, but the offender in no way modified his manner. When Judge Weissman, fat and perspiring and covered with jewelry, whirled past him in a phaeton a moment later, the boy shouted in Russian, "Jew! Dirty Jew!" Judge Weissman regarded the boy with his pop eyes, wiped his mahogany face and muttered to his companion, Lawyer Briggs, "These foreigners are getting too free in their manners. . . . The Harrisons will have trouble at the Mills one of these days. . . . There ought to be a law against letting them into the country."

The Judge was angry, although his anger was stirred not by the shout of Stepan Krylenko but by the fact that Julia Shane had become suddenly blind as his phaeton swept round the corner of the old house. The shout was something upon which to fasten his anger.

III

FROM her point of vantage on the wistaria clad piazza, the old woman watched the little drama at the entrance to the Park, and when the gates had been flung closed once more, she moved back into the cool shadows, still wondering where Lily and Irene and the Governor could have hidden themselves. She settled herself on an iron bench, praying that no one would pass to disturb her, and at the same moment the sound of sobbing reached her ears. It came from the inside of the house, from the library just beyond the tall window. There, in a corner beyond the great silver mounted globe, Irene had flung herself down and was weeping. The half-suppressed sobs shook the girl's frail body. Her muslin dress with the blue sash was crushed and damp. The mother bent over her and drew the girl into a sitting posture against the brocade of the rosewood sofa.

"Come, Irene," said the old woman. "It is no time for tears. There is time enough when this infernal crowd is gone. What is it? What has come over you since yesterday?"

The girl's sobs grew more faint but she did not answer nor raise her head. She was frail and blond with wide blue eyes set far apart. Her thick hair was done low at the back of her neck. She had a small pretty mouth and a rather prominent nose. Her mother must have resembled her before she hardened into a cynical old woman, before the prominent nose became an eagle's beak and the small pretty mouth a thin-lipped sardonic one. The mother, puzzled and silent, sat stiffly beside the sobbing girl, fingering all the while the chain of amethysts set in Spanish silver.

"Are you tired?" she asked presently.

"No."

"Then what is it, Irene? There must be some reason. Girls don't behave like this for nothing. What have you done that has made you miserable?"

9

"Nothing," sobbed the girl. "Nothing!"

The mother sat up a little straighter and began to trace with her ebony stick the outlines of the roses on the Aubusson carpet. At length she spoke again in a clear, hard voice.

"Then you must pull yourself together and come out. I want you to find Lily and the Governor.—Every one is leaving and they should be here. There's no use in giving a party for him if he is going to snub the politicians. . . . Here—sit up! . . . Turn round while I fasten your hair."

With perfect deliberation the mother arranged the girl's hair, smoothed the crumpled muslin of her dress, patted straight the blue ribbon sash, dried her eyes, and bade her stand away to be surveyed.

"Now," she said in the same crisp voice, "You look all right . . . I can't have you behaving like this. . . . You should be out in the garden. Before I die, Irene, I want to see you married. You never will be if you hide yourself where no one can see you. . . . I don't worry over Lily—she can take care of herself. Go and find them and bring them back. . . . Tell them I said to return at once."

The girl, without a word, went out of the room into the big dark hallway and thence into the garden. Her mother's voice was one made to command. It was seldom that any one refused to carry out her orders. When Irene reached the terrace the guests were making their way back toward the house in little groups of two or three, ladies in summer dresses very tight at the waists, shielding their complexions from the June sun with small, bright-colored parasols . . . Mrs. Mills, the rector's wife, Miss Bird, the Town librarian, Mrs. Smyth, wife of the Methodist clergyman, Mrs. Miliken, wife of the sheriff, Miss Abercrombie, Mrs. . . . And behind them, the husbands, and the stray politicians who treated the little arbor over the punch bowl as though it were a corner saloon. The punch was gone now and the last of the pink ices melted. From other parts of the garden more guests made their way toward the house. Irene passed them, bowing and forcing herself to smile though the effort brought her a kind of physical pain. Among the rhododendrons she came upon a little terra cotta Virgin and Child brought by father from Sienna and, remembering her convent training, she paused for a moment and breathed a prayer.

Lily and the Governor were not among the rhododendrons. She ran on to the little pavilion beyond the iris walk. It was empty. The arbor, green with the new leaves of the Concord grapes, was likewise untenanted save by the shadows of the somber, tall cypresses. The girl ran on and on from one spot of shelter to another, distracted and terrified, her muslin dress soiled and torn by the twigs. The little park grew empty and the shadows cast by the setting sun sprawled across the patches of open grass. Two hiding places remained, but these Irene avoided. One was the clump of bushes far down by the iron gates. She dared not go there because the little crowd of aliens peering through the bars terrified her. Earlier in the afternoon she had wandered there to be alone and a big tow headed boy shouted at her in broken English, "There are bones . . . people's bones hidden in your cellar!"

No, she dared not again risk the torment of his shouting.

The other hiding place was the old well behind the stables, a well abandoned now and almost lost under a tangle of clematis. There was a sheltered seat by its side. The girl ran as far as the stables and then, summoning her strength to lie to her mother if the necessity arose, turned back without looking and hastened across the garden toward the piazza. She had not the courage to approach the well because she knew that it was there she would find her sister Lily and the Governor.

When Irene entered the house, she found her mother in the drawing-room seated alone in the twilight. The guests had all departed and the old woman was smoking, a pleasure she had denied herself until the last of the visitors were gone. No one in the Town had ever seen her smoke. It was well enough to smoke at Biarritz or Monte Carlo; smoking in the Town was another matter. Julia Shane smoked quietly and with a certain elegance of manner which removed from the act all trace of vulgarity. She sat in a corner of the big room near one of the tall windows which stood open a little way admitting ghostly fragments of scent, now of iris, now of wistaria, now of lilac. Sometimes there penetrated for a second the acrid tang of soot and gas from the distant furnaces. The diamonds

and amethysts on her thin fingers glittered in the fading light.
She was angry and the unmistakable signs of her anger were
present—the flash in her bright blue eye, the slight trembling
of the veined hands. The ebony stick rested by her side. As
Irene entered she did not move or shift for a second the expression of her face.

"And where are they?—Have you found them?"

The girl's lips grew pale, and when she replied, she trembled
with the awful consciousness of lying to her mother.

"I cannot find them. I have looked everywhere."

The mother frowned. "Bring me an ash tray, Irene, and
do not lie to me. They are in the garden." She crushed out
the ember of her cigarette. "That man is a fool. He has
offended a dozen important men after I took the trouble to
invite them here. God knows, I didn't want them!"

While she was speaking, the sound of footsteps arose in the
open gallery that ran along the far side of the drawing-room,
and two figures, silhouetted against the smoky, setting sun, appeared at the windows moving toward the doorway. They
were the missing Lily and the Governor. He followed her at
a little distance as though they had been quarreling and she
had forbidden him to address her. At the sight of them, Irene
moved toward the door, but her mother checked her escape.

"Irene! Where are you going now? What are you afraid
of? If this behavior does not stop, I shall forbid you to go to
mass. You are already too pious for any good on this earth."

The frightened girl returned silently and sat down with her
usual air of submission on the sofa that stood in the shadows
by a mantelpiece which supported a painting of Venice, flam-
bant and glowing, executed by the hand of Turner. At
the sound of Lily's voice, she shrank back among the cushions
as if to hide herself. There was in the voice nothing to terrify
her. On the contrary it was a voice, low and warm, indolent
and ingratiating—a voice full of charm, one which inspired
affection.

Lily was taller than her sister and two years older; yet
there was an enormous difference between them which had
to do less with age than with manner. There was about
Irene something childish and undeveloped. Lily was a woman,

a young woman, to be sure, tall and lovely. Her hair was the color of honey. It held bright copper lights; and she wore it, in the fashion of Irene, low on a lovely neck that carried a warning of wilfulness. Her skin was the transparent sort which artists love for its green lights, and her eyes were of a shade of violet which in some lights appeared a clear blue. Her arms were laden with irises, azure and pale yellow, which she had plucked on her way from the old well. She too wore a frock of muslin with a girdle of radiant blue. As she entered, she laid the flowers gently among the crystal and silver bibelots of a rosewood table and rang for Sarah, the mulatto wife of Hennery, guardian of the wrought iron gates.

The Governor followed her, a tall man of perhaps forty, strongly built with a fine chest and broad shoulders. His hair was black and vigorous and he wore it cropped close to a well-shaped head. He had the drooping mustaches of the period. His was a figure which commands the attention of mobs. His manner, when he was not too pompous or condescending, was charming. People said there was no reason why he should not one day be president. He was shrewd in the way of politicians, too shrewd perhaps ever to be anything but one who made other men presidents.

He was angry now with a primitive, boiling anger which threatened to burst the bonds of his restraint. His breath came huskily. It was the anger of a man accustomed to dominate, who has encountered suddenly some one who cares not a fig for his powers.

"Madame," he said, "your daughter has refused to marry me."

The mother took up her ebony stick and placed it squarely before her, at the same time leaning forward upon it. For a moment, she smiled, almost secretly, with a sort of veiled amusement at his pompous speech. She did not speak until the mulatto woman, slipping in noiselessly, had taken the flowers and disappeared again into the vast hall. Then she addressed Lily who stood leaning against the mantelpiece, her lovely body slightly balanced, her manner as calm and as placid as if nothing had gone wrong.

"Is this true, Lily?"

The girl nodded and smiled, so slightly that the play of expression could scarcely have been called a smile. It was as though she kept the smile among her other secrets, not to be shared by people who knew nothing of its meaning.

"It is serious, Madame, I promise you," the Governor interrupted. "I love your daughter. She has told me that she loves me." He had grown a little pompous now, as though he were addressing an assembly of constituents. "What else is there?" He turned to Lily suddenly, "It is true, isn't it?"

The girl nodded. "Yes, I have told you that. . . . But I will not marry you. . . . I am not refusing because I want to be unkind. . . . I can't help it. Believe me, I cannot."

The mother began tracing the design on the carpet, round and round the petals of the faded roses. When she spoke she did not raise her head. She kept on tracing . . . tracing. . . .

"There must be some reason, Lily. . . . It is a match not to be cast aside lightly. . . . It would make me very happy."

She was interrupted by the sound of a closing door. Irene had vanished into the gallery on the far side of the drawing-room. The three of them saw her running past the window back into the garden as though she were pursued. The mother fell once more to tracing the outlines on the carpet. In the growing darkness the scent of the lilac grew more and more strong.

The Governor, who had been standing by the window, turned sharply. "I would like to speak to you, Mrs. Shane . . alone, if possible. There are some things which I must tell . . . things which are unpleasant but of tremendous importance, both to Lily and to me." He coughed and the blood mounted to his coarse handsome face. "As an honorable man I must confess them."

At this last statement, a faint sound of mirth came from Lily. She bowed her head suddenly and looked away.

"It would be better if Lily left us," he added savagely.

The girl smiled and smoothed her red hair. "You may speak to mother if you like. It will do you no good. It will only make matters worse. After all, it concerns no one but ourselves."

He shouted at her suddenly. "Please, will you go. Haven't

ou done enough? There is no need to behave like a devil!"

The girl made no reply. She went out quietly, closing the door behind her, and made her way across the terrace to the rhododendrons where she knew she would find Irene. It was almost dark now and the glow from the furnaces below the hill had begun to turn the whole sky to a murky, glowing red. A locomotive whistled shrilly above the steady pounding of the roller mills. Through a gap in the dying hedge, the signal lights began to show, in festoons of jewels. The wind had turned and the soot and smoke were being swept toward Cypress Hill. It meant the end of the flowers. In the rare times when the wind blew from the south the blossoms were scorched and ruined by the gases.

Among the fireflies Lily hastened along the path to the rhododendrons. There, before the terra-cotta Virgin and Child, she found her sister praying earnestly. Lily knelt down and clasped the younger girl in her arms, speaking affectionately to her and pressing her warm cheek against Irene's pale one.

IV

THAT night Irene and Lily had dinner in their ow
rooms. In the paneled dining-room, a gloomy pla
decorated with hunting prints and lighted by ta
candles in silver holders, Julia Shane and the Gove
nor dined alone, served by the mulatto woman who shuffled
and out noiselessly, and was at last dismissed and told not
enter the room again until she was summoned. There fo
lowed a long talk between the Governor and the old lad
during which the handsome Governor pulled his mustach
furiously and sometimes raised his voice until the room sho
and Julia Shane was forced to bid him be more cautious. S
permitted him to do most of the talking, interrupting h
rarely and then only to interject some question or remark
uncanny shrewdness.

At length when he had pushed back his chair and taken
pacing the room, the mother waited silently for a long tin
her gaze fixed upon the tiny goblet of chartreuse which glow
pale gold and green in the light from the dying candl
Presently she leaned back in her chair and addressed him.

"It is your career, then, which is your first consideration
she began. "It is that which you place above everything e
. . . above everything?"

For a moment the tall Governor halted, standing motionl
across the table from her. He made no denial. His fa
grew more flushed.

"I have told you that I love Lily."

The old woman smiled at this evasion and the sharp lc
gleamed for a second in her bright blue eyes. Her thin l
contracted into the faintest of smiles, a mere shadow, mock
and cynical. In the face of his anger and excitement,
was calm, cold, with the massive dignity of an iceberg.

"It is I," she said, "who should be offended. You have

16

use for anger." She turned the rings on her fingers round
ad round. The diamonds and amethysts caught the light,
attering it and sending it forth again in a thousand frag-
ents. "Besides," she added softly, "Love can be so many
ings. . . . Believe me, I know."

Slowly she pushed back her chair and drew herself up, sup-
orted by the ebony stick. "There is nothing to do now but
ear what Lily has to say. . . . It is, after all, her affair."

The library was a square room, high-ceilinged and dark,
alled by books and dominated by a full-length portrait of
ohn Shane, builder of Cypress Hill and the first gentleman
the Western Reserve. The picture had been painted in the
ties soon after he came to the Town and a decade before he
arried Julia MacDougal. In the dark portrait he stood
ainst a table with a white Irish setter at his feet. He was a
ll man, slim and wiry, and wore dove gray trousers and a
ng black coat reaching to the knees. Set rakishly and with
air of defiance on the small well-shaped head was a dove
ay top hat. His neckerchief was bright scarlet but the
rnishings and dust of years had modified its color to a dull
aroon. One hand hung by his side and the other rested on
e table, slender, nervous and blue-veined, the hand of an
istocrat. But it was the face that impressed you above all
se. It was the face of one possessed, a countenance that
mehow was both handsome and ugly, shifting as you regarded
from one phase to the other as though the picture itself
ysteriously altered its character before your eyes. It was a
an face, swarthy and flushed with too much drinking, the
s red and sensual yet somehow firm and cruel. The eyes,
hich followed you about the room, were large and deeply
t and of a strange deep blue like cobalt glass with light
ining through it. It was the portrait of a gentleman,
a duellist, of a sensitive man, of a creature haunted by a
mper verging upon insanity. One moment it was a hor-
ble picture; the next it held great charm. Above all else,
was baffling.

It was in this room that Julia Shane and the Governor
aited in silence for Lily, who came down a little while
ter in response to the message from the mulatto woman.

The sound of her footsteps on the long stairs reached them
before she arrived; it came lightly, almost tripping, until
she appeared all at once at the open door, clad in a black cloak
which she had thrown over her pegnoir.   Her red hair was
piled carelessly atop her head and at the moment her eyes were
blue and not violet.   She carried herself lightly and with
a certain defiance, singularly like the dare-devil defiance of
the tall man in the darkening portrait.   For a moment, she
paused in the doorway regarding her mother who sat beneath
the picture, and the Governor who stood with his hands
clasped behind him, his great chest rising and falling as he
watched her.   Pulling the cloak higher about her white throat
she stepped into the room, closing the door softly behind her.

"Sit down," said the mother, in a strained colorless voice.
"I know everything that has happened. . . . We must talk
it over and settle it to-night one way or another, for good and
all."

The girl sat down obediently and the Governor came over
and stood before her.

"Lily," he said and then halted as though uncertain now
to continue.   "Lily . . . I don't believe you realize what has
happened.   I don't believe you understand."

The girl smiled faintly.   "Oh, yes . . . I know . . . I
am not a child, you know . . . certainly not *now.*"   All the
while she kept her eyes cast down thoughtfully.

The mother leaning forward, interrupted.   "I hadn't
thought it would end in this fashion," she said.   "I had hoped
to have him for a son-in-law.   You know, Lily, you must con-
sider him too.   Don't you love him?"

The girl turned quickly.   "I love him. . . . Yes, . . . I
love him and I've thought of him. . . . You needn't fear
scandal.   There is no need for one.   No one would ever
have known if he hadn't told you.   It was between us alone.
The Governor pulled his mustaches furiously and attempted to
speak but the girl halted him.   "I know . . . I know," she
said.   "You're afraid I might tell some one. . . . You're
afraid there might be a child. . . . Even if there was it would
make no difference."

"But why . . . why?" began her mother.

"I can't tell why . . . I don't know myself. I only know
at I don't want to marry him, that I want to be as I
1. . . ." For a second the shadow of passion entered her
ice. "Why can't I be? Why won't you let me? I have
oney of my own. I can do as I please. It is my affair."

V

FOR a little while the room grew silent save for t‍ distant pounding of the Mills, regular and reverberar‍ monotonous and unceasing. The wind from the Sou‍ bore a smell of soot which smothered the scent of w‍taria and iris. All at once a cry rang out and the Governo‍ very red and handsome in his tight coat, fell on his knees b‍fore her, his arms about her waist. The girl remained sittil‍ quietly, her face quite white now against the black of her cloa‍

"Please . . . please, Lily," the man cried. "I will give ‍everything . . . I will do as you like. I will be your slave‍ He became incoherent and muddled, repeating over and ov‍ again the arguments he had used in the afternoon by the o‍ well. For a long time he talked, while the girl sat as st‍ as an image carved from marble, regarding him curiously‍ though the whole scene were a nightmare and not reality‍ all. At last he stopped talking, kissed her hand and stoc‍ up once more. The old woman seated under the portr‍ said nothing. She regarded the pair silently with wise, na‍ rowed eyes.

It was Lily who spoke. "It is no use. . . . How can ‍ explain to you? I would not be a good wife. I know . ‍ you see, I know because I know myself. I love you, I su‍pose, but not better than myself. It is my affair." A nc‍ almost of stubbornness entered her voice. "Two days ago‍ might have married you. I cannot now, because I know.‍ wanted to know, you see." She looked up suddenly with ‍ strange smile. "Would you have preferred me to take a lov‍ from the streets?"

For the first time the mother stirred in her chair. "Li‍ . . . Lily . . . How can you say such a thing?"

The girl rose and stood waiting in a respectful attitud‍ "There is nothing more to be said. . . . May I go?" The‍ turning to the Governor. "Do you want to kiss me. . . . ‍ think it would please me."

For a second there was a terrific struggle between the de-
re of the man and his dignity. It was clear then beyond all
oubt that he loved her passionately. He trembled. His face
rew scarlet. At last, with a terrible effort he turned sud-
enly from her. He did not even say farewell.

"You see," said the mother, "I can do nothing. There is
o much of her father in her." A shade of bitterness crept
ito her voice, a quality of hardness aroused by a man who no
inger existed save in the gray portrait behind her. "If it had
en Irene," she continued and then, checking herself, "but
hat am I thinking of? It could never have been Irene."

Quietly Lily opened the door and stole away, the black
oak trailing behind her across the polished floor, the sound
: her footsteps dying slowly away as she ascended the stairs.

At midnight Hennery brought the carriage round from the
ables, the Governor climbed in, and from the shelter of the
azza Julia Shane, leaning on her stick, watched him drive
riously away down the long drive through the iron gates
d into the street bordered by the miserable shacks and board-
g houses occupied by foreigners. At the corner the jangling
usic of the mechanical piano drifted through the swinging
ors of the saloon where a mob of steel puddlers, in from
e night shift, drank away the memories of the hot furnaces.
Thus the long association of the Governor with the old
use at Cypress Hill came abruptly to an end.

He left behind him three women. Of these Lily was already
leep in the great Italian bed. In an adjoining room her
other lay awake staring into the darkness, planning how to
ep the knowledge of the affair from Irene. It was impos-
le to predict the reaction which it might have upon the
l. It might drive her, delicate and neurotic, into any one
a score of hysterical paths. The room was gray with the
ht of dawn before Julia Shane at last fell asleep.

As for the third—Irene—she too lay awake praying to the
essed Virgin for strength to keep her terrible secret. She
sed her eyes; she buried her face in her pillow; but none
these things could destroy the picture of the Governor
althily opening the door of Lily's room.

VI

THERE had been a time, within the memory of Lily
though not of Irene who was but two years old
when the first transcontinental railroad stretched it
ribbons of steel through the northern edge of th
Town, when the country surrounding Cypress Hill was ope
marsh land, a great sea of waving green, of cat tails and mars
grasses with a feathery line of willows where a muddy, sluggis
brook called the Black Fork threaded a meandering path. I
those days Cypress Hill had been isolated from the Town,
country place accessible only by the road which John Shan
constructed across the marshes from the Town to the grea
mound of glacial moraine where he set up his fantastic hous
As a young man, he came there out of nowhere in the fifti
when the Town was little more than a straggling double ro
of white wood and brick houses lining a single street. He wa
rich as riches went in those days, and he purchased a grea
expanse of land extending along one side of the single stre
down the hill to the opposite side of the marsh. His purcha
included the site of the Cypress Hill house, which raised itse
under his direction before the astonished eyes of the coun
people.

Brickmakers came west over the mountains to mo
bricks for him in the kilns of the claybanks along the meande
ing Black Fork. Town carpenters returned at night wi
glowing tales of the wonders of the new house. Strange tre
and shrubs were brought from the east and a garden w
planted to surround the structure and shield it from the h
sun of the rolling, fertile, middle west. Gates of wroug
iron were set up and stables were added, and at last Jo
Shane returned from a trip across the mountains to occupy l
house. It gained the name of Shane's Castle and, althou
he called it Cypress Hill, the people of the Town preferr

their own name and it was known as Shane's Castle to the very end.

Who John Shane was or whence he came remained a mystery. Some said he was Irish, which might well have been. Others were certain that he was English because he spoke with the clipped accent of an Englishman. There were even some who held that so swarthy a man could only have come from Spain or Italy; and some were convinced that his love of travel was due to an obscure strain of gipsy blood. As to the light which Shane himself cast upon the subject, no one ever penetrated beyond a vague admission that he had lived in London and found the life there too tame.

He set himself up in the house at Cypress Hill to lead the life of a gentleman, a worldly cynical gentleman, perhaps the only gentleman in the archaic sense of the word in all the Western Reserve. In a frontier community where every one toiled, he alone made, beyond the control of his farms, no pretense at working. He had his horses and his dogs, and because there were no hounds to follow and no hunters to ride with him, he set aside on the land bordering the main street of the Town a great field where he rode every day including the Sabbath, and took the most perilous jumps to the amazement of the farmers and townspeople who gathered about the paddock to watch his eccentric behavior.

Among these were a Scotch settler and his son-in-law, Jacob Barr, who owned jointly a great stretch of land to the west of Shane's farm. They kept horses to ride though they were in no sense sporting men. They were honest stock, dignified and hard-working, prosperous and respected throughout the country as men who had wrested from the wilderness a prosperous living. MacDougal was the first abolitionist in the county. He it was who established the first station of the underground railway and organized the plans for helping slaves to escape across the border into Canada. These two sometimes brought their horses into the paddock at Shane's farm and there, under his guidance, taught them to jump.

The abolitionist activities culminated in the Civil War, and the three men joined the colors, Shane as a lieutenant because somewhere in his mysterious background there was a thorough experience in military affairs. His two friends joined the ranks, rising at length to commands. MacDougal lost his life in the campaign of the Wilderness. Jacob Barr returned stricken by fever, and Shane himself received a bullet in the thigh.

Returning as a colonel from the war he found that in place of the dead MacDougal he had as a riding companion the farmer's youngest daughter, a girl of nineteen. She had taken to the saddle with enthusiasm and was a horsewoman after his own heart. She knew no such thing as fear; she joined him recklessly in the most perilous feats and sat his most unruly horses with the ease and grace of an Amazon. She was not a pretty girl. The word "handsome" would have described her more accurately. She was strong, lithe and vigorous, and her features, though large like the honest MacDougal's, were clearly chiseled and beautiful in a large way.

The strange pair rode together in the paddock more and more frequently until, at last, the astonished county learned that John Shane, the greatest gentleman in the state, had taken MacDougal's youngest daughter east over the mountains and quietly made her mistress of Shane's Castle. It also learned that he had taken his bride to Europe, and that his housekeeper, a pretty middle-aged Irish woman who never mingled with the townspeople, had been sent away, thus ending rumors of sin which had long scandalized the county. It appeared, some citizens hinted, that Julia MacDougal had been substituted for the Irish woman.

For two years the couple remained abroad, but during that time they were separated, for Shane, conscious of his bride's rustic simplicity, sent her to a boarding school for English girls kept by a Bonapartist spinster named Violette de Vaux at St. Cloud on the outskirts of Paris. During those two years he did not visit her, choosing instead to absent himself upon some secret business in the south of Europe; and when he returned, his bride found it difficult to recognize in the man with a thick, blue black beard, the husband she had married two years earlier. The adornment gave him an appearance even more alien and sinister.

The two years were for the girl wretched ones, but in some incomprehensible fashion they hardened her and fitted her to begin the career her mysterious husband had planned. When they returned to Cypress Hill, Shane shaved off his beard once more and entered politics. From then on, great people came to stay at Cypress Hill—judges, politicians, lawyers, once even a president. As for Shane he sought no office for himself. It seemed that he preferred in politics to be the power behind the throne, the kingmaker, the man who advised and planned campaigns; he preferred the intrigues without the responsibilities. And so he became a figure in the state, a strange, bizarre, dashing figure which caught somehow the popular imagination. His face became known everywhere, as well as the stories about his private life, of strange brawls in the growing cities of the middle-west, of affairs with women, of scandals of every sort save those which concerned his personal honesty. Here he was immune. No one doubted his honesty. And the scandals did him little harm save in a small group of his own townspeople who regarded him as the apotheosis of sin, as a sort of Lucifer dwelling in a great brick house in the center of the Black Fork marshes.

In the great house, his wife, whose life it was whispered was far from happy, bore him two daughters, a circumstance which might have disappointed most men. It pleased the perverse John Shane who remarked that he was glad there was no son to carry on "his accursed name."

As he grew older the unpopularity increased until among the poorer residents of the Town strange stories found their way into circulation, tales of orgies and wickedness in the great brick house. The stories at length grew by repetition until they included the unfortunate wife. But Shane went his proud way driving his handsome horses through the Town, riding like mad in the paddock. The Town grew and spread along the outskirts of his farm, threatening to surround it, but Shane would not sell. He scorned the arguments for progress and prosperity and held on to his land. At last there came a second railroad and then a third which crossed the continent, passing on their way along the banks of the sluggish Black Fork through the waving green swamp. Shane found himself powerless because the state condemned the land and it was his own party which promoted the railroad. He gave way and his land doubled and tripled in value. Factories began to appear and the marsh land became precious because in its midst three railroads crossed in a triangle which surrounded the house at Cypress Hill. Shane became older and more perverse. The tales increased, tales of screams heard in the night and of brutalities committed upon his wife; more scandals about a young servant girl leaked out somehow and were seized by the population of the Town. But throughout the state Shane's name still commanded respect. When the great came to the Town they stopped at Shane's Castle where the drawing-room was thrown open and receptions were held with the rag, tag and bobtail permitted to satisfy their curiosity. They found nothing but a handsome house, strange and beautifully furnished in a style unknown in the Town. John Shane and his wife, her face grown hard now as the jewels on her fingers, stood by this judge or that governor to receive, calm and dignified, distinguished by a worldliness foreign to the rugged, growing community.

And at last the master of Shane's Castle was stricken dead by apoplexy one winter night at the top of the long polished stairway; and the wiry, thin old body rolled all the way to the bottom. Irene, who was a neurotic, timid girl, saw him fall and ran screaming from the house. Lily was in Europe at St. Cloud on the outskirts of Paris, a *pensionnaire* in the boarding school of Mademoiselle Violette de Vaux. The wife quietly raised the body, laid it on a sofa under the portrait in the library and summoned a doctor who made certain that the terrible old man at last was dead.

When the news of his death spread through the Town, Italian workmen passing along the railroad at the foot of Cypress Hill crossed themselves and looked away as though the devil himself lay in state inside the wrought iron gates. Governors, judges and politicians attended the funeral and the widow appeared in deep mourning which she wore for three years. She played the rôle of a wife bereft of a devoted husband. The world whispered tales of her unhappiness, but the world *knew* nothing. When great people came to the

Town, they were still entertained at Cypress Hill. The legend of John Shane attained the most fantastic proportions; it became a part of the Town's tradition. The words which Stepan Krylenko, the tow-headed Ukrainian, shouted through the wrought iron gates at the terrified Irene were simply an echo of certain grotesque stories.

After the death of her husband, Julia Shane sold off piecemeal at prodigious prices the land in the marshes traversed by the railroads. Factory after factory was erected. Some built farming implements, some manufactured wooden ware, but it was steel which occupied most of the district. Rolling mills came in and blast furnaces raised their bleak towers until Shane's Castle was no longer an island surrounded by marshes but by great furnaces, steel sheds and a glistening maze of railway tracks. New families grew wealthy and came into prominence, the Harrisons among them. Some of the Shane farm land was sold, but out of it the widow kept a wide strip bordering Main Street where she erected buildings which brought her fat rents. The money that remained she invested shrewdly so that it increased at a startling rate. She became a rich woman and the legend of Shane's Castle grew, spurred on by envy.

To the foreigners who lived in the hovels at the gate of Cypress Hill, the house and the park became the symbols of an oppressing wealth, of a crude relentless power no less savage than the old world which they had deserted for this new one. It was true that Julia Shane had nothing to do with the mills and furnaces; her money came from the land she owned. The mills were owned by the Harrisons and Judge Weissman; but Shane's Castle became an easy symbol upon which to fix a hatred. Its fading grandeur arose in the very midst of the hot and overcrowded kennels of the workers.

VII

SIX weeks after the night the Governor drove furiously away from the house at Cypress Hill, Julia Shane gave her last dinner before sending Lily away. It was small, including only Mrs. Julis Harrison, her son William, and Miss Abercrombie, but it served her purpose clearly as a piece of strategy to deceive the Town. Irene was absent, having gone back to the convent in the east where she had been to school as a little girl. A great doctor advised the visit, a doctor who held revolutionary ideas gained in Vienna. It was, he said, the one means of bringing the girl round, since he could drag from her no sane reason for her melancholy and neurasthenic behavior. Her mother could discover nothing; indeed it appeared that the girl had a strange fear of her which struck her dumb. So Julia Shane overcame her distaste for the Roman Catholic church and permitted the girl to return, thanking Heaven that she had kept from her the truth. This, she believed, would have caused Irene to lose her mind.

In the drawing-room after dinner a discreet battle raged with Julia Shane on one side and Mrs. Julis Harrison and Miss Abercrombie on the other. Lily and William Harrison withdrew to the library. In a curious fashion the drawing-room made an excellent battle-ground for so polite a struggle. It was so old, so mysterious and so delicate. There were no lights save the lamps, three of them, one majolica, one blue faience and one Ming, and the candles in the sconces on each side of the tall mirror and the flaming Venice of Mr. Turner. The only flowers were a bowl of white peonies which Lily had been able to save from the wreck of a garden beaten for three days by a south wind.

"The Governor's visit," observed Mrs. Harrison, "turned out unfortunately. He succeeded in offending almost every one of importance."

"And his sudden going-away," added Miss Abercrombie, eagerly leaning forward.

Julia Shane stirred in her big chair. To-night she wore an old-fashioned gown of black lace, very tight at the waist and very low in the neck, which displayed boldly the boniness of her strong shoulders. "I don't think he intended slighting any one," she said. "He was called away by a telegram. A Governor, you know, has duties. When Colonel Shane was alive . . ." And she launched into an anecdote of twenty years earlier, told amusingly and skilfully, leading Mrs. Julis Harrison and Miss Abercrombie for the time being far away from the behavior of the Governor. She spoke of her husband as she always did, in terms of the most profound devotion.

Mrs. Harrison was a handsome stout woman, a year or two older than Julia Shane but, unlike her, given to following the fashions closely. She preserved an illusion of youth by much lacing and secret recourse to rouge, a vain deception before Julia Shane, who knew rouge in all its degrees in Paris where rouge was used both skilfully and frankly. She moved, the older woman, with a slight pomposity, conscious always of the dignity of her position as the richest woman in the Town; for she was richer by a million or two than Julia Shane, to whom she acceded nothing save the prestige which was Cypress Hill and its tradition.

Miss Abercrombie, a spinster of uncertain age, wore her hair in a pompadour and spoke French, as she believed, perfectly. It was necessary that she believe in her own French, for she it was who instructed the young girls of the Town in French and in history, drawing upon a background derived from a dozen summers spent at one time or another on the continent. Throughout Julia Shane's long anecdote, Miss Abercrombie interrupted from time to time with little fluttering sighs of appreciation, with "Ohs!" and "Ahs!" and sudden observations of how much pleasanter the Town had been in the old days. When the anecdote at last was finished, she it was who brought the conversation by a sudden heroic gesture back to the Governor.

"And tell me, dear Julia," she said. "Is there no news of Lily? . . . Has nothing come of the Governor's devotion?"

There was nothing, Julia replied with a sharp, compressed smile. "Nothing at all, save a flirtation. Lily, you know, is very pretty."

"So beautiful!" remarked Mrs. Harrison. "I was telling my son William so, only to-night. He admires her . . . deeply, you know, deeply." She had taken to fanning herself vigorously for the night was hot. She did it boldly, endeavoring in vain to force some stray zephyr among the rolls of fat inside her tight bodice.

"What I can never understand," continued Miss Abercrombie, "is why Lily hasn't already married. A girl so pretty and so nice to every one . . . especially older people."

Mrs. Shane became falsely deprecating of Lily's charms. "She is a good girl," she said. "But hardly as charming as all that. The trouble is that she's very fastidious. She isn't easy to suit." In her deprecation there was an assumption of superiority, as though she could well afford to deprecate because no one could possibly take her seriously.

"She's had plenty of chances. . . . I don't doubt that," observed Miss Abercrombie. "I can remember that summer when we were all in Aix together. . . . Do you remember the young Englishman, Julia? The nice one with yellow hair?" She turned to Mrs. Julis Harrison with an air of arrogant pride and intimacy. "He was the second son of a peer, you know, and she could have had him by a turn of her finger."

And the association with the peerage placed for the time being Miss Abercrombie definitely on the side of Julia Shane in the drawing-room skirmish.

"And Harvey Biggs was so devoted to her," she babbled on. "Such a nice boy . . . gone now to the war like so many other brave fellows." Then as though remembering suddenly that William Harrison was not at the war but safe in the library across the hall, she veered quickly. "They say the Spanish atrocities in Cuba are beyond comprehension. I feel that we should spread them as much as possible to rouse the spirit of the people."

"I've thought since," remarked Mrs. Harrison, "that you should have had flags for decorations at the garden party, Julia. With a war on and especially with the Governor here.

I only mention it because it has made people talk. It only adds to the resentment against his behavior."

"I thought the flowers were enough," replied Mrs. Shane, making a wry face. "They were so beautiful until cinders from your furnaces destroyed them. Those peonies," she added, indicating the white flowers that showed dimly in the soft light, "are all that is left." There was a moment's pause and the distant throb of the Mills filled the room, proclaiming their eternal presence. It was a sound which never ceased. "The garden party seems to have been a complete failure. I'm growing too old to entertain properly."

"Nonsense!" declared Mrs. Julis Harrison with great emphasis. "But I don't see why you persist in living here with the furnaces under your nose."

"I shan't live anywhere else. Cypress Hill was here before the Mills . . . long before."

Almost unconsciously each woman discovered in the eye of the other a faint gleam of anger, the merest flash of spirit, a sign of the eternal struggle between that which is established and that which is forever in a state of flux, which Mrs. Julis Harrison in her heart called "progress" and Julia Shane in hers called "desecration."

VIII

THE struggle ended here because at that moment the voice of William Harrison, drawling and colorless, penetrated the room. He came in from the hallway, preceded by Lily, who wore a gown of rose-colored satin draped at the waist and ornamented with a waterfall of lace which descended from the discreet V at the neck. He was an inch or two shorter than Lily, with pale blond hair and blue eyes that protruded a little from beneath a high bald forehead. His nose was long and his mouth narrow and passionless. He held himself very straight, for he was conscious that his lack of stature was inconsistent with the dignity necessary to the heir of the Harrison millions.

"It is late, mother," he said. "And Lily is leaving to-morrow for New York. She is sailing, you know, on Thursday."

His face was flushed and his manner nervous. He fingered his watch-chain, slipping the ruby clasp backward and forward restlessly.

"Sailing!" repeated Mrs. Harrison, sitting bolt upright in her chair and suspending her fan in mid-air. "Sailing! Why didn't you tell me, Julia? I should have sent you a going-away present, Lily."

"Sailing," echoed Miss Abercrombie, "to France, my dear! I have some commissions you must do for me. Do you mind taking a package or two?"

Lily smiled slowly. "Of course not. Can you send them down in the morning? I'm afraid I won't get up to the Town to-morrow."

She moved aside suddenly to make way for the mulatto woman, Hennery's wife, for whom Julia Shane had rung at the moment of William Harrison's first speech.

"'Tell Hennery,'" she said, "to send round Mrs. Harrison's carriage." The old woman was taking no chances now.

There followed the confusion which surrounds the collecting of female wraps, increased by the twittering of Miss Abercrombie in her excitement over the thought of a voyage to "the continent." The carriage arrived and the guests were driven off down the long drive and out into the squalid street.

When Miss Abercrombie had been dropped at a little old house which, sheltered by lilacs, elms and syringas, stood in the old part of the Town, William Harrison shifted his position in the victoria, fingered his watch chain nervously and lowered his voice lest the coachman hear him above the rumble of the rubber-tires on the cobble-stones.

"She refused me," he said.

For a time the victoria rumbled along in silence with its mistress sitting very straight, breathing deeply. At length she said, "She may come round. . . . You're not clever with women, William."

The son writhed in the darkness. He must sometimes have suspected that his mother's opinion of him was even less flattering than his own. There was no more talk between them that night. For Mrs. Harrison a great hope had been killed—put aside perhaps expressed it more accurately, for she was a powerful woman who did not accept defeat passively. She had hoped that she might unite the two great fortunes of the Town. Irene had been tried and found impossible. She would never marry any one. One thing puzzled the indomitable woman and so dulled a little the keen edge of her disappointment. It was the sudden trip to Paris. A strange incredible suspicion raised itself in her mind. This she considered for a time, turning it over and over with a perverse pleasure. At last, despite all her desire to believe it, she discarded it as too fantastic.

"It couldn't be," she thought. "Julia would never have dared to invite us to meet the girl. Lily herself could not have been so calm and pleasant. No, it's impossible!"

All the same when she went to her room in the great ugly house of red sandstone, she sat down before undressing and wrote a note to a friend who lived in Paris.

IX

AT Cypress Hill, Julia Shane and her elder daughter returned, when the door had closed on their guests, to the drawing-room to discuss after a custom of long standing the entertainment of the evening. They agreed that Mrs. Harrison had grown much too stout, that she was indeed on the verge of apoplexy; that Miss Abercrombie became steadily more fidgety and affected.

"A woman should marry," said Julia Shane, "even if she can do no better than a day laborer."

Two candles by the side of the tall mirror and one by the flaming Venice of Mr. Turner guttered feebly and expired. Now that she was alone, the old woman lighted a cigarette and blew the smoke quietly into the still air. It was Lily who interrupted the silence.

"Willie proposed to me again," she said presently.

The mother made no answer but regarded the girl quietly with a curious questioning look in her tired eyes. Lily, seated in the glow of light from the majolica lamp, must have understood what was passing in her mind.

"No," she said, "if I had wanted to marry, I could have had a man . . . a real man." For a second her eyes grew dark with emotion and her red lips curved as if she remembered suddenly and with a shameless pleasure the embraces of her lover. "No," she continued, "I wouldn't play such a trick, even on a poor thing like Willie."

The old woman knocked the ashes from her cigarette. The rings flashed and glittered in the candle light. "Sometimes," she said softly, "I think you are hopeless . . . altogether abandoned."

There was a note of melancholy in her voice, so poignant that the girl suddenly sprang from her chair, crossed the little space between them and embraced her mother impulsively.

34

"I'm sorry for your sake, Mama," she said. "I'm sorry. . . ." She kissed the hard, handsome face and the mother returned the embrace with a sudden fierce burst of unaccustomed passion.

"It's all right, Lily dear. I'm only thinking of you. I don't think anything can really hurt me any longer. I'm an old warrior, tough and well-armored." For a second she regarded the girl tenderly and then asked, "but aren't you afraid?"

"No!" The answer was quiet and confident.

"You're a strange, strange girl," said the mother.

X

MADAME GIGON with Fifi lived in a tiny apartment in the Rue de la Assomption. In the summer she went to live at Germigny l'Evec in a curve of the Marne after it has passed Meaux and Trilport, wandering its soft and amiable way between sedges and wild flags under rows of tall plane trees with bark as green and spotted as the backs of salamanders. Here she occupied the lodge of the château belonging to her cousin, a gentleman who inherited his title from a banker of the First Empire and lent the lodge rent free to Madame Gigon, whose father, also a banker, was ruined by the collapse of the Second Empire. M. Gigon, a scholar and antiquarian, one of the curators of the Cluny Museum, was long since dead—an ineffectual little man with a stoop and a squint, who lived his life gently and faded out of it with so little disturbance that even Madame Gigon sometimes examined her conscience and her respectability because there were long periods when she forgot that he had ever existed at all. Fifi was to her far more of a personality—Fifi with her fat waddle, her black and tan coat, and her habit of yapping for gateaux at tea time.

Although Madame Gigon was not English at all, tea was a fixed rite in her life. She came by the custom at the boarding school of Mademoiselle Violette de Vaux at St. Cloud on the edge of Paris where tea was a regular meal because there was always a score of English girls among Mademoiselle's *pensionnaires*. On the passing of Monsieur Gigon she had taken, under the stress of bitter necessity, a place as instructress in art and history at the establishment of the aging Mademoiselle de Vaux, who, like herself was a Bonapartist, a *bourgeoise* and deeply respectable. She saved from her small salary a comfortable little fortune, and at length retired with Fifi to the little flat in the Rue de la Assomption to live upon her interest and the bounty of her cousin the Baron. But above even her respectability and her small fortune, she honored her position, an element which she had preserved through a lifetime of adversity. She was respected still as the daughter of a man who had ruined himself to support Napoleon the Little. She still attended the salons of the Bonapartist families in the houses and apartments of Passy, of the Boulevard Flandrin, and the new Paris of the Place de l'Etoile. She was respected still in the circles which moved about the aging figure of the Prince Bonaparte and, greatest of all, she received a card of admission signed by his own hand whenever the Prince addressed the Geographical Society.

Madame Gigon was in the act of closing her tiny apartment in the Rue de la Assomption for the summer when the letter of Julia Shane arrived. At the news it contained, she suspended the operations necessary to her departure for the lodge of Germigny l'Evec and settled herself to await the arrival of pretty Lily Shane, contenting herself meanwhile with taking Fifi for airings in the Bois de Boulogne, a suitable distance away for one of Madame's age and infirmities. And when the day came, she managed to meet Lily in a fiacre at the Gare du Nord.

There was something touching in Madame Gigon's reception of the girl, something even more touching in Lily's reception by the fat and wheezing Fifi. The shrewd old dog remembered her as the girl who had been generous with gateaux, and when Lily, dressed smartly in a purple suit with a large hat covered with plumes, climbed into the fiacre, the plump Fifi shouted and leapt about with all the animation of a puppy.

Throughout the journey to Meaux and on the succeeding trip by carriage along the Marne to Germigny, the pair made no mention of Julia Shane's letter. They talked of the heat, of the beauty of the countryside, of Mademoiselle de Vaux, who was past ninety and very feeble, of the new girls at the school . . . until the peasant coachman drew up his fat horse before the gate of the lodge and carried their luggage into the vine covered cottage.

XI

AFTER Lily had rested in the room just beneath the dove cote, the pair, assisted by a red-cheeked farm girl, set themselves to putting the place in order. With the approach of evening, Madame Gigon took off her wig, donned a lace cap, and they were settled until the month of October.

When they had finished a supper of omelette, potatoes and wine, they seated themselves on the terrace and Madame Gigon at length approached the matter, delicately and with circumspection. It was a blue, misty evening of the sort frequent in the Isle de France, when the stillness becomes acute and tangible, when the faintest sound is sharply audible for an amazing distance across the waving fields of wheat. From the opposite side of the river arose the faint tinkling of a bell as a pair of white oxen made their way slowly from the farm to the sedge-bordered river. Overhead among the vines on the roof of the lodge, the pigeons stirred sleepily, cooing and preening themselves. The evening was beautiful, unbelievably calm, with the placidity of a marvelous dream.

After a long silence, Madame Gigon began to gossip once more and presently, she said, "To be sure, it has happened before in this world. It will happen again. The trouble is that you are too pretty, dear Lily, and you lose your head. You are too generous. I always told Mademoiselle you were more like our girls than the English or Americans."

Lily said nothing. It appeared that she heard nothing old Madame Gigon said. Wrapped in her black cloak against the chill of the faint mist which swam above the Marne, she seemed lost in the breathless beauty of the evening.

"Why, in my family, it has happened. There was my cousin . . . a sister of the Baron who lives here in the Chateau. . . ." And Madame Gigon moved from one case to another, justifying Lily's strange behavior. When she had finished with a long series, she shook her head gently and said, "I know, I know . . . ," smiling all the while as though she had known many lovers and been as seductive as Cleopatra. She drank the last of her coffee, drying her mustache when she had finished.

"I brought down some fine lawn and some lace from Paris," she said, "I remember that you always sewed beautifully. We shall be busy this winter in the little flat."

And then Lily stirred for the first time, moving her body indolently with her eyes half-closed, her head resting on the back of the chair. "We shan't live in the little flat, Madame Gigon. . . . We shall have a house. . . . I know just the one, in the Rue Raynouard. You see, I am going to live in Paris always. I am never going back to America to live."

The old Frenchwoman said nothing, either in approval or disagreement, but she grew warm suddenly with pleasure. The house in the Rue Raynouard captured her imagination. It meant that she would have the dignity of surroundings suitable to one who received signed cards from the Prince Bonaparte to his lectures. She could have a salon. She knew that Lily Shane, like all Americans, was very rich.

A little while later they went inside and Lily in her room just under the dove-cote lighted a candle and settled herself to writing letters. One she addressed to the convent where Irene was stopping, one to Cypress Hill, and the last, very short and formal, she addressed the Governor. It was the first line she had written him. Also it was the last.

XII

IN the Town the tidings of Lily's sudden departure followed the course of all bits of news from Shane's Castle. It created for a time a veritable cloud of gossip. Again when it became gradually known that she intended living in Paris, heads wagged for a time and stories of her father were revived. Her name became the center of a myriad tales such as accumulate about beautiful women who are also indifferent.

But of one fact the Town learned nothing. It had no knowledge of a cablegram which arrived at Shane's Castle containing simply the words, "John has arrived safely and well." Only the telegraph operator saw it and to him the words could have meant nothing.

It was Mrs. Julis Harrison who kept alive the cloud of rumors that closed over the memory of Lily. When she was not occupied with directing the activities of the Mills through the mouthpiece of her son Willie, she fostered her suspicions. The letter addressed to a friend in Paris bore no fruit. Lily, it seemed, had buried herself. She was unknown to the American colony. But Mrs. Harrison, nothing daunted, managed herself to create a story which in time she came to believe, prefacing it to her choicest friends with the remark that "Shane's Castle has not changed. More things go on there than this world dreams of."

As for the Governor, he visited the Town two years later on the eve of election; but this time he did not stay at Shane's Castle. It was known that he paid old Julia Shane a mysterious visit lasting more than an hour, but what passed between them remained at best a subject for the wildest speculation.

With the departure of Lily, her mother settled slowly into a life of retirement. There were no more receptions and garden-parties. With Lily gone, there appeared to be no reasons for gaiety. Irene, as every one knew, hated festivities of every sort.

"I am growing too old," said Julia Shane. "It tires me to entertain. Why should I?"

It was not true that she was old, yet it was true that she was tired. It was clear that she was letting slip all threads of interest, even more apparent that she actually cherished her solitude.

She still condescended to go to an occasional dinner in the Town, driving in her victoria with Hennery on the box through sweating smelly Halsted street, across the writhing oily Black Fork and up the Hill to the respectable portion of the Town where lived the people of property. It was impossible to have guessed her thoughts on that infrequent journey. They must have been strange . . . the thoughts of a woman not long past middle-age who had seen within her lifetime the most extraordinary metamorphosis in the Town of her birth. She could remember the days when she rode with John Shane in his paddock, now completely buried beneath massive warehouses. She could remember the days when Halsted street was only a private drive across the marshes to Cypress Hill. Indeed it appeared, as the years passed, that Julia Shane was slipping slowly back across all those years into the simplicity that marked her childhood as a farmer's daughter. She talked less and avoided people. She no longer cared for the elegance of her clothes. As though her gaunt and worldly air had been only a mockery she began to slough it off bit by bit with the passing months. The few women who crossed the threshold of Shane's Castle returned with stories that Julia Shane, having closed the rest of the house, had taken to living in two or three rooms.

People said other things too, of Julia and her two daughters, but mostly of Lily, for Lily somehow captured their imagination. In the midst of the Town, born and bred upon the furnace girt hill, she was an exotic, an orchid appearing suddenly in a prosperous vegetable garden.

People said such things as, "Julia Shane gets no satisfaction out of her daughter Irene. . . . I believe myself that the girl is a little queer."

Or it might be that Mrs. Julis Harrison, with a knowing shake of the head would remark, "It's strange that Lily has never married. They say she is enjoying herself in Paris, although she doesn't see anything of the Americans there. It's like John Shane's daughter to prefer the French."

XIII

MEANWHILE the Town grew. The farm where Julia Shane spent her youth disappeared entirely, broken up into checker board allotments, crossed by a fretwork of crude concrete sidewalks. Houses, uniform and unvaryingly ugly in architecture and cheap in construction, sprang up in clusters like fungi to house the clerks and the petty officials of the Mills. In the Flats, which included all that district taken over by the factories, hundreds of alien workmen drifted in to fill the already overcrowded houses beyond endurance. Croats, Slovenes, Russians, Poles, Italians, Negroes took up their abodes in the unhealthy lowlands, in the shadows of the furnace towers and the resounding steel sheds, under the very hedges of Shane's Castle. In Halsted street, next door to the corner saloon, a handful of worthy citizens, moved by the gravity of conditions in the district, opened an establishment which they gave the sentimental name of Welcome House, using it to aid the few aliens who were not hostile and suspicious of volunteer workers from the Town.

All this, Julia Shane, living in another world, ignored. She saw nothing of what happened beneath her very windows.

It was true that she found no satisfaction in her daughter Irene. On the return of the girl from a long rest at the convent, there took place between mother and daughter a terrible battle which did not end in a sudden, decisive victory but dragged its length across many weeks. Irene returned with her thin pretty face pale and transparent, her ash blond hair drawn back tightly from her forehead in severe nunlike fashion. She wore a suit of black stuff, plainly made and ornamented only by a plain collar of white lawn.

On the first evening at home, the mother and daughter sat until midnight in the library, a room which they used after dinner on evenings when they were alone. The little French

clock struck twelve before the girl was able to summo
courage to address her mother, and when at last she succeede
she was forced to interrupt the old woman in the midst of
new book by Collette Willy, sent her by Lily, which she wa
reading with the aid of a silver mounted glass.

"Mother," began Irene gently. "Mother . . ."

Julia Shane put down the glass and looked up. "What i
it?"

"Mother, I've decided to enter the church."

It was an announcement far from novel, a hope expresse
year after year only to be trodden under foot by the will o
the old woman. But this time there was a new quality i
Irene's voice, a shade of firmness and determination that wa
not at all in keeping with the girl's usual humility. Th
mother's face grew stern, almost hard. Cheri slipped gentl
to the floor where it lay forgotten.

"Is this my reward for letting you go back to the con
vent?" The voice was cold, dominating, a voice which alway
brought Irene into a trembling submission. The church t
both meant but one thing—the Roman Catholic church—
which John Shane, a Romanist turned scoffer, had mocked a
his life, a church which to his Presbyterian widow was alway
the Scarlet Woman of Rome.

The girl said nothing but kept her eyes cast down, fingerin
all the while the carving on the arm of her rosewood chai
She had grown desperately pale. Her thin fingers tremblec

"Has this anything to do with Lily?" asked the mother wit
a sudden air of suspicion, and Irene answered "No! No!
with such intensity that Julia Shane, convinced that she sti
knew nothing, tried a new tack.

"You know how I feel," she said. "I am old and I a
tired. I have had enough unhappiness, Irene. This would t
the last."

Tears came into the eyes of the girl, and the tremblin
grew and spread until her whole body was shaking. "It is a
I have," she cried.

"Don't be morbid!"

The eagle look came into Mrs. Shane's face—the look wit
which she faced down all the world save her own family.

"I won't hear of it," she added. "I've told you often
enough, Irene. . . . I won't have a daughter of mine sell herself to the devil if I can prevent it." She spoke with a rising
intensity of feeling that was akin to hatred. "You shall not
do it as long as I live and never after I am dead, if I can
help it."

The girl tried not to sob. The new defiance in her soul
gave her a certain spiritual will to oppose her mother. Never
before had she dared even to argue her case. "If it were
Lily . . ." she began weakly.

"It would make no difference. Besides, it could never be
Lily. That is out of the question. Lily is no fool. . . ."

The accusation of Irene was an old one, secret, cherished
always in the depths of a lonely submissive heart. It was
born now from the depths of her soul, a cry almost of passion,
a protest against a sister whom every one pardoned, whom
every one admired, whom all the world loved. It was an
accusation directed against the mother who was so sympathetic
toward Lily, so uncomprehending toward Irene.

"I suppose they have been talking to you . . . the sisters,"
continued Julia Shane. And when the girl only buried her
face miserably in her arms, she added more gently, "Come here,
Irene. . . . Come over here to me."

Quietly the daughter came to her side where she knelt down
clasping the fingers covered with rings that were so cold
against her delicate, transparent skin. For an instant the
mother frowned as if stricken by some physical pain. "My
God!" she said, "Why is it so hard to live?" But her weakness passed quickly. She stiffened her tired body, sighed,
and began again. "Now," she said gruffly. "We must work
this out. . . . We must understand each other better, my dear.
If you could manage to confide in me . . . to let me help you.
I am your mother. Whatever comes to you comes to me as
well . . . everything. There are three of us, you and Lily
and me." Her manner grew slowly more tender, more af-
fectionate. "We must keep together. You might say that
we stood alone . . . three women with the world against us.
When I die, I want to leave you and Lily closer to each
other than you and I have been. If there is anything that

you want to confess . . . if you have any secret, tell it to me and not to the sisters."

By now Irene was sobbing hysterically, clinging all the while to the hand of her mother. "There is nothing . . . nothing!" she cried, "I don't know why I am so miserable."

"Then promise me one thing . . . that you will do nothing until we have talked the matter out thoroughly." She fell to stroking the girl's blond hair with her thin veined hand slowly, with a hypnotic gesture.

"Yes. . . . Yes. . . . I promise!" And gradually the sobbing ebbed and the girl became still and calm.

For a time they sat thus listening to the mocking frivolous tick-tick of the little French clock over the fireplace. A greater sound, rumbling and regular like the pounding of giant hammers they did not hear because it had become so much a part of their lives that it was no longer audible. The throb of the Mills, working day and night, had become a part of the very stillness.

At last Julia Shane stirred and said with a sudden passion, "Come, Irene! . . . Come up to my room. There is no peace here." And the pair rose and hurried away, the mother hobbling along with the aid of her ebony stick, never once glancing behind her at the portrait whose handsome malignant eyes appeared to follow them with a wicked delight.

XIV

FOR days a silent struggle between the two continued, a struggle which neither admitted, yet one of which they were always conscious sleeping or waking. And at last the mother gained from the tormented girl a second romise . . . that she would never enter the church so long as er mother was alive. Shrewdly she roused the interest of the irl in the families of the mill workers who dwelt at the gates f Cypress Hill. Among these Irene found a place. Like a ister of charity she went into their homes, facing all the deep-ooted hostility and the suspicions of Shane's Castle. She ven went by night to teach English to a handful of laborers in 1e school at Welcome House. For three years she labored hus, and at the end of that time she seemed happy, for there vere a few among the aliens who trusted her. There were mong them devout and simple souls who even came to be-eve that there was something saintly in the lady from hane's Castle.

It was this pale, devout Irene that Lily found when she eturned home after four years to visit her mother at Cypress Iill. Without sending word ahead she arrived alone at the 1ooty brick station in the heart of the Flats, slipping down at 1idnight from the transcontinental express, unrecognized even y the old station master who had been there for twenty years. he entered the Town like a stranger, handsomely dressed ith a thick Parisian veil and heavy furs which hid her face ive for a pair of dark eyes. When one is not expected one not easily recognized, and there were people in the Town who elieved that Lily Shane might never return from Paris.

She remained for a moment on the dirty platform, looking oout her at the new factory sheds and the rows of workmen's ouses which had sprung up since her departure. They ap-eared dimly through the falling snow as if they were not

47

solid and real at all, but queer structures born out of dream
Then she entered one of the station cabs, smelling faintly
mold and ammonia, and drove off. Throughout the journe
up Halsted street to Shane's Castle, she kept poking her hea
in and out of the cab window to regard the outlines of ne
chimneys and new sheds against the glow in the sky. Th
snow fell in great wet flakes and no sooner did it touch th
ground than it became black, and melting, flowed away in
dirty stream along the gutters. At the corner saloon, a crow
of steel workers peered at her in a drunken wonder tinge
with hostility, amazed at the sight of a strange woman
richly dressed driving through the Flats at midnight. Wha
ever else was in doubt, they must have known her destinatio
was the great black house on the hill.

As the cab turned in the long drive, Lily noticed by th
glare of the street light that the wrought iron gates had n
been painted and were clotted with rust. The gaps in th
hedge of arbor vitæ had spread until in spots the desolatio
extended for a dozen yards or more. In the house the windov
all were dark save on the library side where a dull light glowe
through the falling snow. The house somehow appeared dea
abandoned. In the old days it had blazed with light.

Jerry, the cab driver, lifted down her bags, stamped wit
the bright labels of Hotels Royale Splendide and Beau Rivag
of Ritz-Carltons and Metropolitans, in St. Moritz, in Canne
in Sorrento and Firenze, and deposited them on the piazz
with the wrought iron columns. The wistaria vines, she di
covered suddenly, were gone and only the black outline of th
wrought iron supports showed in a hard filigree against th
dull glow of the furnaces.

The door was locked and she pulled the bell a half doze
times, listening to the sound of its distant tinkle, before th
mulatto woman opened and admitted her to the accompan
ment of incoherent mutterings of welcome.

"Mama!" Lily called up the long polished stairwa
"Irene! Mama! Where are you?"

She gave her coat and furs to the mulatto woman and
she untied her veil, the sound of her mother's limping step an

e tapping of her stick echoed from overhead through the si-
nt house. A moment later, Julia Shane herself appeared at
e top of the stairs followed by Irene clad like a deaconess in
 dress of gray stuff with a high collar.

XV

ON the occasion of Lily's first dinner at home, the m
latto woman brought out the heaviest of the silv
candelabra and despatched Hennery into the Tov
for a dozen tall candles and a great bunch of pii
roses which filled the silver épergne when the mother and tl
two daughters came down to dinner; Julia Shane, as usua
wore black with a lace shawl thrown over her gray hair,
custom which she had come to adopt in the evenings and oi
which gave the Town one more point of evidence in the grov
ing chain of her eccentricities. Irene, still clad in the gra
dress with the high collar and looking somehow like a gover
ess or a nurse employed in the house, took her place at tl
side of the table. As for Lily, her appearance so fascinate
the mulatto woman and the black girl who aided her that tl
dinner was badly served and brought a sharp remonstran
from Mrs. Shane. No longer had Lily any claims to gir
hood. Indisputably she was become a woman. A fine figu
of a woman, she might have been called, had she been le
languid and indolent. Her slimness had given way to a del
cate voluptuousness, a certain opulence like the ripeness of
beautiful fruit. Where there had been slimness before the
now were curves. She moved slowly and with the same cv
rious dignity of her mother, and she wore no rouge, for h
lips were full and red and her cheeks flushed with delica
color. Her beauty was the beauty of a peasant girl fro:
which all coarseness had been eliminated, leaving only a r
diant glow of health. She was, after all, the granddaught
of a Scotch farmer; there was nothing thin-blooded abov
her, nothing of the anemia of Irene. To-night she wore
tea-gown from Venice, the color of water in a limestone poc
liquid, cool, pale green. Her reddish hair, in defiance of tl
prevailing fashions, she wore bound tightly about her head ar

astened by a pin set with brilliants. About her neck on a
thin silver cord hung suspended a single pear-shaped emerald
which rested between her breasts, so that sometimes it hung
outside the gown and sometimes lay concealed against the delicate white skin.

Irene throughout the dinner spoke infrequently and kept
her eyes cast down as though the beauty of her sister in some
way fascinated and repelled her. When it was finished, she
stood up and addressed her mother.

"I must go now. It is my night to teach at Welcome
House."

Lily regarded her with a puzzled expression until her
mother, turning to explain, said, "She teaches English to a
class of foreigners in Halsted street." And then to Irene,
"You might have given it up on the first night Lily was
home!"

A look of stubbornness came into the pale face of the younger
sister. "I can't. They are depending on me. I shall see
Lily every day for weeks. This is a duty. To stay would be
to yield to pleasure."

"But you're not going alone into Halsted street?" protested
Lily. "At night! You must be crazy!"

"I'm perfectly safe. . . . They know me and what I do,"
the sister answered proudly. "Besides there is one of the men
who always sees me home."

She came round to Lily's chair and gave her a kiss, the
merest brushing of cool lips against the older sister's warm
cheek. "Good-night," she said, "in case you have gone to
bed before I return."

When Irene had gone, an instant change took place in the
demeanor of the two women. It was as though some invisible barrier, separating the souls of mother and daughter, had
been let down suddenly. Lily leaned back and stretched her
long limbs. The mulatto woman brought cigarettes and the
mother and daughter settled themselves to talking. They
were at last alone and free to say what they would.

"How long has Irene been behaving in this fashion?" asked
Lily.

"It is more than three years now. I don't interfere be-

cause it gives her so much pleasure. It saved her, you kno
from entering the church. Anything is better than that."

Then all at once as though they had suddenly entered anoth
world, they began to talk French, shutting out the mula
woman from their conversation.

"Mais elle est déja religieuse," said Lily, "tout simpleme
You might as well let her enter the church. She already
haves like a nun . . . in that ridiculous gray dress. S
looks ghastly. You should forbid it. A woman has no rig
to make herself look hideous. There's something sinful in i

The mother smiled wearily. "Forbid it? You don't kn
Irene. I'm thankful to keep her out of the church. She
becoming fanatic." There was a pause and Mrs. Sha
added, "She never goes out now . . . not since a year a
more."

"She is like a spinster of forty. . . . It is shameful for
girl of twenty-five to let herself go in that fashion. No m
would look at her."

"Irene will never marry. . . . It is no use speaking to h
I have seen the type before, Lily . . . the religieuse. It tak
the place of love. It is just as ecstatic."

The mulatto woman, who had been clearing away the dish
came and stood by her mistress' chair to await, after her cu
tom, the orders for the following day. "There will only
three of us . . . as usual. That is all, Sarah!"

The woman turned to go but Lily called after h
"Mama," she said, "can't we open the rest of the hou
while I'm here? It's horrible, shut up in this fashion.
hate sitting in the library when there is all the drawing-room

Mrs. Shane did not argue. "Get some one to help you op
the drawing-room to-morrow, Sarah. We will use it wh
Miss Lily is here."

The mulatto woman went out and Lily lighted anoth
cigarette. "You will want it open for the Christmas party
she said. "You can't entertain all the family in the library

"I had thought of giving up the Christmas party this yea
replied the Mother.

"No . . . not this year," cried Lily. "It is such fun, a

haven't seen Cousin Hattie and Uncle Jacob and Ellen for
ears."

Again the mother yielded. "You want gaiety, I see."

"Well, I'm not pious like Irene, and this house is gloomy
ough." At the sight of her mother rising from her chair,
e said . . . "Let's not go to the library. Let's sit here.
hate it in there."

So there they remained while the tall candles burned lower
d lower. Suddenly after a brief pause in the talk, the
other turned to Lily and said, "Et toi."

Lily shrugged her shoulders. "Moi? Moi? Je suis
ntente."

"Et Madame Gigon, et le petit Jean."

"They are well . . . both of them. I have brought a
cture which I've been waiting to show you."

"He is married, you know."

"When?"

"Only three weeks ago. He came here after your letter
offer to do anything he could. He wants the boy to go to
ool in America."

Here Lily smiled triumphantly. "But Jean is mine. I
ill accept nothing from him. He is afraid to recognize
an because it would ruin him. I shall send the boy where
like." She leaned forward, glowing with a sudden en-
usiasm. "You don't know how handsome he is and how
ver." She pushed back her chair. "Wait, I'll get his
ture."

The mother interrupted her. "Bring me the enameled box
m my dressing table. There is something in it that will
erest you."

XVI

IN a moment the daughter returned bearing the photogra[ph] and the enameled box. It was the picture which inte[r]ested Julia Shane. Putting aside the box she took it [up] and gazed at it for a long time in silence while L[ily] watched her narrowly across the polished table.

"He is a handsome child," she said presently. "He [re]sembles you. There is nothing of his father." Her bl[ue] eyes were moist and the tired hard face softened. "Co[me] here," she added almost under her breath, and when t[he] daughter came to her side she kissed her softly, holding h[er] close to her thin breast. When she released Lily from h[er] embrace, she said, "And you? When are you going [to] marry?"

Lily laughed. "Oh, there is plenty of time. I am on[ly] twenty-seven, after all. I am very happy as I am." S[he] picked up the enameled box, smiling. "Show me the secre[t]" she said.

Mrs. Shane opened the box and from a number of yell[ow] clippings drew forth one which was quite new. "There," s[he] said, giving it to the daughter. "It is a picture of him a[nd] his new wife, taken at the wedding."

There was a portrait of the Governor, grown a little m[ore] stout, but still tall, straight and broad shouldered. His flo[w]ing mustache had been clipped; otherwise he was unchang[ed]. In the picture he grinned amiably toward the camera as if [he] saw political capital even in his own honeymoon. By his si[de] stood a woman of medium height and strong build. H[er] features were heavy and she too smiled, although there w[as] something superior in her smile as though she felt a disd[ain] for the public. It was a plain face, intelligent, yet someh[ow] lacking in charm. The clipping identified her as the daugh[ter] of a wealthy middle-western manufacturer and a graduate

54

woman's college. It continued with a short biographical
account of the Governor, predicting for him a brilliant future
and congratulating him upon a marriage the public had long
awaited with interest.

Lily replaced the clipping in the enameled box and closed
the lid with a snap. "He had done well," she remarked.
"She sounds like a perfect wife for an American politician. I
should have been a hopeless failure. As it is we are both
happy."

The look of bewilderment returned to her mother's eyes.
"The boy," she said, "should have a father. You should
marry for his sake, Lily."

"He shall have . . . in time. There is no hurry. Besides, his position is all right. I am Madame Shane, a rich
American widow. Madame Gigon has taken care of that.
My position is excellent. No woman could be more respected."

Gradually she drifted into an account of her life in Paris.
It followed closely the line of pleasant anticipations which
Madame Gigon had permitted herself during the stillness of
that first evening on the terrace above the Marne. The house in
the Rue Raynouard was big and old. It had been built before the Revolution at a time when Passy was a suburb surrounded by open meadows. It had a garden at the back which
ran down to the Rue de Passy, once the open highroad to
Auteuil. Apartments, shops and houses now covered the open
meadows but the old house and the garden remained unchanged, unaltered since the day Lenôtre planned them for the
Marquise de Sevillac. The garden had a fine terrace and a
pavilion which some day Jean should have for his own quarters. The house itself was well planned for entertaining. It
had plenty of space and a large drawing-room which extended
along the garden side with tall windows opening outward upon
the terrace. At a little distance off was the Seine. One could
hear the excursion steamers bound for Sèvres and St. Cloud
whistling throughout the day and night.

As for friends, there were plenty of them . . . more than
she desired. There were the respectable baronnes and com-
tesses of Madame Gigon's set, a group which worshiped the

Prince Bonaparte and talked a deal of silly nonsense about th
Restoration of the Empire. To be sure, they were fuddy
duddy, but their sons and daughters were not so bad. Som
of them Lily had known at the school of Mademoiselle d
Vaux. Some of them were charming, especially the men. Sh
had been to Compiègne to hunt, though she disliked exercis
of so violent a nature. Indeed they had all been very kin
to her.

"After all," she concluded, "I am not clever or brilliant
I am content with them. I am really happy. As for Madam
Gigon, she is radiant. She has become a great figure in he
set. She holds a salon twice a month with such an arra
of gateaux as would turn you ill simply to look at. I giv
her a fat allowance but she gets herself up like the devil.
think she is sorry that crinolines are no longer the fashion
She looks like a Christmas tree, but she is the height of re
spectability." For an instant a thin shade of mockery, almos
of bitterness colored her voice.

Julia Shane reached over suddenly and touched he
daughter's arm. Something in Lily's voice or manner ha
alarmed her. "Be careful, Lily. Don't let yourself grov
hard. That's the one thing."

XVII

THEY sat talking thus until the candles burnt low, guttered and began to go out, one by one, and at last the distant tinkle of a bell echoed through the house. For a moment they listened, waiting for one of the servants to answer and when the bell rang again and again, Lily at last got up languidly saying, "It must be Irene. I'll open if the servants are in bed."

"She always has a key," said her mother. "She has never forgotten it before."

Lily made her way through the hall and boldly opened the door to discover that she was right. Irene stood outside covered with snow. As she stepped in, her sister caught a glimpse through the mist of falling flakes of a tall man, powerfully built, walking down the long drive toward Halsted street. He walked rapidly, for he wore no overcoat and the night was cold.

In the warm lamplighted hall, Irene shook the snow from her coat and took off her plain ugly black hat. Her pale cheeks were flushed, perhaps from the effort of walking so rapidly up the drive.

"Who is the man?" asked Lily with an inquisitive smile. Her sister, pulling off her heavy overshoes, answered without looking up. "His name is Krylenko. He is a Ukrainian . . a mill worker."

An hour later the two sisters sat in Lily's room while she took out gown after gown from the brightly labeled trunks. Something had happened during the course of the evening to soften the younger sister. She showed for the first time traces of an interest in the life of Lily. She even bent over the trunks and felt admiringly of the satins, the brocades, the silks and the furs that Lily lifted out and tossed carelessly upon the big Italian bed. She poked about among the deli-

cate chiffons and laces until at last she came upon a sma
photograph of a handsome gentleman in the ornate unifor
of the cuirassiers. He was swarthy and dark-eyed with
crisp vigorous mustache, waxed and turned up smartly at th
ends. For a second she held it under the light of the be
lamp.

"Who is this?" she asked, and Lily, busy with her unpack
ing, looked up for an instant and then continued her tasl
"It is the Baron," she replied. "Madame Gigon's cousin . .
the one who supports her."

"He is handsome," observed Irene in a strange shrew
voice.

"He is a friend. . . . We ride together in the countr
Naturally I see a great deal of him. We live at his châtea
in the summer."

The younger sister dropped the conversation. She becam
silent and withdrawn, and the queer frightened look showe
itself in her pale blue eyes. Presently she excused herself o
the pretense that she was tired and withdrew to the chast
darkness of her own room where she knelt down before
plaster virgin, all pink and gilt and sometimes tawdry, to pra

XVIII

ON the following night the house, as it appeared from the squalid level of Halsted street, took on in its setting of snow-covered pines and false cypresses the appearance to which the Town had been accustomed in the old days. The drawing-room windows glowed with warm light; wreaths were hung against the small diamond shaped panes, and those who passed the wrought iron gates heard during the occasional pauses in the uproar of the Mills the distant tinkling of a piano played with a wild exuberance by some one who chose the gayest of tunes, waltzes and polkas, which at the same hour were to be heard in a dozen Paris music halls.

Above the Flats in the Town, invitations were received during the course of the week to a dinner party, followed by a ball in the long drawing-room.

"Cypress Hill is becoming gay again," observed Miss Abercrombie.

"It must be the return of Lily," said Mrs. Julis Harrison. "Julia will never entertain again. She is too broken," she added with a kind of triumph.

A night or two after Lily's return Mrs. Harrison again spoke to her son William of Lily's beauty and wealth, subtly to be sure and with carefully concealed purpose, for Willie, who was thirty-five now and still unmarried, grew daily more shy and more deprecatory of his own charms.

It was clear enough that the tradition of Cypress Hill was by no means dead, that it required but a little effort, the merest scribbling of a note, to restore all its slumbering prestige. The dinner and the ball became the event of the year. There was great curiosity concerning Lily. Those who had seen her reported that she looked well and handsome, that her clothes were far in advance of the local fashions. They talked once more of her beauty, her charm, her kindliness.

They spoke nothing but good of her, just as they mocked Irene and jeered at her work among the foreigners in the Flats. It was Lily who succeeded to her mother's place as chatelaine of the beautiful gloomy old house at Cypress Hill.

It was also Lily who, some two weeks before Christmas received Mrs. Julis Harrison and Judge Weissman on the mission which brought them together in a social way for the only time in their lives. The strange pair arrived at Shane's Castle in Mrs. Harrison's victoria, the Jew wrapped in a great fur coat, his face a deep red from too much whiskey and the dowager, in an imperial purple dress with a dangling gold chain, sitting well away to her side of the carriage as if contact with her companion might in some horrid way contaminate her. Lily, receiving them in the big hall, was unable to control her amazement at their sudden appearance. As the Judge bowed, rather too obsequiously, and Mrs. Harrison fastened her face into a semblance of cordiality, a look of intense mirth spread over Lily's face like water released suddenly from a broken dam. There was something inexpressibly comic in Mrs. Harrison's obvious determination to admit nothing unusual in a call made with Judge Weissman at ten in the morning.

"We have come to see your mother," announced the purple clad Amazon. "Is she able to see us?"

Lily led the pair into the library. "Wait," she replied, "I'll see. She always stays in bed until noon. You know she grows tired easily nowadays."

"I know . . . I know," said Mrs. Harrison. "Will you tell her it is important? A matter of life and death?"

While Lily was gone the pair in the library waited beneath the mocking gaze of John Shane's portrait. They maintained a tomb-like silence, broken only by the faint rustling of Mrs. Harrison's taffeta petticoats and the cat-like step of the Judge on the Aubusson carpet as he prowled from table to table examining the bits of jade or crystal or silver which caught his Oriental fancy. Mrs. Harrison sat bolt upright, a little like a pouter pigeon, with her coat thrown back to permit her to breathe. She drummed the arm of her chair with her fat fingers and followed with her small blue eyes the movements of the elk's tooth charm that hung suspended from the Judge's watch chain and swayed with every movement of his obese body. At the entrance of Julia Shane, so tall, so gaunt, so cold, she rose nervously and permitted a nervous smile to flit across her face. It was the deprecating smile of one prepared to swallow her pride.

Mrs. Shane, leaning on her stick, moved forward, at the same time fastening upon the Judge a glance which conveyed both curiosity and an undisguised avowal of distaste.

"Dear Julia," began Mrs. Harrison, "I hope you're not too weary. We came to see you on business." The Judge bobbed his assent.

"Oh, no, I'm quite all right. But if you've come about buying Cypress Hill, it's no use. I have no intention of selling it as long as I live."

Mrs. Harrison sat down once more. "It's not that," she said. "It's other business." And then turning. "You know Judge Weissman, of course."

The Judge gave a obsequious bow. From the manner of his hostess, it was clear that she did not know him, that indeed thousands of introductions could never induce her to know him.

"Won't you sit down?" she said with a cold politeness, and the Judge settled himself into an easy chair, collapsing vaguely into rolls of fat.

"We should like to talk with you alone," said Mrs. Harrison. "If Lily could leave. . . ." And she finished the speech with a nod of the head and a turn of the eye meant to convey a sense of grave mystery.

"Certainly," replied Lily, and went out closing the door on her mother and the two visitors.

For two hours they remained closeted in the library while Lily wandered about the house, writing notes, playing on the piano; and once, unable to restrain her curiosity, listening on tip-toe outside the library door. At the end of that time, the door opened and there emerged Mrs. Julis Harrison, looking old and massively dignified, her gold chain swinging more than usual, Judge Weissman, very red and very angry, and

last of all, Julia Shane, her old eyes lighted by a strange new
spark and her thin lips framed in an ironic smile of triumph.

The carriage appeared and the two visitors climbed in and
were driven away on sagging springs across the soot-covered
snow. When they had gone, the mother summoned Lily into
the library, closed the door and then sat down, her thin smile
growing at the same time into a wicked chuckle.

"They've been caught . . . the pair of them," she said.
"And Cousin Charlie did it. . . . They've been trying to get
me to call him off."

Lily regarded her mother with eyebrows drawn together in
a little frown. Plainly she was puzzled. "But how Cousin
Charlie?" she asked. "How has he caught them?"

The mother set herself to explaining the whole story. She
went back to the very beginning. "Cousin Charlie, you know,
is county treasurer. It was Judge Weissman who elected
him. The Jew is powerful. Cousin Charlie wouldn't have
had a chance but for him. Judge Weissman only backed him
because he thought he'd take orders. But he hasn't. That's
where the trouble is. That's why they're worried now. He
won't do what Judge Weissman tells him to do!"

Here she paused, permitting herself to laugh again at the
discomfiture of her early morning callers. So genuine was her
mirthful satisfaction that for an instant, the guise of the
worldly woman vanished and through the mask showed the
farm girl John Shane had married thirty years before.

"You see," she continued, "in going through the books
Cousin Charlie discovered that the Cyclops Mills owe the
county about five hundred thousand dollars in back taxes.
He's sued to recover the money together with the fines, and
he cannot lose. Judge Weissman and Mrs. Harrison have
just discovered that and they've come to me to call him off because he is set on recovering the money. He's refused to take
orders. You see, it hits their pocket-books. The man who
was treasurer before Cousin Charlie has disappeared neatly.
There's a pretty scandal somewhere. Even if it doesn't come
out, the Harrisons and Judge Weissman will lose a few hundred thousands. The Jew owns a lot of stock, you know."

The old woman pounded the floor with her ebony stick as

hough the delight was too great to escape expression by any
ther means. Her blue eyes shone with a wicked gleam.
"It's happened at last!" she said. "It's happened at last!
've been waiting for it . . . all these years."

"And what did you tell them?" asked Lily.

"Tell them! Tell them!" cried Julia Shane. "What
ould I tell them? Only that I could do nothing. I told
hem they were dealing with an honest man. It is impossible
o corrupt Hattie's husband. I could do nothing if I would,
nd certainly I would do nothing if I could. They'll have to
ay . . . just when they're in the midst of building new fur-
aces." Suddenly her face grew serious and the triumph died
ut of her voice. "But I'm sorry for Charlie and Hattie, just
he same. He'll suffer for it. He has killed himself politically.
The Jew is too powerful for him. It'll be hard on Hattie and
he children, just when Ellen was planning to go away to study.
Judge Weissman will fight him from now on. You've no
dea how angry he was. He tried to bellow at me, but I soon
topped him."

And the old woman laughed again at the memory of her
riumph.

As for Lily her handsome face grew rosy with indignation.
"It can't be as bad as that! That can't happen to a man be-
ause he did his duty! The Town can't be as rotten as that!"

"It is though," said her mother. "It is. You've no idea
ow rotten it is. Why, Cousin Charlie is a lamb among the
volves. Believe me, I know. It's worse than when your
ather was alive. The mills have made it worse."

Then both of them fell silent and the terrible roar of the
Cyclops Mills, triumphant and monstrous, invaded the room
nce more. Irene came in from a tour of the Flats and look-
ng in at the door noticed that they were occupied with their
wn thoughts, and so hurried on to her room. At last Mrs.
Shane rose.

"We must help the Tollivers somehow," she said. "If only
hey weren't so damned proud it would be easier."

Lily, her eyes dark and serious, stood at the window now
ooking across the garden buried beneath blackened snow. "I
know," she said. "I was thinking the same thing."

XIX

FOR thirty years Christmas dinner had been an even at Shane's Castle. John Shane, who had no famil of his own, who was cut off from friends and relatives adopted in the seventies the family of his wife, and es tablished the custom of inviting every relative and connectio to a great feast with wine, a turkey, a goose and a pair of roas pigs. In the old days before the MacDougal Farm wa swallowed up by the growing town, New Year's dinner at th farmhouse had also been an event. The family came in sled and sleighs from all parts of the county to gather round th groaning table of Jacob Barr, Julia Shane's brother-in-law an the companion of John Shane in the paddock now covered b warehouses. But all that was a part of the past. Even th farmhouse no longer existed. Christmas at Cypress Hill wa all that remained.

Once there had been as many as thirty gathered about th table, but one by one these had vanished, passing out of thi life or migrating to the West when the Mills came and th county grew crowded; for the MacDougals, the Barrs and al their connection were adventurers, true pioneers who becam wretched when they were no longer surrounded by a sense o space, by enough air, unclogged by soot and coal gas, for thei children to breathe.

On Christmas day there came to Cypress Hill a little rem nant of seven. These with Julia Shane and her two daughter were all that remained of a family whose founder had crosse the Appalachians from Maryland to convert the wildernes into fertile farming land. They arrived at the portico wit the wrought iron columns in two groups, the first of whic was known as The Tolliver Family. It included Cousi Hattie, her husband Charles Tolliver, their daughter Ellen two sons Fergus and Robert, and Jacob Barr, who made hi

64

come with them and shared with Julia Shane the position of Head of the Family.

They drove up in a sleigh drawn by two horses—good horses, for Jacob Barr and Charles Tolliver were judges of horseflesh—and Mrs. Tolliver got down first, a massive woman, large without being fat, with a rosy complexion and a manner of authority. She wore a black feather boa, a hat rimmed with stubby ostrich plumes perched high on her fine black hair, and a short jacket of astrakhan, slightly *démodé* owing to its leg-of-mutton sleeves. After her descended her father, the patriarch Jacob Barr. The carriage rocked beneath his bulk. He stood six feet three in his stocking feet and for all his eighty-two years was bright as a dollar and straight as a poker. A long white beard covered his neckerchief and fell to the third button of his embroidered waistcoat, entangling itself in the heavy watch chain from which hung suspended a nugget of gold, souvenir of his adventure to the Gold Coast in the Forties. He carried a heavy stick of cherry wood and limped, having broken his hip and recovered from it at the age of eighty.

Next Ellen got down, her dark curls transformed into a pompadour as her mother's concession to a recent eighteenth birthday. She was tall, slim, and handsome despite the awkwardness of the girl not yet turned woman. Her eyes were large and blue and her hands long and beautiful. She had the family nose, prominent and proudly curved, which in Julia Shane had become an eagle's beak. After her, Fergus, a tall, shy boy of fourteen, and Robert, two years younger, sullen, wilful, red-haired like his venerable grandfather, who in youth was known in the county as The Red Scot. The boys were squabbling and had to be put in order by their mother before entering Cousin Julia's handsome house. Under her watchful eye there was a prolonged scraping of shoes on the doormat. She managed her family with the air of a field-marshal.

As for Charles Tolliver, he turned over the steaming horses to Hennery, bade the black man blanket them well, talked with him for a moment, and then followed the others into the house. Him Hennery adored, with the adoration of a

servant for one who understands servants. In the stable
Hennery put extra zeal into the rubbing down of the animal
his mind carrying all the while the picture of a tall gentle
man with graying hair, kindly eyes and a pleasant soft voice.

"Mr. Tolliver," he told the mulatto woman later in th
day, "is one of God's gentlemen."

The other group was known as The Barr Family. The
passing of years had thinned its ranks until there remained
only Eva Barr, the daughter of Samuel Barr and therefor
a niece of the vigorous and patriarchal Jacob. Characteris
tically she made her entrance in a town hack, stopping t
haggle with the driver over the fare. Her thin, spinsteris
voice rose above the roaring of the Mills until at length
she lost the argument, as she always did, and paid reluctantl
the prodigious twenty-five cents. She might easily have com
by way of the Halsted street trolley for five cents, but thi
she considered neither safe nor dignified. As she grew olde
and more eccentric, she had come to exercise extraordinary pre
cautions to safeguard her virginity. She was tall, thin, an
dry, with a long nose slightly red at the end, and hair tha
hung in melancholy little wisps about an equine face; yet sh
had a double lock put on the door of her room at Haines
boarding house, and nothing would have induced her to ventur
alone into the squalid Flats. She was poor and very pious. Int
her care fell the destitute of her parish. She administered
scrupulously with the hard efficiency of a penurious house
keeper.

Dinner began at two and assumed the ceremonial dignity
of a tribal rite. It lasted until the winter twilight, descend
ing prematurely because of the smoke from the Mills, made i
necessary for the mulatto woman and her black helpers t
bring in the silver candlesticks, place them amid the wreck
age of the great feast, and light them to illumine the paneled
walls of the somber dining-room. When the raisins and nut
and the coffee in little gilt cups had gone the rounds, the
room resounded with the scraping of chairs, and the littl
party wandered out to distribute itself at will through the bi
house. Every year the distribution followed the same plan
In one corner of the big drawing-room Irene, in her plai

gray dress, and Eva Barr, angular and piercing in durable and shiny black serge, foregathered, drawn by their mutual though very different interest in the poor. Each year the two spinsters fell upon the same arguments; for they disagreed about most fundamental things. The attitude of Irene toward the poor was the Roman attitude, full of paternalism, beneficent, pitying. Eva Barr in her Puritan heart had no room for such sentimental slop. "The poor," she said, "must be taught to pull themselves out of the rut. It's sinful to do too much for them."

Two members of the family, the oldest, Jacob Barr, and the youngest, his grandson, disappeared completely, the one to make his round of the stables and park, the other to vanish into the library where, unawed by the sinister portrait of old John Shane, he poked about, stuffing himself with the candy sent by Willie Harrison as a token of a thrice renewed courtship. The grandfather, smoking what he quaintly called a cheroot, surveyed scrupulously the stable and the house, noting those portions which were falling into disrepair. These he later brought to the attention of Julia Shane; and the old woman, leaning on her stick, listened with an air of profound attention to her brother-in-law only to forget everything he had advised the moment the door closed upon him. Each year it was the same. Nothing changed.

In the far end of the drawing-room by the grand piano, Lily drew Ellen Tolliver and the tall shy brother Fergus to her side. Here Mrs. Tolliver joined them, her eyes bright with flooding admiration for her children. The girl was plainly fascinated by her glamorous cousin. She examined boldly Lily's black gown from Worth, her pearls, and her shoes from the Rue de la Paix. She begged for accounts of the Opéra in Paris and of Paderewski's playing with the Colonne Orchestra. There was something pitiful in her eagerness for some contact with the glamorous world beyond the Town.

"I'm going to New York to study, next year," she told Lily. "I would go this year but Momma says I'm too young. Of course, I'm not. If I had money, I'd go anyway." And she cast a sudden defiant glance at her powerful mother.

Lily, her face suddenly grave with the knowledge of Judg
Weissman's visit, tried to reassure her. "You'll have plent
of opportunity, Ellen. You're still a young girl . . . onl
eighteen."

"But there's never any money," the girl replied, with a
angry gleam in her wide blue eyes. "Papa's always in debt
I'll never get a chance unless I make it myself."

In the little alcove by the gallery, Julia Shane leaning o
her stick, talked business with Charles Tolliver. This to
was a yearly custom; her nephew, the county treasurer, gav
her bits of advice on investments which she wrote down wit
a silver pencil and destroyed when he had gone. She listene
and begged his advice because the giving of it encouraged hir
and gave him confidence. He was a gentle, honest fellow, an
in her cold way she loved him, better even than she loved h
wife who was her niece by blood. The advice he gave wa
mediocre and uninspired; besides Julia Shane was a shrew
woman and more than a match in business matters for mos
men.

When they had finished this little ceremony, the old woma
turned the conversation to the Cyclops Mill scandal.

"And what's to come of it?" she asked. "Are you going t
win?"

Charles Tolliver smiled. "We've won already. The cas
was settled yesterday. The Mill owes the state some fiv
hundred thousand with fines."

Julia Shane again pounded the floor in delight. "A fin
Christmas present!" she chuckled. "A fine Christma
present!" And then she did an unaccountable thing. With he
thin ringed hand she slapped her nephew on the back.

"You know they came to me," she said, "to get my in
fluence. I told them to go to the Devil! . . . I suppose the
tried to bribe you."

The nephew frowned and the gentleness went out of hi
face. The fine mouth grew stern. "They tried . . . care
fully though, so carefully they couldn't be caught at it."

"It will make you trouble. Judge Weissman is a bad
enemy. He's powerful."

"I know that. I've got to fight him. The farmers are with me."

"But the Town is not, and it's the Town which counts nowadays. The day of the farmer is past."

"No, the Town is not."

The face of Charles Tolliver grew serious and the blue eyes grave and worried. Julia Shane saw that he was watching his tall daughter who sat now at the piano, preparing to play.

"If you need money at the next election," she said, "Come to me. I can help you."

XX

AT the sound of Ellen's music, the conversation in the
long drawing-room ceased save for the two women
who sat the far corner—Irene and Eva Barr. They
went on talking in an undertone of their work among
the poor. The others listened, captivated by the sound, for
Ellen played well, far better than any of the little group save
Lily and Julia Shane knew. To the others it was simply music; to the old woman and her daughter it was something more.
They found in it the fire of genius, the smoldering warmth of a
true artist, a quality unreal and transcendental which raised the
beautiful old room for a moment out of the monotonous slough
of commonplace existence. Ellen, in high-collared shirtwaist and skirt with her dark hair piled high in a ridiculous
pompadour, sat very straight bending over the keys from
time to time in a caressing fashion. She played first of all
a Brahms waltz, a delicate thread of peasant melody raised
to the lofty realm of immortality by genius; and from this
she swept into a Chopin valse, melancholy but somehow brilliant, and then into a polonaise, so dashing and so thunderous
that even Irene and Eva Barr, ignorant of all the beauty of
sound that tumbled flood-like into the old room, suspended
their peevish talk for a time and sat quite still, caught somehow in the contagious awe of the others.

The thin girl at the piano was not in a drawing-room at
all. She sat in some enormous concert hall on a high stage
before thousands of people. The faces stretched out before
her, row after row, until those who sat far back were misty
and blurred, not to be distinguished. When she had finished
the polonaise she sat quietly for a moment as though waiting
for a storm of applause to arise after a little hush from the
great audience. There was a moment of silence and then the
voice of Lily was heard, warm and soft, almost caressing

70

"It was beautiful, Ellen . . . really beautiful. I had no idea you played so well."

The girl, blushing, turned and smiled at the cousin who lay back so indolently among the cushions of the sofa, so beautiful, so charming in the black gown from Worth. The smile conveyed a world of shy and inarticulate gratitude. The girl was happy because she understood that Lily knew. To the others it was just music.

"Your daughter is an artist, Hattie," remarked Julia Shane. "You should be proud of her."

The mother, her stout figure tightly laced, sat very straight in her stiff chair, her work-stained hands resting awkwardly in her lap. Her face beamed with the pride of a woman who was completely primitive, for whom nothing in this world existed save her children.

"And now, Ellen," she said, "play the McKinley Funeral March. You play it so well."

The girl's young face clouded suddenly. "But it's not McKinley's Funeral March, Mama," she protested. "It's Chopin's. It's not the same thing."

"Well, you know what I mean . . . the one you played at the Memorial Service for McKinley." She turned to Lily, her pride written in every line of her strong face. "You know, Ellen was chosen to play at the services for McKinley. Mark Hanna himself made a speech from the same platform."

XXI

AN irrepressible smile swept Lily's face. "They couldn't have chosen better, I'm sure. Do play it, Ellen."

The girl turned to the piano and a respectful silence fell once more. Slowly she swept into the somber rhythms of the *March Funèbre,* beginning so softly that the music was scarcely audible, climbing steadily toward a climax. From the depths of the old Pleyel she brought such music as is seldom heard. The faces in the drawing-room became grave and thoughtful. Lying among the pillows of the divan, Lily closed her eyes and listened through a wall of darkness. Nearby, her mother, leaning on the ebony stick, bowed her head because her eyes had grown dim with tears, a spectacle which she never permitted this world to witness. Presently the music swung again into a somber retarding rhythm; and then slowly, surely, with a weird, unearthly certainty, it became synchronized with the throbbing of the Mills. The steady beat was identical. Old Julia Shane opened her eyes and stared out of the window into the gathering darkness. The music, all at once, made the pounding of the Mills hideously audible.

When the last note echoing through the old house died away, Eva Barr, fidgeting with her embroidered reticule in search of a handkerchief to wipe her lean red nose, rose and said, "Well, I must go. It's late and the hack is already here. He charges extra for waiting, you know."

That was the inevitable sign. The dinner was ended. Grandpa Barr, very rosy from his promenade about the grounds, and the red-haired Robert, much stuffed with Willie Harrison's courting chocolates, reappeared and the round of farewells was begun.

Before Hennery brought round from the stable the Tolliver's sleigh, Lily placing her arm about Ellen's waist, drew her aside and praised her playing. "You must not throw it away," she said. "It is too great a gift." She whispered. Her manner became that of a conspirator. "Don't let them make you settle into the pattern of the Town. It's what they'll try to do, but don't let them. We only live once, Ellen, don't waste your life. The others . . . the ones who aren't remarkable in any way will try to pull you down from your pedestal to their level. But don't let them. Fitting the pattern is the end of their existence. 'Be like every one else,' is their motto. Don't give in. And when the time comes, if you want to come and study in Paris with the great Philippe, you can live with me."

The girl blushed and regarded the floor silently for a moment. "I won't let them," she managed to say presently. "Thank you, Cousin Lily." At the door, she turned sharply, all her shyness suddenly vanished, an air of defiance in its place. "I won't let them. . . . You needn't worry," she added with a sudden fierceness.

"And next week," said Lily, "come here and spend the night. I want to hear more music. There's no music in this Town but the Mills."

By the fireplace under the flaming Venice of Mr. Turner, Julia Shane talked earnestly with her niece, Mrs. Tolliver, who stood warming her short astrakhan jacket by the gentle blaze.

"And one more thing, Hattie," said the old woman. "I've been planning to give you these for some time but the opportunity never arose. I shan't live many more years and I want you to have them."

With an air of secrecy she took from her thin fingers two rings and slipped them into the red, worn hands of her niece. "Don't tell any one," she added. "It's a matter between us."

Mrs. Tolliver's hand closed on the rings. She could say nothing, but she kissed Aunt Julia affectionately and the tears came into her eyes because the old woman understood so well the intricate conventions of pride in matters of money. The

rings were worth thousands. Hattie Tolliver could not have
accepted their value in money.

At the door the little party made its departure with a great
deal of healthy hubbub, colliding at the same time with a
visitor who had driven up unseen. It was Willie Harrison,
come to call upon Lily and to propose a visit to the Mills
to look over the new furnaces that were building. In the
stream of light from the doorway the caller and Charles Tolliver recognized each other and an awkward moment followed.
It was Willie Harrison, overcome with confusion, who bowed
politely. Charles Tolliver climbed into his sleigh without
making any sign of recognition. The feud between the old
and the new, concealed for so many years, was emerging slowly
into the open.

XXII

THE day after Christmas dawned bright and clear, as clear as any day dawned in the Flats where at sunrise the smoke turned the sun into a great copper disk rising indolently toward the zenith of the heavens. The false warmth of the January thaw, precocious that year, brought gentle zephyrs that turned the icicles on the sweeping eaves of the house into streams of water which added their force to the rivulets already coursing down the long drive to leave the gravel bare and eroded, swelling with the upheaval of the escaping frost. But the false warmth brought no beauty; no trees burgeoned forth in clouds of bright green and no crocuses thrust forth their thin green swords and errant blossoms. The January thaw was but a false hope of the northern winter. When the sun of the early afternoon had destroyed all traces of the snow save drifts which hid beneath the rhododendrons or close against the north wall of the stable, it left behind an expanse of black and dessicated lawn, in spots quite bare even of dying grass. The garden stripped of its winter blanket at last stood revealed, a ravaged fragment of what had once been a glory.

Lily, drawn from the house by the warmth of the sun, wandered along the barren paths like a lovely hamadyrad enticed by deceitful Gods from her winter refuge. She ran from clump to clump of shrubbery, breaking off the tender little twigs in search of the green underbark that was a sign of life. Sometimes she found the green; more often she found only dead, dry wood, bereft of all vitality. In the flower garden she followed the brick path to its beginning in the little arbor covered with wistaria vine. Here too the Mills had taken their toll; the vine was dead save a few thin twining stalks that clung to the arbor. In the border along the walk, she found traces of irises—hardy plants difficult to

kill—an occasional thick green leaf of a companula or a foxglove hiding among the shelter of leaves provided by the
careful Hennery. But there were great gaps of bare earth
where nothing grew, stretches which in her childhood had been
buried beneath a lush and flowery growth of sky-blue
delphinium, scarlet poppies, fiery tritomas, blushing peonies,
foxglove, goosefoot, periwinkle, and cinnamon pinks. . . . All
were gone now, blighted by the capricious and fatal south
wind with its burden of gas and soot. It was not alone the
flowers which suffered. In the niches clipped by Hennery
in the dying walls of arbor vitae, the bits of white statuary
were streaked with black soot, their pure bodies smudged and
defiled. The Apollo Belvedere and the Venus of Cydnos were
no longer recognizable.

In the course of her tour about the little park, her red hair
became loosened and disheveled and her cheeks flushed with
her exertion. When she again reentered the house, she discovered that her slippers, high-heeled and delicate, were ruined.
She called the mulatto woman and bade her throw them away.

On the stairs she encountered her mother, whom she
greeted with a little cry of horror. "The garden, Mama, is
ruined. . . . Nothing remains!"

The expression on the old woman's face remained unchanged
and stony.

"Nothing will grow there any longer," she said. "Besides, it does not matter. When I die, there will be no one
to live in the house. Irene hates it. She wants me to take
a house in the Town."

Lily, her feet clad only in the thinnest of silk-stockings,
continued on her way up the long stairs to her room. If
Willie Harrison had ever had a chance, even the faintest
hope, the January thaw, revealing the stricken garden a fortnight too soon, destroyed it once and for all.

XXIII

AT three that afternoon Willie's victoria called to bear Lily and Irene to the Cyclops Mills for the tour which he proposed. Workmen, passing the carriage, regarded the two sisters with curiosity, frowning at the sight of Irene in a carriage they recognized as Harrison's. A stranger might have believed the pair were a great lady and her housekeeper on the way to market, so different and incongruous were the appearances of the two women. Lily, leaning back against the thick mulberry cushions, sat wrapped in a sable stole. She wore a gray tailored suit and the smallest and smartest of black slippers. Around her white throat, which she wore exposed in defiance of fashions which demanded high, boned collars, she had placed a single string of pearls the size of peas. By the side of her opulent beauty Irene possessed the austerity and plainness of a Gothic saint. As usual she wore a badly cut suit, a plain black hat and flat shoes with large, efficient heels. Her thin hands, clad in knitted woolen gloves, lay listlessly in her lap.

Willie Harrison was waiting for them at the window of the superintendent's office just inside the gate. They saw him standing there as the victoria turned across the cinders in through the red-painted entrance. He stood peering out of the window in a near-sighted way, his shoulders slightly stooped, his small hands fumbling as usual the ruby clasp of his watch chain. At the sight of him Lily frowned and bit her fine red lip as though she felt that a man so rich, a man so powerful, a man who owned all these furnaces and steel sheds should have an air more conquering and impressive.

Irene said, "Oh, there's William waiting for us now." And a second later the victoria halted by the concrete steps and Willie himself came out to greet them, hatless, his thin blond hair waving in a breeze which with the sinking of the sun grew rapidly more chilly. The sun itself, hanging over the roseate tops of the furnaces, had become a shield of deep copper red.

"You're just in time," said Willie. "The shifts will be changing in a little while. Shall we start here? I'll show you the offices."

They went inside and Willie, whose manner had become a little more confident at the prospect of such a display, led them into a long room where men sat in uniform rows on high stools at long tables. Over each table hung suspended a half-dozen electric lights hooded by green shades. The lights, so Willie told them, were placed exactly to the sixteenth of an inch eight feet and three inches apart. It was part of his theory of precision and regularity.

"This," said Willie, with a contracted sweep of his arm, "is the bookkeeping department. The files are kept here, the orders and all the paper work."

At the approach of the visitors, the younger men looked up for an instant fascinated by the presence of so lovely a creature as Lily wandering in to shatter so carelessly the sacred routine of their day. There were men of every age and description, old and young, vigorous and exhausted, men in every stage of service to the ponderous mill gods. The younger ones had a restless air and constantly stole glances in the direction of the visitors. The middle-aged ones looked once or twice at Lily and then returned drearily to their columns of figures. The older ones did not notice her at all. They had gone down for the last time in a sea of grinding routine.

Irene, who knew the Town better than Lily, pointed out among the near-sighted, narrow-chested workers men who were grandsons or great-grandsons of original settlers in the county, descendants of the very men who had cleared away the wilderness to make room for banks and lawyers and mills.

"Let's go on," said Lily, "to the Mills. They're more interesting than this, I'm sure. You know I've never been inside a mill-yard." She spoke almost scornfully, as if she thought the counting room were a poor show indeed. A shadow of disappointment crossed Willie's sallow face.

After donning a broadcloth coat with an astrakhan collar and a derby hat, he led the way. For a long time they walked among freight cars labeled with names from every part of North America. . . . Santa Fé, Southern Pacific, Great Northern, Chicago, Milwaukee and St. Paul. . . . They passed between great warehouses and vast piles of rusty pig iron still covered with frost, the dirty snow lying unmelted in the crevasses; and at last they came to an open space where rose a vast, shapeless object in the process of being raised toward the sky.

"Here," said Willie, "are the new furnaces. There are to be six of them. This is the first."

"I like this better," said Lily. "There is spirit here . . . even among the laborers."

The structure bore a strange resemblance to the Tower of Babel. Swarthy workmen, swarming over the mass of concrete and steel, shouted to each other above the din of the Mills in barbaric tongues which carried no meaning to the visitors. Workmen, like ants, pushed wheelbarrows filled with concrete, with fire clay or fire bricks. Overhead a giant crane lifted steel girders with an effortless stride and swung them into place. The figures of the workmen swept toward the tower in a constant stream of movement so that the whole took on a fantastic composition, as if the tower, rushing on its way heavenward, were growing taller and taller before their very eyes, as if before they moved away it might pierce the very clouds.

At the sight of Willie Harrison, the foremen grew more officious in manner and shouted their orders with redoubled vigor, as if the strength of their lungs contributed something toward the speed with which the great tower grew. But the workmen moved no more rapidly. On returning to the mounds of sand and fire brick, they even stopped altogether at times to stare calmly like curious animals at the visitors. One or two nodded in recognition of Irene's "Good-day, Joe," or "How are you, Boris?"—words which appeared to cloud somewhat Willie's proud enjoyment of the spectacle. And every man who passed stared long and hard at Lily, standing wrapped in her furs, a little aloof, her eyes bright neverthe-

less with the wonder of the sight. Neither Lily nor Irene
nor Willie spoke more than was necessary, for in order to be
heard above the din they were forced to scream.

From the growing tower the little party turned west toward
the sunset, walking slowly over a rough roadway made of
cinders and slag. Once a cinder penetrated Lily's frail shoe
and she was forced to lean against Willie while she took it
off and removed the offending particle. He supported her
politely and turned away his face so that he should not offend
her by seeing her shapely stockinged foot.

A hundred yards further on they came upon a dozen
great vats covered by a single roof of sheet iron. From the
vats rose a faint mist, veiling the black bodies of negroes
who, shouting as they worked, dipped great plates of steel in
and out. An acrid smell filled the air and penetrated the
throats of the visitors as they passed rapidly by, causing Lily to
take from her hand bag a handkerchief of the thinnest linen
which she held against her nose until they were once more
beyond the zone of the fumes.

"Those are the tempering vats," said Willie. "Only
negroes work here."

"But why?" asked Irene.

"Because the other workers won't," he said. "The acid
eats into their lungs. The negroes come from South Carolina
and Georgia to do it. They are willing!"

As they walked the sound of pounding, which appeared to
come from the great iron shed lying before them black
against the sunset, grew louder and louder, steadily more dis
tinct. In the fading twilight that now surrounded them the
Mill yard became a fantastic world inhabited by monsters of
iron and steel. Great cranes swung to and fro against the glow
of the sky, lifting and tossing into piles huge plates of steel that
fell with an unearthly slithering din when an invisible hand
concealed somewhere high among the black vertebræ of the
monsters, released a lever. High in the air lights, red and
green, or cold piercing blue-white, like eyes appeared one by
one peering down at them wickedly. Beyond the cranes
in the adjoining yard the black furnaces raised gigantic
towers crowned by halos of red flame that rose and fell, pal

pitating as the molten iron deep in the bowels of the towers churned and boiled with a white infernal heat. Dancing malignant shadows assailed them on every side.

The three visitors, dwarfed by the monsters of steel, made their way across the slag and cinders, deafened by the unearthly noise.

"Yesterday," shouted William Harrison in his thin voice, "there was a terrible accident yonder in the other yard. A workman fell into a vat of molten iron."

Irene turned to her companion with horror stricken eyes. "I know," she said. "It was an Italian named Rizzo. I heard of it this morning. I have been to see his wife and family. There are nine of them."

William shouted again. "They found nothing of him. He became a part of the iron. He is part of a steel girder by now."

Out of the evil, dancing shadows a man blackened by smoke leapt suddenly at them. "Look out!" he cried, and thrust them against the wall of a neighboring shed so roughly that Irene fell forward upon her knees. A great bundle of steel plates—tons of them—swung viciously out of the darkness, so close to the little party that the warmth of the metal touched their faces. It vanished instantly, drawn high into the air by some invisible hand. It was as if the monster had rebelled suddenly against its master, as if it sought to destroy Willie Harrison as it had destroyed the Italian named Rizzo.

Willie lost all power of speech, all thought of action. Irene, her face deathly white, leaned against the wall calling upon Lily to support her. It was Lily, strangely enough, who alone managed to control herself. She displayed no fear. On the contrary she was quiet, fiercely quiet as if a deadly anger had taken complete possession of her soul.

"Great God!" she exclaimed passionately. "This is a nightmare!" Willie fumbled helplessly by her side, rubbing the wrists of the younger sister until she raised her head and reassured them.

"I'm all right," said Irene. "We can go on now."

But Lily was for taking her home. "You've seen enough. I'm not going to have you faint on my hands."

"I'm all right . . . really," repeated Irene, weakly. "I want to see the rest. I must see it. It's necessary. It is part of my duty."

"Don't be a fool! Don't try to make a martyr of yourself!"

But Irene insisted and Lily, who was neither frightened nor exhausted, yielded at last, weakened by her own curiosity. At the same moment her anger vanished; she became completely amiable once more.

Willie led them across another open space shut in on the far side by the great shed which had loomed before them throughout the tour. They passed through a low, narrow door and stood all at once in an enormous cavern glowing with red flames that poured from the mouths of a score of enormous ovens. From overhead, among the tangle of cranes and steel work, showers of brilliant cold light descended from hooded globes. The cavern echoed and reechoed with the sound of a vast hammering, irregular and confused—the very hammering which heard in the House at Cypress Hill took on a throbbing, strongly-marked rhythm. On the floor of the cavern, dwarfed by its very immensity, men stripped to the waist, smooth, hard, glistening and streaked with sweat and smoke, toiled in the red glow from the ovens.

XXIV

BEFORE one of these the little party halted while Lily, and Irene, who seemed recovered though still deathly pale, listened while Willie described the operation. Into a great box of steel and fire clay were placed block after block of black iron until the box, filled at length, was pushed forward, rolling easily on balls of iron, into the fiery mouth of the oven. After a little time, the box was drawn out again and the blocks of whitehot iron were carried aloft and deposited far off, beside the great machines which rolled and hammered them into smooth steel plates.

While they stood there, workmen of every size and build, of a dozen nationalities, toiled on ignoring them. Lily, it appeared, was not deeply interested in the explanation, for she stood a little apart, her gaze wandering over the interior of the tavern. The adventure—even the breathless escape of a moment before—left her calm and indifferent. In her gaze there was a characteristic indolence, an air of absent-mindedness, which frequently seized her in moments of this sort. Nothing of her apparel was disarranged. Her hat, her furs, her pearls, her suit, were in perfect order. The flying dust and soot had gathered in her long eyelashes, but this only gave her a slightly theatrical appearance; it darkened the lashes and made her violet eyes sparkle the more. Her gaze appraised the bodies of the workmen who stood idle for the moment waiting to withdraw the hot iron from the ovens. They leaned upon the tools of their toil, some on shovels, some on long bars of iron, great chests heaving with the effort of their exertions.

Among them there was one who stood taller than the others, a giant with yellow hair and a massive face with features which were like the features of a heroic bust not yet completed by the sculptor. There was in them something of

the unformed quality of youth.   The man was young; he coul
not have been much over twenty, and the muscles of his arr
and back stood out beneath his fair skin like the muscles o
one of Rodin's bronze men in the Paris salons.   Once h
raised a great hand to wipe the sweat from his face and, dis
covering that she was interested in him, he looked at he
sharply for an instant and then sullenly turned away lean
ing on a bar of iron with his powerful back turned to her.

She was still watching the man when Willie approache
her and touched her arm gently.   It seemed that she wa
unable to look away from the workman.

"Come over here and sit down," said Willie, leading her t
a bench that stood a little distance away in the shadow of th
foreman's shack.   "Irene wants to speak to one of the men."

Lily followed him and sat down.   Her sister, looking pal
and tired, began a conversation with a swarthy little Pol
who stood near the oven.   The man greeted her with a sulle
frown and his remarks, inaudible to Lily above the din, ap
peared to be ill-tempered and sulky as if he were ashamed be
fore his fellows to be seen talking with this lady who cam
to the cavern accompanied by the master.

"Do you find it a wonderful sight?" began Willie.

Lily smiled.   "I've seen nothing like it in all my life.
never knew what lay just beyond the garden hedge."

"It will be bigger than this next year and even bigger th
year after."   His eyes brightened and for a moment the droo
of his shoulders vanished.   "We want some day to see th
Mills covering all the Flats.   The new furnaces are the be
ginning of the expansion.   We hope to grow bigger an
bigger."   He raised his arms in a sudden gesture.   "There'
no limit, you know."

But Lily's gaze was wandering again back and forth, u
and down, round and round the vast cavern as if she were no
the least interested in Willie's excitement over bigness.   Iren
had left the swarthy little man and was talking now to th
tow-headed young giant who leaned upon the iron bar.   Hi
face was sulky, though it was plain that he was curiousl
polite to Irene, who seemed by his side less a woman of fles

and blood than one of paper, so frail and wan was her face.
He smiled sometimes in a shy, withdrawn fashion.

Politely Lily turned to her companion. "But you are
growing richer and richer, Willie. Before long you will
own the Town."

He regarded her shyly, his thin lips twisted into a hope-
ful smile. Once more he began to fumble with the ruby clasp
of his watch chain.

"I could give you everything in the world," he said suddenly, as though the words caused him a great effort. "I
could give you everything if you would marry me." He
paused and bent over Lily who sat silently turning the rings
on her fingers round and round. "Would you, Lily?"

"No." The answer came gently as if she were loath to
hurt him by her refusal, yet it was firm and certain.

Willie bent lower. "I would see that Mother had nothing to do with us." Lily, staring before her, continued to
turn the rings round and round. The young workman with
Irene had folded his muscular arms and placed his iron bar
against the wall of the oven. He stood rocking back and
forth with the easy, balanced grace of great strength. When
he smiled, he showed a fine expanse of firm white teeth. Irene
laughed in her vague half-hearted way. Lily kept watching
. . watching. . . .

"You could even spend half the time in Europe if you
liked," continued Willie. "You could do as you pleased. I
would not interfere." He placed one hand gently on her
shoulder to claim her attention, so plainly wandering toward
the blond and powerful workman. She seemed not even to
be conscious of his hand.

The workmen had begun to move toward the oven now, the
young fellow with the others. He carried his iron bar as if
it were a straw. He moved with a sort of angry defiance, his
head thrown back upon his powerful shoulders. He it was
who shouted the orders when the great coffin full of hot iron was
drawn forth. He it was who thrust his bar beneath the
mass of steel and lifting upward shoved it slowly and easily
forward on the balls of iron. His great back bent and the

muscles rippled beneath the skin as if they too were made o
some marvelous flexible steel.

Willie Harrison took Lily's hand and put an end to th
turning of the rings. "Tell me, Lily," he said softly, "i
it no use? Maybe next year or the year after?"

All at once as though she had heard him for the first time
she turned and placed the other hand gently on top of his
looking up at the same time from beneath the wide brim o
her hat. "It's no use, Willie. I'm sorry. I'm really sorry.'
She laughed softly. "But you were wrong in your method
You shouldn't have given me the promise about Europe
When I marry, it will be a man who will not let me leav
his side."

That was all she said to him. The rest, whatever it was
remained hidden, deep within her, behind the dark eyes which
found so little interest in Willie Harrison, which saw nothing
but the blond giant who moved with such uncanny strength
with such incredibly easy grace about his heroic task. Per
haps if Willie had guessed, even for a moment, what wa
passing in her mind, he would have blushed, for Willie was
so people said, a nice young man who had led a respectabl
life. Such things were no doubt incomprehensible to him
Perhaps if she had spoken the truth, if she had bothered her
self to explain, she would have said, "I could not marry you
I could give myself to no man but one who caught my fancy
in whom there was strength and the grace of a fine anima
Beauty, Willie, counts for much . . . far more than yo
guess, living always as you do in the midst of all this savag
uproar. I am rich. Your money means nothing. And you
power! It is not worth the snap of a finger to me. . . . Ah
if you had a face like that workman . . . a face . . . a rea
face, and a body . . . a real body like his, then you might as
with hope. It is hopeless, Willie. You do not interest me
though I am not eager to hurt you just the same."

But she said none of these things, for people seldom sa
them. On the contrary, she was content to put him off wit
a bare denial. It is doubtful whether such thoughts even oc
curred to her, however deep they may have been rooted in he
soul; for she was certainly not a woman given to reflectior

To any one, it was apparent that she did not examine her motives. She was content, no doubt, to be beautiful, to live where there was beauty, to surround herself with beautiful, luxurious things.

She was prevented from saying anything further by the arrival of Irene who had abandoned her workmen to rejoin Willie and her sister. Willie, crimson and still trembling a little with the effort of his proposal, suggested that they leave. It was already a quarter to six. The workmen vanished suddenly into a little shed. Their shift was finished. They were free now to return to their squalid homes, to visit the corner saloon or the dismal, shuttered brothels of Franklin street, free to go where they would in the desolate area of the Flats for twelve brief hours of life.

XXV

THE three visitors made their way back to the office of the superintendent across a mill yard now bright with the cold glare of a hundred arc lights. On the way, Lily turned suddenly to her sister and asked, "Who was the man you were talking to . . . the tall one with the yellow hair?"

Irene, moving beside her, cast a sudden glance at her sister and the old terrified look entered her pale eyes. "His name is Krylenko," she replied in a voice grown subdued and cold. "He is the one who brought me home from Welcome House the other night. He is a bright boy. I've taught him English."

Willie, who had been walking behind them, quickened his pace and came abreast. "Krylenko?" he said. "Krylenko? Why, that's the fellow who's been making trouble. They've been trying to introduce the union." He addressed Irene. "Your Welcome House is making trouble I'm afraid, Irene. There's no good comes of educating these men. They don't want it."

Lily laughed. "Come now," she said, "that's what your mother says, isn't it? I can hear her saying it."

Willie failed to answer her, but a sheepish, embarrassed look took possession of his sallow face, as if the powerful figure of his mother had joined them unawares. And Irene, walking close to Lily, whispered to her sister, "You shouldn't have said that. It was cruel of you."

At the office of the superintendent they found Willie's victoria waiting, the horses covered with blankets against the swift, piercing chill of the winter night. The coachman shivered on the box. The three of them climbed in and Willie bade the man drive to Halsted street where he would get down, leaving the carriage to the ladies. When Lily protested, he answered, "But I want to walk up the hill to the Town. I need the exercise."

They drove along between two streams of mill workers, one entering, one leaving the Mill yards with the change of shifts. The laborers moved in two columns, automatons without identity save that one column was clean and the men held their heads high and the other was black with oil and soot and the heads were bent with a terrible exhaustion. It was a dark narrow street bordered on one side by the tall blank walls of warehouses and on the other by the Mill yard. The smells of the Black Fork, coated with oil and refuse, corrupted the damp air. On the Mill side a high fence made of barbed wire strung from steel posts was in the process of construction. To this Willie called their attention with pride. "You see," he said, "we are making the Mills impregnable. If the unions come in there will be trouble. It was my idea . . . the fence. A stitch in time saves nine." And he chuckled softly in the darkness.

At Halsted street Willie got down and, removing his hat, bade the sisters a dry and polite good-night. But before the carriage drove on, Lily called out to him, "You're coming to the ball to-night, aren't you? Remember, there's a quadrille and you can't leave us flat at the last minute."

"I'm coming," said William. "Certainly I'm coming." And he turned away, setting off in the opposite direction toward the Hill and Mrs. Julis Harrison who sat in the ugly house of red sandstone awaiting news of the proposal. He walked neatly, placing his small feet firmly, his hands clasped behind his back, his head bowed thoughtfully. The umbrella, held in the crook of his arm, swung mournfully as he walked. His shoulders drooped wearily. He had shown Lily all his wealth, all his power; and she treated it as if it were nothing at all. In the brownstone house, Mrs. Harrison sat waiting.

The carriage drove up Halsted street past the corner saloon now thronged with mill workers, toward the house at Cypress Hill. In a tenement opposite the wrought iron gates a nostalgic Russian sat on the front stoop squeezing mournfully at a concertina which filled the winter evening with the somber music of the steppes.

Irene, leaning back pale and exhausted on the mulberry cushions, said, "Why did you ask Willie whether he was coming? You know he never misses anything if he can help it."

"I only wanted to make him feel welcome," her sister replied absently. "Since this affair over the taxes, Mama and Mrs. Harrison haven't been very thick. . . . I feel sorry for Willie. He doesn't know what it's all about."

XXVI

INSIDE the old house, Irene went to her room, and Lily, instead of seeking out her mother for their usual chat, went quietly upstairs. She ignored even the preparations for the ball. After she had taken off her clothes, she lay for a long time in a hot bath scented with verbena salts, drowsing languidly until the hot water had eliminated every soiling trace of the Mills. Returning to her room, she sat clad in a thin satin wrapper for a long time before the mirror of her dressing table, polishing her pink nails, examining the tiny lines at the corners of her lips,—lines which came from smiling too much. Then she powdered herself all over with scented powder and did up her red hair, fastening it with the pin set in brilliants. And presently, the depression having passed away, she began to sing in her low warm voice, *Je sais que vous êtes gentil.* It was a full-throated joyous song. At times her voice rose in a crescendo that penetrated the walls of the room where Irene lay in the darkness on her narrow white bed.

As she dressed for dinner, she continued to sing one song after another; most of them piquant and racy, songs of the French cuirassiers. She sang *Sur la route á Montauban, Toute la longe de la Tamise* and *Auprés de ma Blonde.* The dressing was the languid performance which required an hour or more, for she took the most minute care with every detail. The chemise must not have a wrinkle; the peacock blue stockings must fit as if they were the skin itself; the corsets were drawn until the result, examined for many minutes before the glass, was absolutely perfect. At the last she put on a gown of peacock blue satin with a long train that swept about her ankles, and rang for one of the black servants to hook it. Before the slavey arrived, Lily had discovered a wrinkle beneath the satin and began all over again the process of dressing, until at the end of the second attempt she stood before the mirror *soignée* and perfect in the soft glow from the open fire by her bed. The tight-fitting gown of peacock blue followed the curves of her figure flawlessly. Then she hung about her fine throat a chain of diamonds set in a necklace of laurel leaves wrought delicately in silver, lighted a cigarette and stood regarding her tall figure by the light of the lamps. Among the old furniture of the dark room she stood superbly dressed, elegant, *mondaine*. A touch to the hair that covered her small head like a burnished helmet, and she smiled with satisfaction, the face in the mirror smiling back with a curious look of elation, of abundant health, of joy; yet there was in it something too of secrecy and triumph.

XXVII

IRENE'S room was less vast and shadowy. In place of
brocade the windows were curtained with white stuff.
In one corner stood a *prie dieu* before a little paint and
plaster image of the Virgin and child—all blue and pink
and gilt,—which Lily had sent her sister from Florence. The
bed was small and narrow and the white table standing near by
was covered with books and papers neatly arranged—the
paraphernalia of Irene's work among the people of the Flats.
Here Lily discovered her when she came in, flushed and
radiant, to sit on the edge of the white bed and talk with her
sister until the guests arrived.

She found Irene at the white table, the neat piles of books
and papers pushed aside to make room for a white tray laden
with food, for Irene was having dinner alone in her room.
There had been no question of her coming to the ball. "I
couldn't bear it," she told her mother. "I would be miserable.
I don't want to come. Why do you want to torture me?"
She had fallen, of late, into using the most exaggerating words,
out of all proportion with truth or dignity. But Julia Shane,
accustomed more and more to yielding to the whims of her
younger daughter, permitted her to remain away.

"Have you anything to read?" began Lily. "Because if you
haven't, my small trunk is full of books."

"I've plenty, and besides, I'm going out."

"Where?" asked Lily, suddenly curious.

"To Welcome House. It's my night to teach. I should
think you would have remembered that." Her voice sounded
weary and strained. She turned to her sister with a look of
disapproval, so intense that it seemed to accuse Lily of some
unspeakable sin.

"I didn't remember," Lily replied. "How should I?" And
then rising she went to her sister's side and put one arm

about her shoulders, a gesture of affection which appeared to inspire a sudden abhorrence in the woman, for she shivered suddenly at the touch of the warm bare arm. "You shouldn't go out to-night. You are too tired!"

"I must go," Irene replied. "They're counting on me."

"What are you eating? . . ." remarked Lily, picking up a bit of cake from the tray, "Peas, potatoes, rice, dessert, milk. . . . Why you've no meat, Irene. You should eat meat. It is what you need more than anything. You're too pale."

Irene's pale brow knitted into a frown. "I've given it up," she said. "I'm not eating meat any longer."

"And why not?" Lily moved away from her and stood looking down with the faintest of mocking smiles. The transparent cheek of her sister flushed slightly.

"Because I don't believe in it. I believe it's wrong."

"Well, I'm going to speak to Mama about it. It's nonsense. You'll kill yourself with such a diet. Really, Irene . . ." Her voice carried a note of irritation, but she got no further for Irene turned on her suddenly, like a beaten dog which after long abuse snaps suddenly at the offending hand.

"Why can't you leave me in peace? You and Mama treat me like a child. I am a grown woman. I want to do as I please. I am harming no one but myself . . . no one . . . I'm sick of it, I tell you. I'm sick of it!"

And suddenly she began to weep, softly and hysterically, her thin shoulders shaking as the sobs tore her body. "I want to go away," she moaned. "I want to be alone, where I can think and pray. I want to be alone!" Her sobbing was at once pitiful and terrible, the dry, parched sobbing of a misery long pent up. For a moment Lily stood helplessly by her side and then, all at once, she went down on her knees in the peacock blue gown and put her lovely bare arms about her sister, striving to comfort her. The effort failed strangely. Irene only drew away and sobbed the more. "If you would only let me have peace . . . I could find it alone!"

Lily said nothing but knelt by her sister's side kissing and caressing the thin white hands until Irene's sobbing subsided a little and she fell forward among the books and papers, burying her head in her arms. The misery of the soul and spirit in some way appalled Lily. She watched her sister with a look of bewilderment in her eyes as if she had discovered all at once a world of which she had been ignorant up to now. The spectacle stifled quickly the high spirits of a moment before. The bawdy French ballads were forgotten. She had become suddenly grave and serious, the lines in her beautiful face grown hard. She was sitting on the floor, her head in Irene's lap, when a knock and the sound of her name roused her.

"Miss Lily," came the mulatto woman's voice, "Mis' Shane says the guests are a-coming and you must come down."

"All right Sarah. . . . I'll be down at once."

Lily, struggling with the tight satin dress, rose slowly, kissed her sister and said, "Please, dear, stay home to-night and rest."

But Irene, still sobbing softly as if entranced by the sensual satisfaction of weeping, did not answer her. She remained leaning over the table, her face buried in her arms. But she was more quiet now, with the voluptuous stillness of one who has passed through a great emotional outburst.

Lily, once more before the mirror in her own room, re-arranged her ruffled hair listening to the murmur of talk that arose from the well of the stairs. It was not until she had fastened the pin set with brilliants for a second time that she discovered with sudden horror that the peacock blue gown was split and ripped at one side from the arm to the waist. In the sudden outburst of affection for her sister, she had flung herself to her knees abandoning all thought of vanity. The gown was ruined.

From below stairs the murmur grew in volume as carriage after carriage arrived. Lily swore beneath her breath in French, tore off the gown and brought from her closet another of a pale yellow-green, the color of chartreuse. The process of dressing began all over again and in half an hour, after the mulatto woman had called twice and been sent away and the guests had gone in to dinner, Lily stood once more before the mirror, radiant and beautiful. The gown was cut lower than

the one she had tossed aside, and the yellow-green blended
with the tawny red of her hair so that there was something
nude and voluptuous in her appearance. The smile returned
to her face, a smile which seemed to say, "The Town will see
something the like of which it has never seen before."

Before going down she went to Irene's room once more,
only to find it dark and empty. Clad in the gray suit and the
plain black hat Irene had made her way silently to the stairs
at the back of the house and thence through the gallery that
led past the drawing-room windows into the dead park. The
austere and empty chamber appeared to rouse a sudden shame
in Lily, for she returned to her room before descending the
long stairs and took from the trunk a great fan of black
ostrich feathers to shield her bare breasts alike from the stares
of the impudent and the disapproving.

The ball was a great success. The orchestra, placed in the
little alcove by the gallery, played a quadrille followed by
waltzes, two-steps and polkas. Until ten o'clock the carriages
made their way along Halsted street past the Mills and the
squalid houses through the wrought iron gates into the park;
and at midnight they began to roll away again carrying the
guests to their homes. Lily, all graciousness and charm, moved
among the dancers distributing her favors equitably save in the
single instance of Willie Harrison, who looked so downcast
and prematurely old in his black evening clothes that she
danced with him three times and sat out a waltz and a polka.
And all the Town, ignorant of the truth, whispered that
Willie's chances once more appeared good.

Ellen Tolliver was there, in a dress made at home by her
mother, and she spent much of the evening by the side of
her aunt Julia who sat in black jet and amethysts at one end
of the drawing-room leaning on her stick and looking for
all the world like a wicked duchess. At the sound of the
music and the sight of the dancers, the old gleam returned
for a little time to her tired eyes.

Ellen was younger than the other guests and knew most of
them only by sight but she had partners none the less, for she
was handsome despite her badly made gown and her absurd
pompadour, and she danced with a barbaric and energetic grace.

When she was not dancing her demeanor carried no trace of the drooping wall-flower. She regarded the dancers with a expression of defiance and scorn. None could have taken her for a poor relation.

XXVIII

A LITTLE while before midnight Irene, accompanied by Krylenko, returned from the Flats and hurried quietly as a moth through the gallery past the brightly lighted windows and up the stairway to her room. The mill worker left her at the turn of the drive where he stood for a time in the melting snow fascinated by the sound of music and the sight of the dancers through the tall windows. Among them he caught a sudden glimpse of Irene's sister, the woman who had watched him at work in the mill shed. She danced a waltz with the master of the Mills, laughing as she whirled round and round with a wild exuberance. Amid the others who took their pleasures so seriously, she was a bacchante, pagan, utterly abandoned. The black fan hung from her wrist and the pale yellow-green ball gown left all her breast and throat exposed in a voluptuous glow of beauty. Long after the music stopped and she had disappeared, Krylenko stood in the wet snowbank staring blindly at the window which she had passed again and again. He stood as if hypnotized, as if incapable of action. At length a coachman, passing by, halted for a moment to regard him in astonishment, and so roused him into action. Murmuring something in Russian, he set off down the long drive walking well to one side to keep from under the wheels of the fine carriages which had begun to leave.

The last carriage, containing Willie Harrison and two female cousins, passed through the wrought iron gates a little after one o'clock, leaving Lily, her mother and Ellen Tolliver who, having no carriage of her own, had chosen this night to spend at Cypress Hill, alone amid the wreckage of crumpled flowers and forgotten cotillion favors. With the departure of the last carriage and the finish of the music, the gleam died out of Julia Shane's eyes. She became again an old woman with a tired bent figure, her sharp eyes half closed by dark swellings which seemed to have appeared all at once with the death of the last chord.

"I'm going to bed," she said, bidding the others good-night. "We can discuss the party in the morning."

She tottered up the stairs leaving her daughter and grand-niece together in the long drawing-room. When she had gone, Lily rose and put out the lamps and candles one by one until only three candles in a sconce above the piano remained lighted.

"Now," she said, lying back among the cushions of the divan and stretching her long handsome legs, "play for me . . . some Brahms, some Chopin."

The girl must have been weary but the request aroused all her extraordinary young strength. She sat at the piano silhouetted against the candle light . . . the curve of her absurd pompadour, the more ridiculous curve of her corseted figure. From the divan Lily watched her through half-closed eyes. She played first of all two études of Chopin and then a waltz or two of Brahms, superbly and with a fine freedom and spectacular fire, as if she realized that at last she had the audience she desired, a better audience than she would ever have again no matter how celebrated she might become. Above the throbbing of the Mills the thread of music rose triumphant in a sort of eternal beauty, now delicate, restrained, now rising in a tremendous, passionate crescendo. The girl invested it with all the yearnings that are beyond expression, the youth, the passionate resentment and scorn, the blind gropings which swept her baffled young soul. Through the magic of the sound she managed to convey to the woman lying half-buried among the cushions those things which it would have been impossible for her to utter, so high and impregnable was the wall of her shyness and pride. And Lily, watching her, wept silently at the eloquence of the music.

Not once was there a spoken word between them, and at last the girl swung softly and mournfully into the macabre beauties of the Valse Triste, strange and mournful music, not great, even a little mediocre, yet superbly beautiful beneath her slim fingers. She peopled the shadowy room with ghostly unreal figures, of tragedy, of romance, of burning, unimagined desires. The dancing shadows cast by the candles among the old furniture became through the mist of Lily's tears fantastic, yet familiar, like memories half-revealed that fade before they can be captured and recognized. The waltz rose in a weird unearthly ecstasy, swirling and exultant, the zenith of a joy and a completion yearned for but never in this life achieved . . . the something which lies just beyond the reach, sensed but unattainable, something which Ellen sought and came nearest to capturing in her music, which Irene, kneeling on the *prie dieu* before the Sienna Virgin, sought in a mystic exaltation, which Lily sought in her own instinctive, half-realized fashion. It was a quest which must always be a lonely one; somehow the music made the sense of loneliness terribly acute. The waltz grew slower once more and softer, taking on a new and melancholy fire, until at last it died away into stillness leaving only the sound of the Mills to disturb the silence of the old room.

After a little pause, Ellen fell forward wearily upon the piano, her head resting upon her arms, and all at once with a faint rustle she slipped gently to the floor, the home-made ball dress crumpled and soiled beneath her slim body. Lily sprang from among the pillows and gathered the girl against her white, voluptuous breasts, for she had fainted.

XXIX

THE visit of Ellen was extended from one night to three. The piano was a beautiful one, far better than the harsh-toned upright in the Tolliver parlor in the Town, and Ellen gladly played for hours with only Lily, lying among the cushions, and old Julia Shane, lost in her own fantastic memories, for an audience.

On the third night, long after twelve o'clock, as Lily and her cousin climbed the long stairway, the older woman said, "I have some clothes, Ellen, that you may have if you like. They have been worn only a few times and they are more beautiful than anything you can find in America."

The girl did not answer until they had reached Lily's room and closed the door behind them. Her face was flushed with the silent struggle between a hunger for beautiful things and a fantastic pride, born of respectable poverty. In some way, her cousin sensed the struggle.

"They are yours if you want them," she said. "You can try them on if you like at any rate."

Ellen smiled gratefully. "I'd like to," she said timidly. "Thank you."

While the girl took off her shirtwaist and skirt, Lily busied herself among the shadows of her closet. When she returned she bore across her arms three gowns, one dull red, one black and one yellow. The girl stood waiting shyly, clad only in her cheap underclothing coarsened and yellowed by many launderings.

"You must take those things off," said Lily. "I'll give you others." And she brought out undergarments of white silk which Ellen put on, shivering a little in the chill of the big room.

Then Lily took the pale yellow gown and slipped it over her cousin's head. It belonged to no period of fashion. It hung from the shoulders in loose folds of shining silk, clinging close to the girl's slim body. There was a silver girdle which fastened over the hips. Ellen turned to regard herself in the mirror.

"But wait," said Lily, laughing, "you've only begun. We've got to change your hair and do away with that ridiculous rat. Why do you spoil such beautiful hair with a wad of old wire?"

She took out the pins and let the hair fall in a clear, black shower. It was beautiful hair of the thick, sooty-black color that goes with fair skin and blue eyes. It fell in great coils over the pale yellow gown. Lily, twisting it into loose strands, held it against the light of the lamp.

"Beautiful hair," she said, "like the hair of Rapunzel."

Then she twisted it low about Ellen's head, loosely so that the light, striking the free ends created a kind of halo. With a supreme gesture of scorn, she tossed the "rat" into the scrap basket.

"There," she said, turning her cousin to face the long mirror. "There . . . Behold the great pianist . . . the great artist."

In the magical mirror stood a tall lovely woman. The ridiculous awkward girl had vanished; it was another creature who stood there transfigured and beautiful. And in her frank blue eyes, there was a new look, something of astonishment mingled with determination. The magical mirror had done its work. From that moment the girl became a stranger to the Town. She had come of age and slipped all unconsciously into a new world.

With shining eyes she turned and faced her cousin.

"May I really have the clothes, Lily?"

"Of course, you silly child!"

And Lily smiled because the clothes had never been worn at all. They were completely new.

XXX

A T breakfast on the following morning, the mulatto woman laid before Lily's plate a cablegram. It read simply, "Jean has measles."

Trunks were packed with desperate haste. The ntire household was thrown into an uproar, all save old Julia Shane who continued to move about with the same unruffled alm, with the same acceptancy of whatever came to her. At nidnight Lily boarded the express for the East. It was not intil the middle of the week, when the drawing-room had been vrapped once more in cheesecloth and scented with camphor, hat the Town learned of Lily's sudden return to Paris. It vas impossible, people decided, to calculate the whims of her xistence.

Three months after her sudden departure, she sat one early pring afternoon on the terrace of her garden in the Rue Ray-ouard, when old Madame Gigon, in a bizarre gown of naroon poplin, with the fat and aging Fifi at her heels, brought er a letter from Julia Shane.

Tearing it open, Lily began to read,

"Of course the biggest bit of news is Ellen's escapade. She as eloped with a completely commonplace young man named Clarence Murdock, a traveling salesman for an electrical ompany, who I believe was engaged to May Seton . . . the etons who own the corset factory east of the Harrison Mills. They have gone to New York to live and now, I suppose, Ellen will have her chance to go on with her music. Know-ng Ellen, I am certain she does not love this absurd man. As or Hattie she is distraught and feels that Ellen has committed ome terrible sin. Nothing I can say is able to alter her mind. Γo be sure, the fellow has nothing to commend him, but I'm villing to let Ellen work it out. She's no fool. None of ur family is that. Hattie thinks it was the gowns you gave

Ellen which turned her head. But I suspect that Ellen saw this young drummer simply as a means of escape . . . a way out of all her troubles. Of course the Town is in a buzz. Miss Abercrombie says nothing so unrespectable has happened in years. More power to Ellen . . . !"

For a moment Lily put down the letter and sat thinking. In the last sentence there was a delicious echo of that wicked chuckle which had marked the departure of the discomfited Judge Weissman and Mrs. Julis Harrison from Cypress Hill . . . the merest echo of triumph over another mark in the long score of the old against the new.

For a time Lily sat listening quietly to the distant sounds from the river . . . the whistling of the steamer bound for St. Cloud, the faint clop-clop of hoofs in the Rue de Passy and the ugly chug-chug of one of the new motor wagons which were to be seen with growing frequency along the boulevards. Whatever she was thinking, her thoughts were interrupted suddenly by a little boy, very handsome and neat, in a sailor suit, who dragged behind him across the flagged terrace a stuffed toy bear. He climbed into her lap and began playing with the warm fur piece she had thrown over her shoulders.

"Mama," he cried. "J'ai faim. . . . Je veux un biscuit!"

Lily gathered him into her arms, pressing his soft face against hers. "Bien, petit . . . va chercher la bonne Madame Gigon."

She seized him more closely and kissed him again and again with all the passion of a savage, miserly possession.

"Je t'aime, Mama . . . tellement," whispered the little fellow, and climbed down to run into the big house in search of kind Madame Gigon and her cakes. The gaze of Lily wandered after his sturdy little body and her dark eyes grew bright with a triumphant love.

When he had disappeared through one of the tall windows, she took up the letter once more and continued her reading.

"Irene," wrote her mother, "seems more content now that you are gone. I confess that I understand her less and less every day. Sometimes I think she must be not quite well . . . a little touched perhaps by a religious mania. She is giving her life, her strength, her soul, to these foreigners in the Flats.

What for? Because it brings her peace, I suppose. But still I cannot understand her. There is one man . . . Krylenko, by name, I believe, whom she has made into a sort of disciple. I only hope that news of him won't reach the Town. God knows what sort of a tale they would make out of it. I'm afraid too of her becoming involved in the troubles at the Mills. Some day there will be open warfare in the Flats."

When Lily had finished reading, she tore the letter slowly into bits after a custom of long standing and tossed the torn fragments into one of the stone urns that bordered the terrace. . . . Then she rose and pulling her fur cloak closer about her began to walk up and down restlessly as if some profound and stirring memory had taken possession of her. The rain began to fall gently and darkness to descend upon the garden. In the house behind her the servants lighted the lamps. Still she paced up and down tirelessly.

After a time she went down from the terrace to the gravel path of the garden and there continued her walking until the gate in the garden wall opened suddenly and a man stepped in, his erect soldierly figure black against the lamps of the Rue de Passy. It was the Baron, Madame Gigon's cousin. He came toward her quickly and took her into his arms, embracing her passionately for a long time in silence.

When at last he freed her, a frown crossed his dark face, and he said, "What is it? What is distracting you? Are you troubled about something?"

Lily thrust her arm through his and leaned against him, but she avoided his gaze. "Nothing," she said. "It's nothing."

And thus they walked through the rain until they reached the pavilion designed by Lenôtre which stood at a distance from the house. Here they halted and the Baron, taking from his pocket a key, unlocked the door and they went in silently.

Once inside, he kissed her again and presently he said, "What is it? There is something between us. There is a difference."

"Nothing," she murmured stubbornly. "It is nothing. You must be imagining things."

XXXI

ALL that Julia Shane had written her daughter was true enough. The escapade of Ellen shocked the Town, not altogether unwillingly however, for it opened a new field for talk and furnished one more evidence of the wildness of a family which had never been content with conformity, a clan which kept bursting its bonds and satisfying in a barbarous fashion its hunger after life.

When Hattie Tolliver, tearful and shaken, came to her aunt for consolation, Julia Shane received her in the vast bedroom she occupied above the Mill yard. The old woman said, "Come, Hattie. You've no reason to feel badly. Ellen is a good girl and a wise one. It's the best thing that could have happened, if you'll only see it in that light."

But Mrs. Tolliver, so large, so energetic, so emotional, was hurt. She kept on sobbing. "If only she had told me! . . . It's as if she deceived me."

At which Julia Shane smiled quietly to herself. "Ah, that's it, Hattie. She couldn't have told you, because she knew you so well. She knew that you couldn't bear to have her leave you. The girl was wise. She chose the better way. It's your pride that's hurt and the feeling that, after all, there was something stronger in Ellen than her love for you." She took the red work-stained hand of her niece in her thin, blue-veined one and went on, "We have to come to that, Hattie . . . all of us. It's only natural that a time comes when children want to be free. It's like the wild animals . . . the foxes and the wolves. We aren't any different. We're just animals too, helpless in the rough hands of Nature. She does with us as She pleases."

But Mrs. Tolliver continued to sob helplessly. It was the first time in her life that she had refused to accept in the end what came to her.

"You don't suppose I wanted Lily to go and live in Paris?

You don't suppose I wanted to be left here with Irene who is like a changeling to me? It's only what is bound to come. If Lily *did* help Ellen it was only because all youth is in conspiracy against old age. All children are in a conspiracy against their parents. When we are old, we are likely to forget the things that counted so much with us when we were young. We take them for granted. We see them as very small troubles after all, but that's because we are looking at them from a long way off. The old are selfish, Hattie . . . more selfish than you imagine. They envy even the life and the hunger of the young."

For a moment the old woman paused, regarding her red-eyed niece silently. "No," she continued presently, "You don't understand what I've been saying, yet it's all true . . . as true as life itself. Besides, life is hard for our children, Hattie. It isn't as simple as it was for us. Their grandfathers were pioneers and the same blood runs in their veins, only they haven't a frontier any longer. They stand . . . these children of ours . . . with their backs toward this rough-hewn middle west and their faces set toward Europe and the East. And they belong to neither. They are lost somewhere between."

But Mrs. Tolliver understood none of this. With her there were no shades of feeling, no variations of duty. To her a mother and child were mother and child whether they existed in the heart of Africa or in the Faubourg St. Germain. After tea she went home, secretly nursing her bruised heart. She told her husband that no woman in the world had ever been called upon to endure so much.

As for Charles Tolliver, his lot was not the happiest. At the next election, despite the money which old Julia Shane poured into his campaign, he was defeated. His ruin became a fact. The Mills were too strong. The day of the farmer was past. After floundering about helplessly in an effort to make ends meet, he took at last a place as clerk in one of the banks controlled by his enemy Judge Weissman . . . a cup of humiliation which he drank for the sake of his wife and children, goaded by the sheer necessity of providing food and shelter for them. So he paid for his error, not of honesty but of judgment. Because he was honest, he was sacrificed to the

Mills. He settled himself, a man of forty-five no longer young
behind the brass bars of the Farmer's Commercial Bank, a
name which somehow carried a sense of irony because it had
swallowed up more than one farm in its day.

In the Town tremendous changes occurred with the passing
of years. There was a panic which threatened the banks.
There were menacing rumors of violence and discontent in the
Flats; and these things affected the Town enormously, as de-
pressions in the market for wheat and cattle had once affected
it. No longer was there any public market. On the Square
at the top of Main Street, the old scales for weighing hay and
grain were removed as a useless symbol of a buried past, a
stumbling block in the way of progress. Opposite the site
once occupied by the scales, the Benevolent and Protective
Order of Elks purchased the Grand Western Hotel and made
it into a club house with a great elk's head in cast iron over the
principal doorway. Through its windows, it was possible in
passing to see fat men with red faces, coats off and perspiring,
while they talked of progress and prosperity and the rising place
of the Town among the cities of the state. One by one the
old landmarks of the Square vanished, supplanted by "smoke-
houses," picture palaces with fronts like frosted pastries, candy
shops run by Greeks, a new element in the growing alien population of the Town. On the far side of the square the tower
of the courthouse, itself a monument to graft, was at last
completed to the enrichment of Judge Weissman and other politicians who had to do with the contract.

In the early evening after the sun had disappeared, the figure
of the Judge himself might be seen, ambulating about the
square, hugging the shadows; for the heat was bad for a man
so red-faced and apoplectic. For all his avoidance of the sun,
he walked arrogantly, with the air of one proud of his work.
When he had tired of the promenade, it was his custom to
return to the Elks' club to squeeze his body between the arms
of a rocking chair and sit watching the passers-by and the noisy
bustle of trade. At such moments one might hear the sound
of money dripping into tills as one heard the distant sound of
the Mills which in the evening penetrated as far as the square
itself. He gloated openly over the prosperity to which he had

contributed so much. He went his way, petty, dishonest, corrupt . . . traits which even his enemies forgave him because he had "done so much to make the Town what it was." Not since the piggish obstinacy of Charles Tolliver had he been thwarted, and even in the matter of the taxes the sympathy of the Town had been on his side, because the decision in the case had delayed the building of new furnaces for more than two years and thus halted the arrival of hundreds of new alien workers who would have made the Town the third largest in the state. Charles Tolliver, most people believed, had been piggish and obstinate. He had put himself between his own Town and its booming prosperity.

XXXII

IN the Flats, as the years passed, new tides of immigran
swept in, filling the abominable dirty houses to suffocatio
adding to the garbage and refuse which already clogge
the sluggish waters of the Black Fork. The me
worked twelve hours and sometimes longer in the Mills. Th
women wore shawls over their heads and bore many childre
most of whom died amid the smoke and filth. Here the Tow
overlooked one opportunity. With a little effort it might hav
saved the lives of these babies to feed to the Mills later or
but it was simpler to import more cheap labor from Europ
Let those die who could not live.

And none of these new residents learned to speak Englis
They clung to their native tongues. They were simply col
nists transplanted, unchanged and unchanging, from Polan
Ukrainia, South Italy and the Balkans—nothing more, nothin
less. The Town had nothing to do with them. They we
pariahs, outcasts, "Hunkies," "Dagos," and the Town held
against them that they did not learn English and join in th
vast chorus of praise to prosperity.

But trouble became more frequent nowadays. Willie Harr
son no longer dared take his exercise by walking alone up th
hill to the Town. The barricade of barbed wire was comple
now. It surrounded the Mills on all sides, impregnable, me
acing. It crowded the dead hedges of arbor vitæ that enclose
the park at Shane's Castle. There had been no need for
yet. It was merely waiting.

Welcome House, the tentative gesture of a troubled civ
conscience, went down beneath the waves of prosperity. Volu
teer citizens no longer ventured into the troubled area of th
Flats. Money ceased to flow in for its support. It droppe
at length from the rank of an institution supported by a con
munity to the rank of a school supported by one woman ar

e man. The woman was Irene Shane. The man was
epan Krylenko. The woman was rich. The man was a
ill worker who toiled twelve hours a day and gave six hours
ore to the education of his fellow workers.

The years and the great progress had been no more kind to
ene than they had been to the Town. She aged . . . dryly,
ter the fashion of spinsters who have diverted the current of
fe from its wide course into a single narrow channel of fever-
h activity. She grew thinner and more pale. There were
mes when the blue veins showed beneath the transparent skin
ke the rivers of a schoolboy's map. Her pale blond hair lost
s luster and grew thin and straight, because she had not time
nd even less desire to care for it. Her hands were red and
orn with the work she did in helping the babies of the Flats
 live. She dressed the same, always in a plain gray suit and
gly black hat, which she replaced when they became worn and
abby. But in replacing them, she ignored the changing styles.
he models remained the same, rather outmoded and grotesque,
 that in the Town they rewarded her for her work among the
or by regarding her as queer and something of a figure of
n.

Yet she retained a certain virginal look, and in her eye there
as a queer exalted light. Since life is impossible without
mpensations of one sort or another, it is probable that Irene
ad her share of these. She must have found peace in her
ork and satisfaction in the leader she molded from the
w haired boy who years before had shouted insults at her
rough the wrought iron gates of Shane's Castle.

For Krylenko had grown into a remarkable man. He spoke
nglish perfectly. He worked with Irene, a leader among his
wn people. He taught the others. He read Jean Jacques
ousseau, John Stuart Mill, Karl Marx, and even Voltaire
 . . books which Irene bought him in ignorance of their flaming
ntents. At twenty-five Stepan Krylenko was a leader in the
istrict, and in the Town there were men of property who had
eard vaguely of him as a disturber, an anarchist, a madman, a
ocialist, a criminal.

Although Irene seldom penetrated the Town any longer and
er mother never left the confines of Shane's Castle, their

affairs still held an interest for those who had known Cypre
Hill in the days of its vanished splendor. For women wl
had long since ceased to take any part in the life of a communi
the names of old Julia Shane and her two daughters came u
with startling frequency at the dinners and lunches and t
parties in the Town. It may have been that in a communi
where life was so noisy, so banal, so strenuous, so redolent
prosperity, the Shanes and the old house satisfied some profou
and universal hunger for the mysterious, the beautiful, t'
bizarre, even the mystic. Certainly in the midst of so m
terialistic a community the Shanes were exotic and worthy
attention. And always in the background there was the tr
dition of John Shane and the memories of things which it w
whispered had happened in Shane's Castle. It was Lily wl
aroused the most talk, perhaps because she was even more wit
drawn and mysterious than her mother and sister, because
was so easy to imagine things about her. . . . Lily who cou
come back and bring all the Town once more to Shane's Castl
Lily, the generous, the good-natured, the beautiful Lily.

Mrs. Julis Harrison discussed them; and her son, the r
jected Willie; and Miss Abercrombie, who with the passing
years had developed an affection of the nerves which made h
face twitch constantly so that always, even in the midst of t
most solemn conversations, she had the appearance of winki
in a lascivious fashion. It was a trial which she bore, with
truly noble fortitude.

XXXIII

ON the evening of the day that Mrs. Harrison called
for the last time at Cypress Hill, Miss Abercrombie
was invited to dine with her in the ugly sandstone
house on the Hill. The call was Mrs. Harrison's
final gesture in an effort to patch up the feud which had grown
furiously since the affair over the taxes. Of its significance
Miss Abercrombie had been told in advance, so it must have
been with a beating, expectant heart that she arrived at the
Harrison mansion.

The two women dined alone in a vast dining-room finished
in golden oak, beneath a gigantic brass chandelier fitted with a
score of pendant brass globes. They sat at either end of a
table so long that shouting was almost a necessity.

"William is absent," explained Mrs. Harrison in a loud,
deep voice. "There is a big corporation from the east that
wants to buy the Mills. It wants to absorb them at a good
price with a large block of stock for William and me. Of
course, I oppose it . . . with all my strength. As I told
William, the Mills *are* the Harrisons . . . I will never see
them out of the family . . . Judge Weissman has gone east
with William to see that he does nothing rash. Neither of
them ought to be away, I told Willie, with all this trouble
brewing in the Flats." Here she paused for a long breath.
"Why, only this afternoon, some of those Polish brats threw
stones at my victoria, right at the foot of Julia's drive. . . .
Imagine that in the old days!"

This long and complicated speech, she made with but a single
pause for breath. She had grown even more stout, and her
stupendous masculine spirit had suffered a certain weakening.
A light stroke of paralysis she had passed over heroically, dis-
missing it by sheer force of her tremendous will. The mis-
fortune left no trace save a slight limp as she dragged her body

across the floor and settled it heavily in the plush covered ar
chair at one end of the table.

The butler—Mrs. Harrison used a butler as the symbol
her domination in the Town, wearing him as a sort of crest-
noiselessly brought the thick mushroom soup, his eye gleamir
at the sight of the two women. He was an old man with whi
hair and the appearance of a gentleman.

"How dreadful!" exclaimed Miss Abercrombie, and the
unable longer to restrain herself, she said, "Tell me! Do te
me about Julia!"

Mrs. Harrison drank from her water glass, set it dow
slowly and then said impressively, "She did not receive me!"

"I feared so," rejoined Miss Abercrombie, winking wi
nervous impatience.

"It is the end! No one can say that I have not done m
part toward a reconciliation." This statement she uttered wit
all the majesty of an empress declaring war. "And to think
she added mournfully, "that such an old friendship should con
to such an end."

"It's just the way I feel," replied Miss Abercrombie. "A
you know, my friendship was even older. I knew her befo
you. Why, I can remember when she was only a farmer girl
Here her illness forced her to wink as if there were somethir
obscene in her simple statement.

"Well," said Mrs. Harrison, "I don't suppose any one i
the Town was ever closer to Julia than I was. D'you know
That mulatto woman actually turned me away today, and
must say her manner was insolent. She said Julia was n
feeling well enough to see me. Imagine, not well enough t
see *me,* her oldest friend!" This statement the sycophant
Miss Abercrombie allowed to pass unchallenged. "Heave
knows," continued Mrs. Harrison. "It was only friendsh
that prompted me. I certainly would not go prying about f
the sake of curiosity. You know that, Pearl. Why, I wasn
allowed to set my foot inside the door. You'd have thoug
I was diseased."

After this a silence descended during which the room v
brated with unsaid things. At the memory of her receptio

Mrs. Harrison's face grew more and more flushed. The gentlemanly butler removed the soup and brought on whitefish nicely browned and swimming in butter.

"It's a queer household," remarked Miss Abercrombie, with an air of hinting at unspeakable things and feeling her way cautiously toward a letting down of all bars. Undoubtedly it was unfortunate that they had disputed the position of "oldest friend." In a way it tied both their hands.

"It has always been queer," replied the hostess. "Even since the house was built."

Again a pregnant silence, and then Miss Abercrombie with another unwilled and obscene wink added, "I must say I can't understand Irene's behavior." About this effort, there was something oblique and yet effective. It marked another step.

"Or Lily's," rejoined Mrs. Harrison, taking a third step.

"They say," said Miss Abercrombie, pulling fishbones from her mouth, "that there is a common mill worker who is very attentive to Irene. Surely she can't be considering marriage with *him*."

"No, from what I hear, she *isn't*," observed Mrs. Harrison. After this dark hint she paused for a moment tottering upon the edge of new revelations with the air of a swimmer about to dive into cold water. At last she plunged.

"They say," she murmured in a lowered voice, "that there is more between them than most people guess . . . more than is proper."

Miss Abercrombie leaned forward. "You know," she said, "that's funny. I've heard the same thing."

"Well, I heard it from Thomas, the coachman. Of course, I reproved him for even hinting at such things. I must say he only hinted . . . very delicately. He was discreet. If I hadn't guessed there was something of the sort going on, I would never have known what he was driving at."

Miss Abercrombie bridled and leaned back for the butler to remove her fish plate. "Imagine!" she said, "Imagine a child of yours being the subject of gossip among servants!"

Her hostess gave a wicked chuckle. "You've forgotten John Shane. When he was alive, his behavior was the talk of

every one. But how could you have forgotten the talk th
went the rounds? It was common property . . . comm
property."

Miss Abercombie sighed deeply. "I know . . . I kno
Julia's life has not been happy." And into the sigh she put
thousand implications of the superior happiness of virgins.

"Of course," said Mrs. Harrison, "he was insane. There
no doubt about it. People may talk, but facts are facts. Joh
Shane was insane . . . certainly toward the end he was insane

The butler brought the roast fowl, and until his back w
turned once more both women kept silence. When he ha
gone out of the room, they found themselves striving for fir
place in the race. Both spoke at once but Mrs. Harrison ove
whelmed the sycophantic Abercrombie.

"Of course," she said, "I think Julia herself is a litt
queer at times. I've noticed it for years . . . ever since . .
well . . . ever since Lily went to Paris to live."

"Yes," observed Miss Abercrombie, moving toward som
thing more definite. "Ever since the Governor's garden part
All that was very queer . . . very queer."

Here again they found themselves halted by the immensi
of the unspoken. Mrs. Harrison veered aside.

"The house has gone to ruin. Even the gate is hanging h
one hinge. Nothing is kept up any longer."

"Have you seen this lover of Irene's?" asked Miss Abe
crombie, calling a spade a spade and endeavoring to keep to or
thing at a time.

"I've seen him once . . . William pointed him out to me a
the Mills. He's one of the men who have been making troub
there."

"Is he good looking?" asked Miss Abercrombie.

"Yes and no," replied her companion.

"Well, what does that mean?"

"Well, he's tall and has a handsome face . . . a little ev
perhaps. The real trouble is that I should call him commo
Yes, common is the word I should use, decidedly common."

Miss Abercrombie raised her eyebrows and smiled. "Bu
my dear, after all he is nothing but a workman."

"Yes," replied Mrs. Harrison, "he *is*." In a manner which
t an end to all doubt in the matter.

'Do you really think," asked Miss Abercrombie, "that there
nything in it?"

Mrs. Harrison poised her fork and gave her guest a knowing
k. "Well, of course I can't see what he sees in her . . .
e and haggard as she is. Now with him it's different.
's . . . well." She halted suddenly, adding, "This fowl is
gh, Pearl . . . I'm sorry it happened when you were dining
h me." And then, "I suppose it's money he's after. She
st be very rich."

The butler, after bringing more rich food, disappeared again
l this time, Miss Abercrombie, casting to the winds all re-
int, rose and said, "I'm going to bring my chair nearer,
le. I can't talk all the way from this end of the table."

And she moved her chair and plate to a more strategic posi-
a so that when the butler returned, he found the two women
ing quite close to each other, their heads together, their
es lowered to the most confidential of pitches. Fragments
heir talk reached an ear long trained to eavesdropping upon
women.

But Lily is the one," drifted to the ear. "I'd really like
now the truth about her. Of course blood is thicker than
er. They say she . . ." Mrs. Harrison rattled the ice in
glass, thus destroying the remainder of the sentence.

o they sat until near midnight—two old women, one of
n at the end of a life barren of love, the other abandoned
love forever and cast aside, a slowly decaying mass of fat
awing over the affairs of two women for whom the force
ove in some manifestation or other was still a radiant reality.
y knew nothing; they possessed only suspicions and frag-
its of gossip, but out of these they succeeded in patching
ther a mosaic which glowed with all the colors of the most
norous sin and the most romantic passion.

XXXIV

AND at the same moment in the house at Cypress H
Julia Shane lay propped up in her bed reading
French novel. It was an enormous bed with a v
dusty canopy supported by two ironical wood-gilt
pids who hung suspended from the ceiling; and Julia Sha
reading by the light of her night lamp, appeared lost in it lik
woman tossing on the waves of the sea. To-night, feel
more ill than usual, she had her dinner in bed, wrapped i
peignoir of mauve ribbon and valenciennes, her bony neck
posed above the linen of her night dress.

She read, as usual, with the aid of a silver mounted read
glass which tossed the sentences in enormous capitals well i
the range of her fading vision. On the table beside her st
one of the gilt coffee cups, a mute witness to the old woma
disobedience of the doctor's orders. Beside it lay two pa
backed French novels and on the floor in the shadow of
table a half dozen more tossed aside carelessly, some ly
properly, others open and sprawled, exposing the ragged ed
of the hastily cut pages.

In the fashion of the ill and aging, she lived nowadays
memories . . . memories of her girlhood when she had rid
John Shane's wildest mare Doña Rita recklessly about the p
dock of the farm, memories of Mademoiselle Violette de V
and the picnics with French and English girls in a neatly k
wood at Sèvres, memories of Cypress Hill in the days
mediately after her return when John Shane was still more
passionate lover than the husband. As she grew older,
memories became clearer and more vivid, but they were neit
vivid nor diverse enough to occupy all her time. What
mained she divided between the game of patience and
French novels which Lily supplied faithfully, shipping t
from Paris in lots of a dozen at a time.

The old woman had evolved her own scheme of reading, a plan which Irene condemned by the word "skimming," but which satisfied Julia Shane because it revealed the plot without an unnecessary waste of time over long, involved descriptions of scenery and minute analyses of incomprehensible Gallic passions. Under the skimming system she read a few pages at the beginning and then turned to the end to learn the outcome of the tale. After this, she plunged into the middle of the book and read a page or two here and there until her curiosity was satisfied and her interest flagged. And at last the book was tossed aside to be carried off by the mulatto woman, who never failed to go through each volume carefully as though by looking at the words frequently enough she would be able at length to unlock the secrets of foreign tongues. The books which lay on the floor beside the bed had been "skimmed." They lay prostrate and sprawled like the dead soldiers of an army. The titles served as an index of the old woman's favorite authors. They appeared some in black ink, some in red, some even in blue . . . Paul Marguerite, Marcel Prévost, Pierre Loti, Paul Bourget, Collette Willy and, strange to relate, Anatole France represented by *L'Ile des Penguins* which, it seemed, had baffled the "skimming" system, for of all the lot it was the only volume in which every page had been cut.

After she grew weary, she tossed aside *Les Anges Gardiens* which she had been reading and sat leaning back with her eyes closed. Perhaps she pondered the doings of the four evil governesses in the Prévost tale; perhaps she turned her thoughts to the Town and Mrs. Julis Harrison whom she had sent away because she "was not in a mood to be bored." It is even possible that she knew at this very moment that in the sandstone house of the Harrisons, they were discussing her affairs. She was too wise and too worldly not to have known what Belle Harrison would say of her. Yet she appeared calm and content enough, completely indifferent to the opinions of her acquaintances, of the Town—indeed of all the world. She had reached the time when such things are no longer of any importance.

So great was her indifference that in more than three months she had left the house only once and then to follow the coffin

of Jacob Barr to the cemetery on the hill. The old man was
dead at last, after an illness which had drained with a bitter,
heart-breaking slowness all the vigor of his strong and energetic body. On the day of the funeral the foreign women in
Halsted street caught a swift glimpse of the mistress of Cypress
Hill as she drove through on her way to the cemetery. They
must have guessed that it was an event of great importance
which drew her from her seclusion; and indeed it was such
an event, for it was the funeral of the oldest member of the
family, the last of all his generation save Julia Shane.

And after the funeral Julia Shane returned and shut herself
in, resolved to see no one but Irene and her niece, Hattie
Tolliver.

XXXV

WHATEVER her thoughts and memories may have been, they were interrupted presently by the knock of the mulatto woman who came to bear away the gilt coffee cup and pile of ravaged novels. The sound of the woman's shuffling approach aroused Julia Shane who opened her eyes and said, "Here, Sarah. Give me a hand. I've slipped down."

Sarah helped lift her once more into a sitting posture. The old woman raised herself scornfully as if there was between her indomitable spirit and her wrecked body no bond of any sort, as if she had only contempt for the body as a thing unworthy of her, a thing which had failed her, over which she had neither control nor responsibility.

The mulatto woman bent to pick up the scattered novels, and as she stood up, her mistress, chuckling, said, "My God. They're tiresome, Sarah. They never write about anything but *l'amour*. You'd think there was nothing else in the world. Even *l'amour* gets to be a bore after a time."

The mulatto woman waited obediently. "Yes, Mis' Shane. I guess you're right," she said presently. At which the old woman smiled.

"And Sarah," the mistress continued. "When Miss Irene comes in, tell her I should like to see her. It's important."

The servant hesitated for an instant. "But Miss Irene don't come in till after midnight, Mis' Shane." She spoke with the manner of concealing something. In her soft voice there was a thin trace of insinuating suspicion, almost of servile accusation. "That foreign fella brings her home," she added.

"It's all right," replied the old woman. "I shall be awake." And then in a cold voice she added, "I'm sure it's good of him to bring her home. I shouldn't want her wandering about alone at that hour of the night. It's very thoughtful of him."

At midnight, true to her word, she was still awake. She had even managed to gain her feet painfully and to make her way with unsteady step across the room to the drawer which held her cigarettes. These too the doctor had forbidden her.

On the way back to her vast bed, she passed by the window and, drawing aside the curtain for a moment, she looked out over the hot panorama of glowing furnaces and tall black chimneys. As she stood there, she saw entering the wrought iron gates two figures sharply outlined against the glare of the white arc light in Halsted Street. The woman was Irene. She was accompanied by Krylenko.

Quietly the old woman extinguished the candle on the table beside her. The room became a vault of darkness. Beneath her window at the turn in the drive, the pair halted and stood talking in voices so low that what they said was inaudible even through the open window. After a time Irene seated herself wearily on the horseblock. Her frail body sagged with fatigue. She leaned against the cast iron Cupid who held in one outstretched hand an iron ring. Krylenko bent over her and his hands, with the curious, eloquent gestures of an alien, pantomimed their tale against the distant arc light. Above them in the recessed window the mother, clinging all the while to the heavy curtains for support, watched silently. She could hear nothing. She could only keep watch. At length Irene arose and lifting the ugly black hat from her head, ran her finger through her loose hair all damp with the terrible heat. Now was the moment. The old woman, awaiting proof, leaned against the table by her side.

But there was no proof. There was no embrace, not even the faintest exchange of intimacies. Krylenko chastely took Irene's hand, bade her good-night and turned with his swinging powerful stride down the long drive. Irene, passing along the gallery by the drawing room, slipped her key into the lock and entered the house.

Above stairs she found her mother sitting up in bed, lost again in the midst of *Les Anges Gardiens*. Still carrying the worn hat in her hand, the daughter came over to the bed. With the increasing illness of the old woman, Irene's manner had become more gentle. She even smiled a tired smile.

"What?" she said playfully. "Are you still awake? Skimming again, I see."

Yet her manner was not the manner of a daughter with a mother. Rather it was that of a casual friend. It was too playful, too forced. The chasm of thirty years and more was not to be bridged by any amount of strained cordiality.

Julia Shane put down her reading glass. "I couldn't sleep, so I tried to read," she said.

Irene drew up a chair and sat by the bed. She appeared worn and exhausted, as though the August heat had drained to the dregs all her intense, self-inspired vitality.

"How are you feeling?"

"Better . . . much better except for the ache in my back."

Irene's face grew serious. "You've been smoking again," she said, "after the doctor forbade you." The old woman, quite prepared to lie, started to protest, shaking her head in negation. "It's no use, Mama . . . I saw you . . . I saw the glow of your cigarette at the window."

(So Irene knew that she had been watched, and there was no need to protest.) The old woman sat still for a moment twisting the silver reading glass round and round, her brow contracted in an angry frown as though she resented bitterly the decay of body which gave any one authority over her. (That Julia Shane should ever take orders from a doctor or stand reproved by her own daughter!) It was this angry emotion that stood revealed and transparent in every line of her face, in the very defiance of her thin body. At length the frown melted slowly away.

"What sort of a man is he, Irene?" she asked looking straight into her daughter's tired eyes. Irene moved uneasily.

"What man?" she asked, "I don't know who you mean."

"That foreigner . . . I don't remember his name. You've never told me. . . . You might have told your mother." There was a note of peevishness in her voice which sounded queer and alien, almost a portent.

"Oh, Krylenko," said Irene, twisting her black hat with her thin hands. "Krylenko." Then she waited for a moment. "He's a fine man . . . a wonderful man. He has given up everything for his people."

"But they are not *your* people," observed her mother looking at her sharply.

"They are my people," replied Irene softly. "All of them down to the last baby. If they are not my people, who are?"

The old woman, opposed once more by the inevitable wall of Irene's obsessions, frowned. "You are wealthy," she said. "You were born to a position."

In Irene's smile there was a shade of bitterness. "In this Town?" she inquired scornfully. "Oh! No! Position in this Town! That's almost funny." She leaned forward a little, pressing her hand against her forehead. "My people?" she said in a hushed voice. "My people. . . . Why, I don't even know where my father came from."

The mother, half-buried among the heavy pillows raised herself slowly as if a wave of new vigor had taken possession of her worn-out body. "Get me a cigarette, Irene."

The girl opened her lips to protest, but her mother silenced her. "Please, Irene, do as I say. It can't possibly matter what I do now."

"Please, Mama," began Irene once more. "The doctor has forbidden it." Then Julia Shane gave her daughter a terrible look pregnant with all the old arrogance and power.

"Will you do as I say, Irene, or must I send for Sarah? She at least still obeys me."

For a second, authority hung in the balance. It was the authority of a lifetime grounded upon a terrific force of will and sustained by the eternal and certain precedent of obedience. It was the old woman who won the struggle. It was her last victory. The daughter rose and obediently brought the cigarettes, even holding the candle to light it. She held the flame at arm's length with a gesture of supreme distaste as if she had been ordered to participate in some unspeakable sin. After she had replaced the candle, her mother puffed thoughtfully for a time.

"Your father," she said presently, "was born in Marseilles. His mother was Spanish and his father Irish. He came to this country because he had to run away. That's all I know. He might have told me more if he had not died suddenly. It's not likely that any of us will ever know his story, no matter how hard we try. Life isn't a story book, you know."

In life there are some things that we never know, even about our own friends, our own children. Each man's soul is a secret, which even himself is not able to reveal."

For an instant the light of triumph swept Irene's pale countenance. "You see!" she said. "I am just like the rest . . . like Stepan Krylenko and all the others. My father was a foreigner."

The mother's lips curved in a sudden, scornful smile. "But he was a gentleman, Irene. . . . That is something. And your mother was an American. Her grandfather was the first settler in the wilderness. . . . The Town was named for him. Have you no pride?"

"No," replied Irene, "to be proud is a vice. . . . I have killed it. I am not proud. I am like all the others." And yet there was a fierce pride in her voice, a smug, fierce, pride in not being proud.

"You are perverse," said her mother. "You are beyond me. You talk like a fool. . . ." Irene raised her head to speak but the will of the old woman swept her back. "I know," she continued. "You think it is saintly. Does it ever occur to you that it might only be smugness?"

The old eyes flashed with anger and resentment, emotions which merely shattered themselves against the barrier of Irene's smiling and fanatic sense of righteousness. A look of obstinacy entered her face. (She regarded herself as superior to Julia Shane! Incredible!)

"You amaze me, Irene. Your hardness is beyond belief. If you could be soft for a moment, gentle and generous . . . like Lily."

The daughter's hands tightened about the battered old hat. "It's always Lily," she said bitterly. "It's always Lily . . . Lily this and Lily that. She's everywhere. Every one praises her . . . even Cousin Hattie." The stubborn look of smugness again descended upon her face. "Well, let them praise her . . . I know that it is I who am right, I who am good in the sight of God." And then for the first time in all the memory of Julia Shane, a look of anger, cold and unrelenting came into the eyes of her daughter. "Lily! Lily!" she cried scornfully, "I hate Lily. . . . May God forgive me!"

XXXVI

THEN for a long time a silence descended upon the room. Julia Shane crushed out the embers of her cigarette and fell once more to turning the silver mounted reading glass round and round, regarding it fixedly with the look of one hypnotized. At last she turned again to her daughter.

"Are you going to marry him?" she asked.

"No, of course not."

"I should be satisfied, if he is as fine as you say he is. I would rather see you married before I die, Irene."

The daughter shook her head stubbornly. "I shall never marry any one."

The old woman smiled shrewdly. "You are wrong, my girl. You are wrong. I haven't had a very happy time, but I wouldn't have given it up. It is a part of life, knowing love and having children. . . . Love can be so many things, but at least it is part of life . . . the greatest part of all. Without it life is nothing."

For a long time Irene remained silent. She kept her eyes cast down and when she spoke again it was without raising them. "But Lily . . ." she began shrewdly. "She has never married." It was the old retort, always Lily. Her mother saw fit to ignore it, perhaps because, knowing what she knew, it was impossible to answer it.

"You've been seeing a great deal of this Krylenko," she said. "It's been going on for years . . . since before Lily was here the last time. That's years ago."

Irene looked up suddenly and a glint of anger lighted her pale eyes. "Who's been talking to you about me? . . . . I know. It's Cousin Hattie. She was here to-day. Oh, why can't people let me alone? I harm no one. I want to be left in peace."

Then Julia Shane, perhaps because she already knew too well the antipathy between her coldly virginal daughter and her niece whose whole life was her children, deliberately lied.

"Cousin Hattie did not even mention it." She turned her eyes away from the light. "I would like to see you married, Irene," she repeated. It was clear that for some reason the old hope, forgotten since that tumultuous visit of the Governor, was revived again. It occupied the old woman's mind to the exclusion of all else.

"There is nothing between us, Mama," said Irene. "Nothing at all. Can't you see. We've been friends all along. I taught him to read English. I got him books." Her voice wavered a little and her hands trembled. It was as if she had become a little girl again, the same girl who, in a white muslin dress with a blue sash, sobbed alone on the sofa in the library beneath John Shane's portrait. "I've made him what he is," she continued. "Don't you see. I'm proud of him. When I found him, he was nothing . . . only a stupid Ukrainian boy who was rebellious and rude to me. And now he works with me. He's willing to sacrifice himself for those people. We understand each other. All we want is to be left alone. Don't you understand? I'm just proud of him because I've made him what he is. I'm nothing," she stammered. "I'm nothing to him in that way at all. That would spoil everything . . . like something evil, intruding upon us."

The pale tired face glowed with a kind of religious fervor. For an instant there was something maternal and exalted in her look. All the plainness vanished, replaced suddenly by a feverish beauty. The plain, exhausted old maid had disappeared.

"Why haven't you told me this before?" asked the old woman.

"You never asked me. . . . You never wanted to know what I was doing. You were always interested in Lily. How could you ever have thought I'd marry him? I'm years older." Suddenly she extended her arms with a curious exhibitive gesture like a gesture Lily sometimes made when she was looking her loveliest. "Look at me. I'm old and battered and ugly. How could he ever love me in that way? He is young."

The thin hands dropped listlessly into her lap and lay against the worn black serge. She fell silent, all exhausted by the emotion. Her mother stared at her with the look of one who has just penetrated the soul of a stranger. Irene, it appeared, was suddenly revealed to her.

"Why, you know he's never looked at a woman," Irene continued in a lowered voice. "He's lived in the Flats all these years and he's never looked at a woman. Do you know what that means in the Flats?" Her voice dropped still lower. "Of course, you don't know, because you know nothing about the Flats," she added with a shade of bitterness.

At this her mother smiled. "The rest of the world is not so different, Irene."

But Irene ignored her. "He's worked hard all these years to make himself worth while and to help his people. He's never had time to be bad." Her mother smiled faintly again. Perhaps she smiled at the spinsterish word by which Irene chose to designate fornication.

"He's pure," continued Irene. "He's fine and noble and pure. I want to keep him so."

"You are making of him a saint," observed the old woman drily.

"He is a saint! That's just what he is," cried Irene. "And you mock him, you and Lily. . . . Oh, I know . . . I know you both. He's been driven from the Mills for what he's done for the people in the Flats. He's been put on a black list so he can never get work in any other Mill. He told me so to-night. That's what he was telling me when you stood watching us." A look of supreme triumph came into her face once more. "But it's too late!" she cried. "It's too late. . . . They've voted to strike. It begins to-morrow. Stepan is the one behind it."

It was as if a terrible war, long hanging in the balance, had suddenly become a reality. Julia Shane, propped among the pillows, turned restlessly and sighed.

"What fools men are!" she said, almost to herself. "What fools!" And then to Irene. "It won't be easy, Irene. It'll be cruel. You'd best go to bed now, dear. You look desperately tired. You'll have plenty of work before you."

Irene pressed a cold, distant kiss on the ivory cheek of her mother and turned to leave.

"Shall I put out the light?"

"Yes, please."

The room subsided into darkness and Irene, opening the door, suddenly heard her mother's voice.

"Oh, Irene." The voice was weary, listless. "I've written for Lily to come home. The doctor told me to-day that I could not possibly live longer than Christmas. I forced it out of him. There was no use in having nonsense. I wanted to know."

And Irene, instead of going to her own room, returned and knelt by the side of her mother's bed. The hardness melted and she sobbed, perhaps because the old woman who faced death with such proud indifference was so far beyond the need of prayer and comfort.

Yet when the smoky dawn appeared at last, it found Irene in her own chaste room still kneeling in prayer before the pink and blue Sienna Virgin.

"Oh, Blessed Virgin," she prayed, from the summit of her complacency. "Forgive my mother her sins of pride and her lack of charity. Forgive my sister her weakness of the flesh. Enter into their hearts and make them good women. Make them worthy to enter the Kingdom of Heaven. Enter into the heart of my sister and cleanse her. Make her a good woman . . . a pure woman, loving only those things which are holy. Cleanse her of the lusts of the flesh!"

Her pale eyes were wet with tears. Although she prayed to a plaster Virgin in pink gilt, she used the sonorous rolling words drawn all unconsciously from the memories of a Presbyterian childhood. And the Lily for whom she prayed . . . the Lily who had been sent for . . . was there in the old house just as she was always in the Town and in the memories of those who knew her beauty, her tolerance and her charm. There were, indeed, times when Krylenko, caught perhaps in the memory of a night when he stood in the melting snow peering into the windows of Shane's Castle, spoke of her; and these were times when Irene turned away from him, frightened by the shadow of something in his eyes.

XXXVII

IT became known as the Great Strike and it served to mark an epoch. Long afterward people in the Town said, "It was the year of the Great Strike" as they said "It was the year of the Spanish-American War" or "the year that Bryan was a candidate for the first time." Willie Harrison found a use for his enclosures of barbed wire and his heavily barricaded gates. As the strike progressed and the violence increased, other machines of warfare were set up . . . such things as machine guns and searchlights which at night fingered the Flats and the sky above with shafts of white light, rigid and unbending as steel.

In one sense the strike was a Godsend. When the Mills shut down there were no more fires in the ovens and the furnaces; no more soot fell in clouds like infernal snow over the low eminence of Cypress Hill and the squalid expanse of the Flats. For the first time in a score of years the sun became clearly visible. Instead of rising and setting as a ball of hot copper immersed in smoke, it appeared and disappeared quite clear and white, a sun such as God intended it to be. But even more remarkable was the blanket of silence which descended upon all the district. With the banking of the fires, there was no more hammering, and in place of the titanic clamor there was a stillness so profound and so unusual that people noticed it as people notice a sudden clap of loud thunder and remark upon it to each other. The silence became noisy.

In the house at Cypress Hill the world of Julia Shane narrowed from the castle itself to a single room and at last to the vast Italian bed. It was seldom that she gathered sufficient strength to struggle to her feet and make her way, leaning on the ebony and silver stick, to the window where the Mill yards and the Flats lay spread out beneath her gaze. During those last months she knew again the stillness which enveloped the Cypress Hill of her youth. But there was a difference; the green marshes were gone forever, buried beneath the masses of cinders, clay and refuse upon which the Mills raised their sheds and towers and the Flats its flimsy, dirty, matchwood houses, all smoke stained and rotting at the eaves. The lush smell of damp growing things was replaced by the faint odor of crowded, sweating humanity. Not one slim cat-tail, not one feathery willow remained in all the desert of industry. There was, however, a sound which had echoed over the swamps almost a hundred years earlier, a sound which had not been heard since the days when Julia Shane's grandfather built about what was now the public square of the Town a stockade to protect the first settlers from the redskins. It was the sound of guns. Sometimes as she sat at the window, there arose a distant rat-tat-tat like the noise of a typewriter but more staccato and savage, followed by a single crack or two. She discovered at length the origin of the sound. In the Mill yard beneath her window a target had been raised, and at a little distance off men lay on their stomachs pointing rifles mounted upon tripods. Sometimes they fired at rusty buckets and old tin cans because these things did not remain stupid and inanimate like the target, but jumped and whirled about in the most tortured fashion when the bullets struck them, as though they had lives which might be destroyed. It made the game infinitely more fascinating and spirited. The men who indulged in this practise were, she learned from Hennery, the hired guards whom the Harrisons and Judge Weissman had brought in to protect the Mills, riff-raff and off-scourings from the slums of New York, Chicago, Pittsburgh and Cleveland.

There came a day, after the sights and sounds of the Mill yard had become a matter of indifference to the old woman, when the doctor forbade her to leave her bed if she wished to survive the day set for Lily's arrival. It was October, and the park remained unchanged save that the atmosphere was less hot and the sun shone more clearly; for the trees and shrubs on the low hill were long since dead and far beyond the stage of sending out new leaves to fall at the approach of winter. It was bald now and very old. The brick house, dominating all the horizon, stood out day after day gaunt and blackened by soot against the brilliant October sky.

Lily had been delayed. Before leaving Paris she wrote to her mother and Irene that it was necessary for her to take a small boy, the son of a friend, to England. After placing him in school there, she wrote, she would sail at once for America and come straight to Cypress Hill. There were also matters of business which might delay her; but she would not arrive later than the middle of November. So Julia Shane set herself to battling with Death, bent upon beating Him off until she had seen Lily once more.

XXXVIII

IN those days, because it was difficult and dangerous for any
one to visit Cypress Hill and because, after all, no one
had any particular reason to visit it, there was at the old
house, only one caller beside the doctor. This was
Hattie Tolliver, whose strength had given way a little to an
increasing stoutness but whose pride and spirit flagged not at
all. To the police and the hired guards at the Mills, she became as familiar a figure as the doctor himself. She came on
foot, since all service on the clanging trolley cars of Halsted
street was long since suspended, her large powerful body clad
in black clothes of good quality, a basket suspended over one
arm and the inevitable umbrella swinging from the other. She
walked with a sort of fierce disdain directed with calculated
ostentation alike at the Mill guards, the police, and the dwellers
of the Flats who viewed her bourgeois approach with a sullen
hostility. The basket contained delicacies concocted by her own
skilled and housewifely hand . . . the most golden of custards,
the most delicate of rennets, fragile biscuits baked without
sugar—in short, every sort of thing which might please the
palate of an invalid accustomed to excellent food.

In effect, Cypress Hill fell slowly into a state of siege. Surrounded on three sides by the barrier of barbed wire, the sole
means of egress was the long drive turning into Halsted street.
Here there was danger, for disorders occurred frequently at
the very wrought iron gates, now rusted and broken. Stones
were hurled by the strikers and shots fired by the police. The
wagons of the Town no longer delivered goods at a spot so
isolated and dangerous, and the duties of supplying the place
with food came gradually to be divided between Irene and
Hattie Tolliver, whose lack of friendliness and understanding
toward each other approached an open hatred. They alone of
the little garrison went in and out of the wrought iron gates;

for Hennery and the mulatto woman were far too terrified by the disorders outside ever to venture into the Town.

On the day of Lily's letter Hattie Tolliver, bearing a well-laden basket, arrived and went at once to Aunt Julia's room She brooked no interference from the mulatto woman.

After bidding Sarah place the contents of the basket in a cool place she swept by the servant with a regal swish of black skirts.

Upstairs in the twilight Julia Shane lay in the enormous bed, flat on her back staring at the ceiling. At the approach of her niece she raised herself a little and asked in a feeble voice to be propped up. It was as though the approach of her vigorous rosy-faced niece endowed her with a sudden energy.

"And how are you?" asked Hattie Tolliver when she had smoothed the pillows with an expert hand and made the old woman more comfortable than she had been in many days.

"The same . . . just the same," was the monotonous answer. "Lily is a long time in coming."

Cousin Hattie went to the windows and flung back the curtains. "Light and air will do you good," she said. "There's nothing like light and air." And then turning, "Why don't you make Sarah keep the windows open?"

Julia Shane sat up more straightly, breathing in the crisp air. "I tell her to . . . but she doesn't like air," she said weakly.

"You let her bully you! She needs some one to manage her. I'm surprised Irene doesn't put her in her place."

The old woman smiled. "Irene," she said. "Irene . . . Why she's too meek ever to get on with servants. It's no use . . . her trying anything."

"I've brought you a custard and some cakes," continued her niece, at the same time flicking bits of dust from the dressing table with her handkerchief and setting the pillows of the chaise longue in order with a series of efficient pats. "There's going to be trouble . . . real trouble before long. The strikers are getting bolder."

"They're getting more hungry too, Irene says," replied the old woman. "Perhaps that's why."

Cousin Hattie came over to the bed now and sat herself

down, at the same time taking out a pillow-case which she set herself to hemming. "You know what they're saying in the Town," she remarked. "They're saying that Irene is helping the strike by giving the strikers money."

To this the old woman made no reply and Cousin Hattie continued. "I don't see the sense in that. The sooner every one gets to work, the better. It isn't safe in Halsted street any longer. I'm surprised at Irene helping those foreigners against the Harrisons. I didn't think she had the spirit to take sides in a case like this."

Julia Shane moved her weary body into a more comfortable position. "She doesn't take sides. She only wants to help the women and children. . . . I suppose she's right after all. . . . They are like the rest of us."

At this Cousin Hattie gave a grunt of indignation. "They didn't have to come to this country. I'm sure nobody wants 'em."

"The Mills want them," said her aunt. "The Mills want them and the Mills want more and more all the time."

"But I don't see why we have to suffer because the Mills want foreigners. There ought to be some law against it."

As though there seemed to be no answer to this, Julia Shane turned on her side and remarked. "I had a letter from Lily to-day."

Her niece put down the pillow case and regarded her with shining eyes. Her heavy body became alive and vibrant. "What did she say? Was there any news of Ellen? Shall I read it?"

"No, go on with your work. If you prop me a little higher and give me my glass, I'll read it."

This operation completed, she read the letter through. It was not until Ellen's name occurred that Cousin Hattie displayed any real interest. At the sound of her daughter's name, the woman put down her sewing and assumed an attitude of passionate listening.

"Ellen," ran the letter, "is doing splendidly. She is contented here and is working hard under Philippe. She plays better than ever . . . if that is possible, and plans to make her début in London next year. She has every reason to make a great success. I am leaving her in my house when I come to America. She gets on beautifully with Madame Gigon. That was my greatest worry, for Madame Gigon has grown worse as she has grown older. But she has taken a fancy to Ellen . . . fortunately, so everything is perfect. Tell Cousin Hattie that one day she will be proud of her daughter."

Julia Shane, when she had finished, put down the letter, and regarded her niece. "You see, Hattie," she said, "there is no need to worry. Everything is going splendidly. Ellen couldn't be in better hands. Lily knows her way about the world a great deal better than most. Some day your daughter will be famous."

There came no response from her niece. Mrs. Tolliver sat upright and thoughtful. Presently she took up the pillow case and set to work again.

"These débuts," she said. "They cost money, don't they?"

"Yes," replied her aunt.

"Well where is Ellen to get it? Clarence's life insurance must all be gone by this time."

"I suppose Lily has found a way. Lily is clever. Besides Ellen isn't altogether helpless."

Again there was a thoughtful pause and the old woman said, "I don't think you'd be pleased if Ellen *was* a great success."

"I don't know. I'd be more pleased if I had her nearer to me. I don't like the idea of her being in Paris. It's not a healthy place. It's the wickedest city in the world."

"Come, Hattie. You mustn't forget Ellen was made to live in the world. You brought her up to be successful and famous. It's your fault if you have reason to be proud of her."

Into this single sentence or two Julia Shane managed to condense a whole epic. It was an epic of maternal sacrifices, of a household kept without servants so that the children might profit by the money saved, of plans which had their beginning even before the children were born, of hopes and ambitions aroused skilfully by a woman who now sat deserted, hemming a pillow-case to help dispel her loneliness. She had, in effect, brought about her own sorrow. They were gone now, Ellen to Paris, Fergus and Robert to New York. It was in their very blood. All this was written, after all, in the strong proud face bent low over the pillow-case . . . an epic of passionate maternity.

"We have to expect these things of our children," continued Aunt Julia. "I'm old enough to know that it's no new story, and I've lived long enough to know that we have no right to demand of them the things which seem to us the only ones worth while. Every one of us is different from the others. There are no two in the least alike. And no one ever really knows any one else. There is always a part which remains secret and hidden, concealed in the deepest part of the soul. No husband ever knows his wife, Hattie, and no wife ever really knows her husband. There is always something just beyond that remains aloof and untouched, mysterious and undiscoverable because we ourselves do not know just what it is. Sometimes it is shameful. Sometimes it is too fine, too precious, ever to reveal. It is quite beyond revelation even if we chose to reveal it. . . ."

XXXIX

AT the close of this long speech, the old woman fell into a fit of coughing and her niece rose quickly to bring more medicine and water. If Hattie Tolliver had understood even for a moment these metaphysical theories, they were forgotten in the confusion of the coughing fit. It is more than probable that she understood nothing of the speech and probable that she was too far lost in thoughts of Ellen to have heard it. In any case, she was, like most good mothers and housewives, a pure realist who dealt in terms of the material. At least she gave no sign, and when the coughing fit was over, she returned at once to the main thread of the conversation.

"These careers," she said, "may be all right but I think that Ellen might be happier if she had something more sound . . . like a husband and children and a home."

It was useless to argue with her. Like all women whose domestic life has been happy and successful, she could not be convinced that there was anything in the world more desirable than the love of a good husband and children. With her it was indeed something even stronger—a tribal instinct upon which life itself is founded. She was a fundamental person beside whom Irene and Lily, even her own daughter Ellen, were sports in the biological sense. They were removed by at least two generations from the soil. In them the struggle for life had become transvalued into a pursuit of the arts, of religion, of pleasure itself.

In the gathering twilight, Hattie Tolliver brought a lamp and lighted it to work by. Julia Shane watched her silently for a time, observing the strong neck, the immaculate full curve of her niece's figure, the certainty with which the strong worn fingers moved about their delicate work.

"You remember," she said, "that Lily mentioned a boy . . . a young boy, in her letter?"

138

"Yes," replied Hattie Tolliver, without glancing from her work. "The child of a friend. I thought she might have passed him by to come home to her mother. . . . Funny how children can forget you."

Julia Shane stirred softly in the deep bed. "I thought you might be thinking that," she said. "I thought it would be better to tell you the truth. I wanted you to know anyway. The truth is, Hattie, that the child is her own. She is more interested in him than in me, and that's natural enough and quite proper."

The strong fingers paused abruptly in their work and lay motionless against the white linen. Hattie Tolliver's face betrayed her amazement; yet clearly she was a little amused.

"Charles always said there was something mysterious about Lily," she said. "But I never guessed she'd been secretly married."

The old woman, hesitating, coughed before she replied, as though the supremely respectable innocence of her niece somehow made her inarticulate. At last she summoned strength.

"But she's never been married, Hattie. There never was any ceremony."

"Then how . ." In Mrs. Tolliver's face the amazement spread until her countenance was one great interrogation.

"Children," interrupted her aunt in a voice filled with tremulous calm, "can be born without marriage certificates. They have nothing to do with legal processes."

For a long time the niece kept silent, fingering the while the half finished pillow case. It appeared that she found some new and marvelous quality in it. She fingered the stuff as though she were in the act of purchasing it across a counter. At last she raised her head.

"Then it was true . . . that old story?" she asked.

"What story?"

"The one they told in the Town . . . about Lily's *having* to go away to Paris."

"Yes. . . . But no one ever really knew. They only guessed. They knew nothing at all. And they know nothing more to-day." The old woman paused for a second as though to give her words emphasis. "I'm trusting you never to tell,

Hattie. I wanted you to know because if ever it was necessary, I wanted Lily to come to you for help. It never will
be. It isn't likely."

Hattie Tolliver sat up very stiff and red. "Tell!" she said,
"Tell! Who should I ever tell in the Town? Why should
I tell any of them?" The tribal instinct rose in triumph.
It was a matter of her family against the Mills, the Town, all
the world if necessary. Torture could not have dragged from
her the truth.

Yet Hattie Tolliver was not unmoved by the confession. It
may even have been that she herself long ago had suspicions
of the truth which had withered and died since from too much
doubt. To a woman of her nature the news of a thousand
strikes, of murder and of warfare was as nothing beside the
thing Julia Shane revealed. For a long time she said nothing
at all, but her strong fingers spoke for her. They worked faster
and more skilfully than ever, as if all her agitation was pouring
itself out through their tips. The fingers and the flying needle
said, "That this should have happened in our family! I can't
believe it. Perhaps Aunt Julia is so sick that her mind is
weakened. Surely she must imagine this tale. Such things
happen only to servant girls. All this is unreal. It cannot
be true. Lily could not be so happy, so buoyant if this were
true. Sinners can only suffer and be miserable."

All this time she remained silent, breathing heavily, and
when at last she spoke, it was to ask, "Who was the man?" in
so terrible a voice that the old woman on the bed started for a
moment and then averted her face lest her niece see the ghost
of a smile which slipped out unwilled.

"It was the Governor," the aunt replied at last.

And then, "Why would he not marry her?" in a voice filled
with accumulations of hatred and scorn for the ravishers of
women.

This time Julia Shane did not smile. Her pride,—the old
fierce and arrogant pride—was touched.

"Oh," she replied, "it was not that. It was Lily who refused to marry him. He begged her . . . on his knees he
begged her. I saw him. He would have been glad enough to
have her."

And this led only to a "Why?" to which the old woman answered that she did not know except that Lily had said she wished to be herself and go her own way, that she was content and would not marry him even if he became president. "Beyond that, I do not know," she said. "That is where a mother does not know even her own daughter. I don't believe Lily knows herself. Can you tell why it is that Ellen must go on studying and studying, why she cannot help it? Can I know why Irene wants only to be left in peace to go her own way? No, we never really know any one."

All this swept over the head of Hattie Tolliver. She returned to one thing. "It would not have been a bad match. He is a senator now."

It had grown quite dark during their talk and from inside the barrier of the Mills the searchlights began to operate, at first furtively and in jerky fashion and then slowly with greater and greater deliberation, sweeping in gigantic arcs the sky and the squalid area of the Flats. A dozen times in their course the hard white beams swept the walls of the barren old house, penetrating even the room where Julia Shane lay slowly dying. The flashes of light came suddenly, bathing in an unearthly glow and with a dazzling clarity the walls and the furniture. At last, as the beams swept the face of the ormulu clock, Hattie Tolliver, rising, folded her pillow case and thrust it into the black bag she carried.

"I must go now," she said. "Charlie will be wanting his supper."

The old woman asked her to bend down while she kissed her. It was the first time she had ever made such a request and she passed over the extraordinary event by hastily begging her niece to draw the curtains.

"The lights make me nervous," she said. "I don't know why, but they are worse than the noise the Mills used to make."

And when this operation was completed she summoned her niece again to her side. "Would you like to see a picture of Lily's boy?"

Hattie Tolliver nodded.

"It is in the top drawer of the chiffonier. Will you fetch it to me?"

Her niece brought the picture and for a time the two women regarded it silently. It was the photograph of a handsome child, singularly like Lily although there was something of the Governor's rather florid good looks, particularly about the high sweeping forehead.

"He is a fine child, isn't he?" the old woman remarked. "I never expected to have a grandchild named Shane."

Still regarding the picture with a sort of fascination, Mrs. Tolliver replied, "He is a darling, isn't he? Does she call him that?"

"Of course. What would she call him?"

"Yes, he is a fine lad. He looks like our family." And then after a long pause she added, "I'm glad you told me all the story. I'm glad Lily did what she did deliberately. I should hate to think that any of us would be weak enough to let a man take advantage of her. That makes a great difference."

After she had put on her small black hat trimmed with worn and stubby ostrich plumes, she turned for the last time. "If you have another of those pictures, Aunt Julia, I would like to have one. I'd like to show it to Charles. He's always admired Lily. It's funny what a way she has with men."

There was no sting in the remark. It was a simple declaration, spoken as though the truth of it had occurred to her for the first time. She was too direct and vigorous to be feline.

As she closed the door the voice of her aunt trailed weakly after. "You needn't worry about Ellen. All her strength and character is your strength and character, Hattie. She can take care of herself."

The niece turned in the doorway, her thick strong figure blocking the shower of dim light from the hall. "No," she said. "It's not as though Lily were bad. She isn't bad. I've always had an idea that she knew what she was about. I suppose she has her own ideas on life. Perhaps she lives up to them. I can't say they're my ideas." For a second she leaned against the frame of the door, searching with an air of physical effort for words to express her thoughts. "No, she isn't bad," she continued. "No one who ever knew her can say she is a bad woman. I can't explain what I mean, but I suppose she believes in what she does."

And with this wise and mysterious observation Mrs. Tolliver returned to the world of the concrete—her own world—swept down the long stairway and into the kitchen where she reclaimed her basket, and left the house without waiting for the hostile mulatto woman to open the door.

XL

PERHAPS because she was so dazed and fascinated by the story which Julia Shane had poured into her astonished ears, she walked in a sort of dream to the foot of the long drive where she found herself suddenly embroiled in a waking nightmare. On all sides of her there rose a great tumult and shouting. Stones were thrown. Cries rang out in barbaric tongues. Men struggled and fought, and above the men on foot rose the figures of the constabulary mounted on wild and terrified horses who charged and curvetted as their masters struck about them with heavy clubs.

Through all this, Hattie Tolliver passed with an air of the most profound detachment and scorn, somewhat in the manner of a great sea-going freighter riding the waves of an insignificant squall. She carried her head high, despising the Irish constabulary as profoundly as she despised the noisy alien rabble Clearly it was none of her affair. This embroiled rabble had nothing to do with her, nothing to do with her family, nothing to do with her world. The riot was as nothing beside the tale that kept running through her mind, blinding her senses to all the struggle that took place at her very side.

And then, suddenly and without warning, the crack of a pistol tore the air; then another and another, and there fell at the feet of Hattie Tolliver, completely blocking her overwhelming progress, the body of a swarthy man with heavy black mustaches. Before she was able to move, one of the constabulary, rushing up, kicked the prostrate body of the groaning man.

But he did not kick twice, for he was repulsed a second later by the savage thrust in the stomach from the umbrella of Mrs Tolliver who, rushing to the attack, cried out, "Get away, you filthy brute! . . . You dirty coward!"

And the trooper, seeing no doubt that she was not one of the foreigners, retired sheepishly before the menace of the angry mob to join his fellows.

The basket and umbrella were cast aside and Mrs. Tolliver, bending over the writhing man, searched for the wound. When she looked up again she found, standing over her, the gigantic steel worker who she knew was Irene's friend. She did not know his name.

"Here," she said, with the manner of a field marshal. "Help me get this fellow into the house over there."

Without a word, Krylenko bent down, picked up the stricken workman and bore him, laid across his brawny shoulders, into the corner saloon whither Hattie Tolliver with her recovered basket and umbrella followed him, surrounded by a protecting phalanx of excited and gibbering strikers.

The saloon was empty, for all the hangers-on had drifted long before into the streets to watch the riot from a safe distance. But the electrical piano kept up its uncanny uproar playing over and over again, Bon-Bon Buddy, the Chocolate Drop and I'm Afraid to go Home in the Dark.

There on the bar, among the empty glasses, Krylenko laid the unconscious striker and Hattie Tolliver, with the scissors she had used but a moment before in hemstitching a pillow-case, cut away the soiled shirt and dressed the wound. When her work was done she ordered Krylenko to take down one of the swinging doors and on this the strikers bore the wounded man to his own house.

When the little procession had vanished around a corner, Mrs. Tolliver brushed her black clothes, gathered up her basket and umbrella and set out up the hill to the Town. It was the first time she had ever set foot inside an establishment which sold intoxicating liquors.

Behind her in the darkened room at Cypress Hill, the sound of shots and cries came distantly to Julia Shane as through a high impenetrable wall, out of another world. At the moment she was alive in a world of memories, a world as real and as tangible as the world of the Mills and the Flats, for the past may be quite as real as the present. It is a vast country full of trees and houses, animals and friends, where people may go on having adventures as long as they live. And the sounds

she heard in her world bore no relation to the sounds in sordi
Halsted street.   They were the sounds of pounding hoofs or
hard green turf, and the cries of admiration from a little group
of farmers and townspeople who leaned on the rail of John
Shane's paddock while his wife, with a skilful hand sent hi
sleek hunter Doña Rita over the bars—first five, then six and
last of all and marvelous to relate, a clean seven!

A stained and dusty photograph slipped from her thin fingers
and lost itself among the mountainous bedclothing which she
found impossible to keep in order.   It was the portrait of a
youngish man with a full black beard and eyes that were wild,
passionate, adventurous . . . the portrait of John Shane, the
lover, as he returned to his wife at the school of Mademoiselle
Violette de Vaux at St. Cloud on the outskirts of Paris.

XLI

AS Julia Shane grew weaker, it was Cousin Hattie
Tolliver who "took hold" of the establishment at
Shane's Castle. It was always Mrs. Tolliver, capable
and housewifely, who "took hold" in a family crisis.
he managed funerals, weddings and christenings. Cousins
ame to die at her shabby house in the Town. She gathered
nto her large strong hands the threads of life and death that
tretched themselves through a family scattered from Paris to
Australia. Her relatives embroiled themselves in scrapes, they
rew ill, they lost or made fortunes, they succumbed to all the
weaknesses to which the human flesh is prone; and always, at
he definitive moment, they turned to Hattie Tolliver as to a
ouse built upon a rock.

Irene, so capable in succoring the miserable inhabitants of the
'lats, grew helpless when death peered in at the tall windows
f Shane's Castle. Besides, she had her own work to do. As
he strike progressed she came to spend days and nights in
he squalid houses of Halsted street, returning at midnight to
nquire after her mother. She knew nothing of managing a
ouse and Hattie Tolliver knew these things intimately. More
han that, Mrs. Tolliver enjoyed "taking hold"; and she ex-
racted, beyond all doubt, a certain faintly malicious satisfaction
n taking over the duties which should have fallen upon Irene,
while Irene spent her strength, her very life, in helping people
nrelated to her, people who were not even Americans.

So it was Hattie Tolliver, wearing a spotless apron and
earing a dustcloth, who opened the door when Hennery, re-
urning from his solitary and heroic venture outside the gates,
drove Lily up from the dirty red brick station, bringing this
ime no great trunks covered with gay labels of Firenze and
Sorrento but a pair of black handbags and a small trunk neatly
trapped. It may have been that Hennery, as Irene hinted

bitterly, made that perilous journey through the riots of Halste
street only because it was Mis' Lily who was returning. Ce:
tainly no other cause had induced him to venture outside th
barren park.

The encounter, for Hattie Tolliver, was no ordinary on
From her manner it was clear that she was opening the door t
a woman . . . her own cousin . . . who had lived in sin, wh
had borne a child out of wedlock. Indeed the woman migh
still be living in sin. Paris was a Babylon where it was im
possible to know any one's manner of living. Like all th
others, Mrs. Tolliver had lived all her life secure in the belie
that she knew Lily. She remembered the day of her cousin
birth . . . a snowy blustering day. She knew Lily throughou
her childhood. She knew her as a woman. "Lily," she un
doubtedly told herself, "was thus and so. If any one know
Lily, I know her." And then all this knowledge had been up
set suddenly by a single word from Lily's mother. It wa
necessary to create a whole new pattern. The woman wh
stood on the other side of the door was not Lily at all—a
least not the old Lily—but a new woman, a stranger, whom sh
did not know. There might be, after all, something in wha
Aunt Julia said about never really knowing any one.

All this her manner declared unmistakably during the fev
strained seconds that she stood in the doorway facing her cousin
For an instant, while the two women, the worldly and th
provincial, faced each other, the making of family history hun;
in the balance. It was Mrs. Tolliver who decided the issue
Suddenly she took her beautiful cousin into her arms, encirclin;
her in an embrace so warm and so filled with defiance of al
the world that Lily's black hat, trimmed with camelias, wa:
knocked awry.

"Your poor mother!" were Cousin Hattie's first words. "Sh
is very low indeed. She has been asking for you."

And so Lily won another victory in her long line of con
quests, a victory which she must have known was a real triumpl
in which to take a profound pride.

Then while Lily took off her hat and set her fine hair ir
order, her cousin poured out the news of the last few days. I

was news of a sort that warmed the heart of Mrs. Tolliver . . . news of Julia Shane's illness delivered gravely with a vast embroidery of detail, a long account of the mulatto woman's insolence and derelictions which increased as the old woman grew weaker; and, last of all, an eloquent and denunciatory account of Irene's behavior.

"She behaves," said Mrs. Tolliver, "as though a daughter had no obligations toward her own mother." Her face grew scarlet with indignation at this flouting of family ties. "She spends all her time in the Flats among those foreigners and never sees her own mother more than a minute or two a day. There she lies, a sick and dying woman, grieving because her daughter neglects her. You'd think Irene loved the strikers more . . . specially one young fellow who is the leader," she added darkly.

Lily, knowing her mother, must have guessed that Cousin Hattie's account suffered from a certain emotional exaggeration. The picture of old Julia Shane, grieving because her daughter neglected her, was not a convincing one. The old woman was too self reliant for that sort of behavior. She expected too little from the world.

But Lily said nothing. She unstrapped her bag and brought out a fresh handkerchief and a bottle of scent. Then she raised her lovely head and looked sharply at her cousin. "I suppose it's this same Krylenko," she said. "D'you think she's in love with him?"

"No," replied Mrs. Tolliver shrewdly, "I don't think she loves anybody or anything but her own soul. She's like a machine. She has an idea she loves the strikers but that's only because she thinks she's saving her soul by good works. I suppose it makes her happy. Only yesterday I told her, thinking it would be a hint, that charity begins at home." For a moment Mrs. Tolliver waited thoughtfully, and then she added, "You know, sometimes Irene looks at her mother as if she wanted her to make haste with her dying. I've noticed the look—more than once."

And so they talked for a time, as people always talked of Irene, as if she were a stranger, a curiosity, something which stood outside the realm of human understanding. And out of

the ruin of Irene's character, Hattie Tolliver rose phoenix-like
triumphant, as the heroine who had seen Irene's duty and taken
it upon herself.

"You know, I'm nursing your mother," she continued.
"She wouldn't have a nurse because she couldn't bear to have
a stranger in the house. She has that one idea now . .
seeing no one but the doctor and her own family. Now that
you've come, I suppose she won't even see the doctor any
more. She's asleep now, so I came down-stairs to put the
house into some sort of order. Heaven knows what it would
have been like if the drawing-room had been open too. That
mulatto woman," she added bitterly, 'hasn't touched a thing
in weeks."

Silently, thoughtfully, Lily pushed open the double doors into
the drawing-room.

"It's not been opened since you left," continued Mrs. Tolliver. "Not even for the Christmas party. But that wasn'
necessary because there aren't many of us left. You could put
all of us into the library. There's only Eva Barr and Charley
and me. The old ones are all dead and the young ones have
gone away." For a moment she paused, for Lily appeared not
to be listening. Then she added softly, "But I guess you know
all that. I'd forgotten Ellen was living with you."

For the time being, the conversation ended while the two
women, Lily in her smart suit from the Rue de la Paix and
Hattie Tolliver in shiny black alpaca with apron and dustcloth
stood in the doorway reverently surveying the vast old room, so
dead now and so full of memories. The rosewood chairs
shrouded like ghosts, appeared dimly in the light that filtered
through the curtained windows. In the far end, before the
long mirror, the piano with its shapeless covering resembled
some crouching, prehistoric animal. Above the mantelpiece
the flaming Venice of Mr. Turner glowed vaguely beneath
layers of dust. Cobwebs hung from the crystal chandeliers and
festooned the wall sconces; and beneath the piano the Aubusson
carpet, rolled into a long coil, waited like a python. The
room was the mute symbol of something departed from the
Town.

Silently the two women regarded the spectacle and when

Lily at length turned away, her dark eyes were shining with
tears. She was inexpressibly lovely, all softened now by the
melancholy sight.

"I suppose it will never be opened again," observed Mrs
Tolliver in a solemn voice. "But I mean to clean it thoroughly
the first time I have an opportunity. Just look at the dust."
And with her competent finger she traced her initials on the top
of a lacquer table.

For a moment Lily made no reply. At last she said, "No.
I suppose it is closed for good."

"You wouldn't come back here to live?" probed her cousin
with an air of hopefulness.

"No. Why should I?" And a second later Lily added,
"But how quiet it is. You can almost hear the stillness."

Mrs. Tolliver closed the door, seizing at the same time the
opportunity to polish the knobs on the hallway side. "Yes, it's
a relief not to hear the Mills. But there are other noises now
. . . riots and machine guns, and at night there are searchlights. Only last night the police clubbed an old woman to
death at the foot of the drive. She was a Polish woman . . .
hadn't been harming any one. I wonder you didn't see the
blood. It's smeared on the gates. Irene can tell you all about
it." For a moment she polished thoughtfully; then she
straightened her vigorous body and said, "But I got back at
them. I gave one of the hired policeman a poke he won't soon
forget. It's a crime the way they behave. . . . It's murder.
No decent community would allow it." And she told Lily the
story of the rescue at the corner saloon.

As Lily made her way up the long stairway, Mrs. Tolliver
paused in her work to watch the ascending figure until it
reached the top. Her large honest face was alive with interest,
her eyes shining as if she now really saw Lily for the first
time, as if the old Lily had been simply an illusion. The beautiful stranger climbed the stairs languidly, the long, lovely
lines of her body showing through the trim black suit. Her
red hair glowed in the dim light of the hallway. She was incredibly young and happy, so unbelievably fresh and lovely that
Mrs. Tolliver, after Lily had disappeared at the turn of the
stair, moved away shaking her head and making the clucking

sound which primitive women use to indicate a disturbance of their suspicions.

And when she returned to dusting the library under the handsome, malignant face of John Shane she worked in silence, abandoning her usual habit of humming snatches of old ballads. After the Ball was Over and The Baggage Coach Ahead were forgotten. Presently, when she had finished polishing the little ornaments of jade and crystal, she fell to regarding the portrait with a profound interest. She stood thus, with her arms akimbo, for many minutes regarding the man in the picture as if he too had become a stranger to her. She discovered, it appeared, something more than a temperamental and clever old reprobate who had been indulgent toward her. Her manner was that of a person who stands before a suddenly opened door in the presence of magnificent and incomprehensible wonders.

Lily found her there when she came down-stairs.

"You know," observed Mrs. Tolliver, "I must be getting old. I have such funny thoughts lately . . . the kind of thoughts a normal healthy woman doesn't have."

XLII

ROOM by room, closet by closet, Mrs. Tolliver and Lily put the big house in order. They even set Hennery to cleaning the cellar, and themselves went into the attic where they poked about among old boxes and trunks filled with clothing and photographs, bits of yellow lace and brocade for which no use had ever been found. There were photographs of Lily and Irene as little girls in tarlatan dresses much ornamented with artificial pansies and daisies; pictures of John Shane on the wrought iron piazza, surrounded by men who were leaders in state politics; dim photographs of Julia Shane in an extremely tight riding habit with a bustle, and a hat set well forward over the eyes; pictures of the annual family gatherings at Christmas time with all its robust members standing in the snow outside the house at Cypress Hill. There were even pictures of Mrs. Tolliver's father, Jacob Barr, on the heavy hack he sometimes rode, and one of him surrounded by his eight vigorous children.

From the sentimental Mrs. Tolliver, this collection wrenched a tempest of sighs. To Lily she said, "It's like raising the dead. I just can't believe the changes that have occurred."

The arrival of Lily brought a certain repose to the household. The mulatto woman who behaved so sulkily under the shifting dominations of the powerful Mrs. Tolliver and the anemic Irene, began slowly to regain her old respectful attitude. It appeared that she honored Miss Lily with the respect which servants have for those who understand them. Where the complaints of Irene and the stormy commands of Mrs. Tolliver had wrought nothing, the amiable smiles and the interested queries of Lily accomplished miracles. For a time the household regained the air of order and dignity which it had known in the days of Julia Shane's domination. Lily was unable to explain her success. After all, there was nothing new in the process. Servants had always obeyed her in the same fashion. She charmed them whether they were her own or not.

Although her arrival worked many a pleasant change in the house and appeared to check for a time the inward sweeping waves of melancholy, there was one thing which she was unable, either consciously or unconsciously, to alter in any way. This was the position of Irene. The sister remained an outsider. It was as if the old dwelling were a rooming house and she were simply a roomer, detached, aloof . . . a roomer in whom no one was especially interested. She was, in fact, altogether incomprehensible. Lily, to be sure, made every effort to change the condition of affairs; but her efforts, it appeared, only drove her sister more deeply into the shell of taciturnity and indifference. The first encounter of the two sisters, for all the kisses and warmth of Lily, was an awkward and soulless affair to which Irene submitted listlessly. So apparent was the strain of the encounter that Mrs. Tolliver, during the course of the morning's work, found occasion to refer to it.

"You mustn't mind Irene's behavior," she said. "She has been growing queerer and queerer." And raising her eyebrows significantly she continued, "You know, sometimes I think she's a little cracked. Religion sometimes affects people in that way, especially the sort of popery Irene practises."

And then she told of finding Irene, quite by accident, prostrate before the pink-gilt image of the Virgin, her hair all disheveled, her eyes streaming with tears.

Once Mrs. Tolliver had reconciled herself to Lily's secret, her entire manner toward her cousin suffered a change. The awe which had once colored her behavior disappeared completely. She was no longer the provincial, ignorant of life outside the Town, face to face with an experienced woman of the world. She was one mother with an understanding for another. Before many days had passed the pair worked and gossiped side by side, not only as old friends might have gossiped but as old friends who are quite the same age, whose interests are identical. In her manner there was no evidence of any strangeness save in the occasional moments when she would cease working abruptly to regard her lovely cousin with an expression of complete bewilderment, which did not vanish until Lily, attracted by her cousin's steady gaze, looked up and caused Mrs. Tolliver to blush as if it were herself who had sinned.

XLIII

IT was Lily who in the end mentioned the affair. She spoke of it as they sat at lunch in the paneled dining room.

"Mama," she said suddenly, "tells me that you know all about Jean."

"Yes," replied Mrs. Tolliver, in a queer unearthly voice. "She told me."

"I'm glad, because I wanted to tell you before, only she wouldn't let me. She said you wouldn't understand."

There was an awesome little pause and Mrs. Tolliver, her fork poised, said, "I don't quite understand, Lily. I must say it's puzzling. But I guessed you knew what you were doing. It wasn't as if you were a common woman who took lovers." She must have seen the faint tinge of color that swept over Lily's face, but she continued in the manner of a virtuous woman doing her duty, seeing a thing in the proper light, being fair and honest. "I guessed there was some reason. Of course, I wouldn't want a daughter of mine to do such a thing. I would rather see her in her grave."

Her manner was emphatic and profound. It was clear that however she might forgive Lily in the eyes of the world, she had her own opinions which none should ever know but herself and Lily.

Lily blushed, the color spreading over her lovely face to the soft fringe of her hair. "You needn't worry, Cousin Hattie," she said. "Ellen would never do such a thing. You see, Ellen is complete. She doesn't need anything but herself. She's not like me at all. She isn't weak. She would never do anything because she lost her head."

Ellen's mother, who had stopped eating, regarded her with a look of astonishment. "But your mother said you hadn't lost your head. She said it was you who wouldn't marry the Governor."

156

Lily's smile persisted. She leaned over to touch her cousin's hand, gently as though pleading with her to be tolerant.

"It's true," she said. "Some of what mother told you. It's true about my refusing to marry him. You see the trouble is that I'm not afraid when I should be. I'm not afraid of the things I should be afraid of. When there is danger, I can't run away. If I could run away I'd be saved, but I can't. Something makes me see it through. It's something that betrays me . . . something that is stronger than myself. That's what happened with the Governor. It was I who was more guilty than he. It is I who played with fire. If I was not unwilling, what could you expect of him . . . a man. Men love the strength of women as a refuge from their own weakness." She paused and her face grew serious. "When it was done, I was afraid . . . not afraid, you understand of bearing a child or even afraid of what people would say of me. I was afraid of losing myself, because I knew I couldn't always love him. . . . I knew it. I knew it. I knew that something had betrayed me. I couldn't give up all my life to a man because I'd given an hour of it to him. I was afraid of what he would become. Can you understand that? That was the only thing I was afraid of . . . nothing else but that. It was I who was wrong in the very beginning."

But Mrs. Tolliver's expression of bewilderment failed to dissolve before this disjointed explanation. "No," she said, "I don't understand. . . . I should think you would have wanted a home and children and a successful husband. He's been elected senator, you know, and they talk of making him president."

Lily's red lip curved in a furtive, secret, smile. "And what's that to me?" she asked. "They can make him what they like. A successful husband isn't always the best. I could see what they would make him. That's why I couldn't face being his wife. I wasn't a girl when it happened. I was twenty-four and I knew a great many things. I wasn't a poor innocent seduced creature. But it wasn't so much that I thought it out. I couldn't help myself. I couldn't marry him. Something inside me wouldn't let me. A part of me was wise. You see, only half of me loved him . . . my body, shall we say, desired

him. That is not enough for a lifetime. The body changes."
For a second she cast down her eyes as if in shame and Mrs.
Tolliver, who never before had heard such talk, looked away,
out of the tall window across the snow covered park.

"Besides," Lily continued, after a little silence, "I have a
home and I have a child. Both of them are perfect. I am a
very happy woman, Cousin Hattie . . . much happier than if
I had married him. I know that from what he taught
me . . . in that one hour."

Mrs. Tolliver regarded her now with a curious, prying,
look. Plainly it was a miracle she had found in a woman
who had sinned and still was happy. "But you have no husband," she said presently, with the air of presenting a final
argument.

"No," replied Lily, "I have no husband."

"But that must mean something."

"Yes, I suppose it does mean something."

And then the approach of the mulatto woman put an end to
the talk for the time being. When she had disappeared once
more, it was Mrs. Tolliver who spoke. "You know," she said,
"I sometimes think Irene would be better off if such a thing
had happened to her. It isn't natural, the way she carries on.
It's morbid. I've told her so often enough."

"But it couldn't have happened to Irene. She will never
marry. You see Irene's afraid of men . . . in that way.
Such a thing I'm sure would drive her mad." And Lily
bowed her lovely head for a moment. "We must be good to
Irene. She can't help being as she is. You see she believes
all love is a kind of sin. Love, I mean, of the sort you and I
have known."

At this speech Mrs. Tolliver grew suddenly tense. Her
large, honest face became scarlet with indignation. "But it
isn't the same," she protested. "What I knew and what you
knew. They're very different things. My love was conse-
crated."

Lily's dark eyes grew thoughtful. "It would have been the
same if I had married the Governor. People would have said
that we loved each other as you and Cousin Charles love each

other. They wouldn't have known the truth. One doesn't
wash one's dirty linen in public."

Her cousin interrupted her abruptly. "It is not the same.
I could not have had children by Charlie until I was married to
him. I mean there could have been nothing like that between
us beforehand."

"That's only because you were stronger than me," said Lily.
"You see I was born as I am. That much I could not help.
There are times when I cannot save myself. You are more
fortunate. Irene is like me. That is the reason she behaves
as she does. After all, it is the same thing in us both."

But Mrs. Tolliver, it was plain to be seen, understood none
of this. It was quite beyond her simple code of conduct.
Her life bore witness to her faith in the creed that breaking
the rules meant disaster.

"I know," continued Lily, "that I was lucky to have been
rich. If I had been poor it would have been another matter.
I should have married him. But because I was rich, I was free.
I was independent to do as I wished, independent . . . like
a man, you understand. Free to do as I pleased." All at once
she leaned forward impulsively. "Tell me, Cousin Hattie
. . . it has not made me hard, has it? It has not made me
old and evil? It has not made people dislike me?"

Mrs. Tolliver regarded her for a moment as if weighing
arguments, seeking reasons, why Lily seemed content and
happy despite everything. At length, finding no better retort,
she said weakly, "How could they dislike you? No one ever
knew anything about it."

A look of triumph shone in Lily's dark eyes. "Ah, that's
it!" she cried. "That's it! They didn't know anything, so
they don't dislike me. If they had known they would have
found all sorts of disagreeable things in me. They would
have said, 'We cannot speak to Lily Shane. She is an immoral
woman.' They would have made me into a hard and unhappy
creature. They would have created the traits which they
believed I should possess. It is the knowing that counts and
not the act itself. It is the old story. It is worse to be found
out in a little sin than to commit secretly a big one. There is

only one thing that puzzles them." She raised her slim, soft hands in a little gesture of badinage. "Do you know what it is? They can't understand why I have never married and why I am not old and rattly as a spinster should be. It puzzles them that I am young and fresh."

For a time Mrs. Tolliver considered the dark implications of this speech. But she was not to be downed. "Just the same, I don't approve, Lily," she said. "I don't want you to think for a minute that I approve. If my daughter had done it, it would have killed me. It's not right. One day you will pay for it, in this world or the next."

At this threat Lily grew serious once more and the smoldering light of rebellion came into her eyes. She was leaning back in her old indolent manner. It was true that there was about her something inexpressibly voluptuous and beautiful which alarmed her cousin. It was a dangerous, flaunting beauty, undoubtedly wicked to the Presbyterian eyes of Mrs. Tolliver. And she was young too. At that moment she might have been taken for a woman in her early twenties.

After a time she raised her head. "But I am happy," she said, defiantly, "completely happy."

"I wish," said Mrs. Tolliver with a frown, "that you wouldn't say such things. I can't bear to hear you."

And presently the talk turned once more to Irene. "She is interested in this young fellow called Krylenko," said Mrs. Tolliver. "And your mother is willing to have her marry him, though I can't see why. I would rather see her die an old maid than be married to a foreigner."

"He is clever, isn't he?" asked Lily.

"I don't know about that. He made all this trouble about the strike. Everything would be peaceful still if he hadn't stirred up trouble. Maybe that's being clever. I don't know."

"But he must be clever if he could do all that. He must be able to lead the workers. I'm glad he did it, myself. The Harrison crowd has ruled the roost long enough. It'll do them good to have a jolt . . . especially when it touches their pocketbooks. I saw him once, myself. He looks like a powerful fellow. I should say that some day you will hear great things of him."

Mrs. Tolliver sniffed scornfully. "Perhaps . . . perhaps. If he is, it will be because Irene made him great. All the same I can't see her marrying him . . . a common immigrant . . . a Russian!"

"You needn't worry. She won't. She could never marry him. To her he isn't a man at all. He's a sort of idea . . . a plaster saint!" And for the first time in all her discussion of Irene a shade of hard scorn colored her voice.

XLIV

FOR an hour longer they sat talking over the coffee while Lily smoked indolently cigarette after cigarette beneath the disapproving eye of her cousin. They discussed the affairs of the household, the news in the papers of Mrs. Julis Harrison's second stroke, of Ellen, and Jean from whom Lily had a letter only that morning.

"Has the Governor ever asked for him?" inquired Mrs. Tolliver, with the passionate look of a woman interested in details.

"No," said Lily, "I have not heard from him in years. He has never seen the boy. You see Jean is mine alone because even if the Governor wanted him he dares not risk a scandal. He is as much my own as if I had created him alone out of my own body. He belongs to me and to me alone, do you see? I can make him into what I will. I shall make him into a man who will know everything and be everything. He shall be stronger than I and cleverer. He is handsome enough. He is everything to me. A queen would be proud to have him for her son."

As she spoke a light kindled in her eyes and a look of exultation spread over her face. It was an expression of passionate triumph.

"You see," she added, "it is a wonderful thing to have some one who belongs to you alone, who loves you alone and no one else. He owns me and I own him. There is no one else who counts. If we were left alone on a desert island, we would be content." The look faded slowly and gave place to a mocking smile that arched the corners of her red lips. "If I had married the Governor, the boy might have become anything. . . . I should have seen him becoming crude and common under my very eyes. I should have hated his father and I could have done nothing. As it is, his father is only a

162

memory . . . pleasant enough, a handsome man who loved me, but never owned me . . . even for an instant . . . not even the instant of my child's conception!"

During this speech the manner of Mrs. Tolliver became more and more agitated. With each bold word a new wave of color swept her large face, until at the climax of Lily's confession she was struck mute, rendered incapable of either thought or action. It was a long time before she recovered even a faint degree of her usual composure. At last she managed to articulate, "I don't see, Lily, how you can say such things. I really don't. The words would burn my throat!"

Her cousin's smile was defiant, almost brazen. "You see, Cousin Hattie, I have lived among the French. With them such things are no more than food and drink . . . except perhaps that they prefer love to everything else," she added, with a mischievous twinkle in her dark eyes.

"And besides," continued Mrs. Tolliver, "I don't know what you mean. I'm sure Charles has never *owned* me."

"No, my dear," said Lily, "He never has. On the contrary it is you who have always owned him. It is always one thing or the other. The trouble is that at first women like to be owned." She raised her hand. "Oh, I know. The Governor would have owned me sooner or later. There are some men who are like that. You know them at once. I know how my father owned my mother and you know as well as I that she was never a weak, clinging woman. If she had been as rich as I, she would have left him . . . long ago. She could not because he owned her."

"But that was different," parried Mrs. Tolliver. "He was a foreigner."

They were treading now upon that which in the family had been forbidden ground. No one discussed John Shane with his wife or children because they had kept alive for more than thirty years a lie, a pretense. John Shane had been accepted silently and unquestioningly as all that a husband should be. Now the manner of Mrs. Tolliver brightened visibly at the approach of an opening for which she had waited more years than she was able to count.

"But he was a man and she was a woman," persisted Lily. "I know that most American women own their husbands, but the strange thing is that I could never have married a man whom I could own. You see that is the trouble with marriage. It is difficult to be rid of a husband."

Mrs. Tolliver shifted nervously and put down her coffee cup. "Really, Lily," she said, "I don't understand you. You talk as though being married was wrong." Her manner, for the first time, had become completely cold and disapproving. She behaved as though at any moment she might rise and turn her back forever upon Lily.

"Oh, don't think, Cousin Hattie, that people get married because they like being tied together by law. Most people get married because it is the only way they can live together and still be respected by the community. Most people would like to change now and then. It's true. They're like that in their deepest hearts . . . far down where no one ever sees."

She said this so passionately that Mrs. Tolliver was swept into silence. Books the good woman never read because there was no time; and even now with her children gone, she did not read because it was too late in life to develop a love for books. Immersed always in respectability, such thoughts as these had never occurred to her; and certainly no one had ever talked thus in her presence.

"I don't understand," she was able to articulate weakly after a long pause. "I don't understand." And then as if she saw opportunity escaping from her into spaces from which it might never be recovered, she said, "Tell me, Lily. Have you ever had any idea from where your father came?"

The faint glint of amusement vanished from her cousin's eyes and her face grew thoughtful. "No. Nothing save that his mother was Spanish and his father Irish. He was born in Marseilles."

"And where's that?" asked Mrs. Tolliver, aglow with interest.

"It's in the south of France. It's a great city and an evil one . . . one of the worst in the world. Mamma says we'll never know the truth. I think perhaps she is right."

After this the conversation returned to the minutiae of the

household for a time and, at length, as the bronze clock struck three the two women rose and left the room to make their way upstairs to the chamber of the dying old woman. In the hall, Lily turned, "I've never talked like this to any one," she said. "I'd never really thought it all out before. I've told you more than I've ever told any one, Cousin Hattie . . . even my mother."

Upstairs Mrs. Tolliver opened the door of the darkened room, Lily followed her on tiptoe. In the gray winter light, old Julia Shane lay back among the pillows sleeping peacefully.

"Will you wake her for her medicine?" whispered Lily.

"Of course," replied her cousin, moving to the bedside, where she shook the old woman gently and softly called her name.

"Aunt Julia! Aunt Julia!" she called again and again. But there was no answer as Mrs. Tolliver's powerful figure bent over the bed. She felt for the weakened pulse and then passed her vigorous hand over the face, so white now and so transparent. Then she stood back and regarded the bony, relentless old countenance and Lily drew nearer until her warm full breasts brushed her cousin's shoulder. The hands of the two women clasped silently in a sort of fearful awe.

"She has gone away," said Mrs. Tolliver, "in her sleep. It could not have been better."

And together the two women set about preparing Julia Shane for the grave, forgetful of all the passionate talk of an hour before. In the face of death, it counted for nothing.

XLV

A LITTLE while later, Lily herself went down the snow covered drive and summoned a passing boy whom she sent into the Flats in search of Irene, since she herself dared not venture among the sullen strikers. After two hours, he returned to say he could find no trace of the sister. So it was not until Irene returned at midnight that she learned her mother was dead. She received the news coldly enough, perhaps because in those days death and suffering meant so little to her; but even Lily must have seen the faint glimmer of triumph that entered her sister's pale, red-rimmed eyes at the news that she was free at last.

Just before dawn when the searchlights, swinging their gigantic arcs over the Flats, pierced the quiet solitude of Lily's room and wakened her, she heard through the mist of sleep the voice of Irene praying in her room for mercy upon the soul of their mother. For a second, she raised her head in an attitude of listening and then sank back and quickly fell asleep, her rosy face pillowed on her white bare arm, her bright hair all loose and shining in the sudden flashes of reflected light.

The Town newspapers published long obituaries of Julia Shane, whole columns which gave the history of her family, the history of John Shane, so far as it was known, and the history of Cypress Hill. In death it seemed that Julia Shane reflected credit in some way upon the Town. She gave it a kind of distinction just as the Cyclops Mills or any other remarkable institution gave it distinction. The newspapers treated her as if she were good advertising copy. The obituaries included lists of celebrated people who had been guests at Cypress Hill. Presidents were mentioned, an ambassador, and the Governor who was now a senator. They remarked that Julia Shane was the granddaughter of the man who gave the Town its name. For a single day Cypress Hill regained its lost and splendid prestige.   Newcomers in the Town, superintendents and clerks from the idle Mills, learned for the first time the history of Shane's Castle, all but the scandalous stories about John Shane which were omitted as unsuitable material for an obituary. Besides no one really knew whether they were true or not.

And despite all this vulgar fanfare, it was clear that a great lady had passed, one who in her day had been a sovereign, but one whose day had passed with the coming of the Mills and the vulgar, noisy aristocracy of progress and prosperity.

The obituaries ended with the sentence, "Mrs. Shane is survived by two unmarried daughters, Irene, who resides at Cypress Hill, and Lily who for some ten years has made her home in Paris.   Both were with their mother at the time of her passing."

It was this last sentence which interested the older residents. *Lily, who for some ten years has made her home in Paris.   Both were with their mother at the time of her passing.*   How much lay hidden and mysterious in those two lines.   Until the publishing of the obituary, the Town had known nothing of Lily's return.

At five o'clock on the afternoon of the funeral Willie Harrison sat in his mother's bedroom in the sandstone house giving her a detailed account of the funeral.   Outside the snow fell in drifting clouds, driven before a wind which howled wildly among the ornamental cupolas and projections of the ugly house.   Inside the air hung warm and stifling, touched by the pallid odor of the sickroom.   It was a large square room constructed with a great effect of solidity, and furnished with heavy, expensive furniture upholstered in dark red plush.   The walls were tan and the woodwork of birch stained a deep mahogany color.   Above the ornate mantelpiece hung an engraved portrait of the founder of the Mills and of the Harrison fortune . . . Julis Harrison, coarse, powerful, beetle-browed, his heavy countenance half-buried beneath a thick chin beard. The engraving was surrounded by a wide frame of bright German gilt; it looked down upon the room with the gaze of one who has wrought a great success out of nothing by the sweat of his brow and labor of bulging muscles, as once he had hammered crude metal into links and links into chains in the blacksmith shop which stood upon the spot now occupied by the oldest of the furnaces. It was a massive awkward room, as much like a warehouse as like a boudoir or a bedroom. It suited admirably the face in the portrait and the heavy body of the old woman who lay in the mahogany bed, helpless and ill-tempered beneath a second stroke of paralysis.

The son sat awkwardly on the edge of the red plush sofa near the mother. As he grew older, his manner became more and more uneasy in the presence of the old woman. His hair had grown thinner and on the temples there were new streaks of gray. There was something withered about him, something incomplete and unfinished like an apple that has begun to shrink before it has reached maturity. In the massive room, beneath the gaze of the overwhelming portrait, beside the elephantine bed in which he was conceived and born of the heavy old woman, Willie Harrison was a curiosity, a mouse born of a mountain in labor. He was the son of parents who were both quite masculine.

In a strange fit of forgetfulness he had worn his heavy overshoes into the sacred precincts of his mother's bedroom and they now lay beside him on the floor where he had placed them timidly when his mother commanded him to remove them lest his feet become overheated and tender, thus rendering him liable to sudden colds. Indeed, since the very beginning of the strike Willie had not been well. The struggle appeared to weigh him down. Day by day he grew paler and more nervous. He rarely smiled, and a host of new fine lines appeared upon his already withered countenance. Yet he had gone through the blowing snow and the bitter cold to the cemetery, partly at the command of his mother who was unable to go and partly because he had hoped to see Lily once more, if only for a moment by the side of an open grave.

And now Mrs. Julis Harrison, lying helpless upon her broad back, waited to hear the account of the funeral. She lay with her head oddly cocked on one side in order to see her son. Her speech came forth mumbled and broken by the paralysis.

"Were there many there?" she asked.

"Only a handful," replied her son in his thin voice. "Old William Baines . . . you know, the old man, the Shane's family lawyer. . . ."

"Yes," interrupted his mother. "An old fogy . . . who ought to have died ten years ago."

William Harrison must have been used to interruptions of this sort from his mother. He continued, "One or two church people and the two girls. It was frightfully cold on top of that bald hill. The coffin was covered with snow the moment it was lowered into the grave."

"Poor Julia," muttered the woman on the bed. "She lived too long. She lost interest in life." This remark she uttered with the most mournful of intonations. On the verge of the grave herself, she still maintained a lively interest in deaths and funerals.

"I'm glad you went," she added presently. "It shows there was no feeling, no matter how bad Julia treated me. It shows that I forgave her. People knew I couldn't go."

There was a long pause punctuated by the loud monotonous ticking of the brass clock. Outside the wind whistled among the cornices.

"She must have left a great deal of money," observed Mrs. Harrison. "More than a couple of millions, I shouldn't wonder. They haven't spent anything in the last ten years."

Willie Harrison lighted a cigarette. "Except Irene," he said. "She has been giving money to the strikers. Everybody knows that."

"But that's her own," said his mother. "It has nothing to do with what Julia left." She stirred restlessly. "Please, Willie, will you not smoke in here. I can't bear the smell of tobacco."

Willie extinguished the cigarette and finding no place in the whole room where he might dispose of the remains, he thrust them silently into his pocket.

"I asked her at the funeral if it was true," he said. "And she told me it was none of my business . . . that she would give everything she possessed if she saw fit."

Mrs. Harrison grunted. "It's that Krylenko," she observed

"That's who it is. Don't tell me she'd give away her money for love of the strikers. No Shane ever gave his fortune to the poor."

The clock again ticked violently and without interruption for a long time.

"And Lily," said Mrs. Harrison presently.

Willie began fumbling with the ruby clasp on his watch chain, slipping it backward and forward nervously.

"She's just the same," he said. "Just the same. . . . Younger if anything. It's surprising how she keeps so young. I asked her to come and see you and she wanted to know if you had asked her to. I said you had and then she smiled a little and asked, 'Is it for curiosity? You can tell her how I look. You can tell her I'm happy.' That was all. I don't suppose she'll ever come back to the Town again after this time."

This Mrs. Harrison pondered for a time. At last she said, "I guess it's just as well she wouldn't have you. There's something bad about her. She couldn't be so young and happy if she was just an old maid. I guess after all you're better off. They have bad blood in 'em. It comes from old John Shane."

Willie winced at the bluntness of his mother's speech and attempted to lead her into other paths. "There was no trouble in the Flats to-day. None of the strikers came into Halsted street. Everything was quiet all day. The superintendent says it was on account of the old woman's funeral."

"You see," said Mrs. Harrison. "It's that Krylenko. I can't understand it . . . how a frumpish old maid like Irene can twist him around her finger."

Willie stopped fumbling with his chain. "She's made a weapon of him to fight us."

Mrs. Harrison shook her massive head with a negative gesture.

"Oh, no," she said, speaking slowly and painfully. "It may look like that, but she never thought it out. She isn't smart enough. Neither of them is, Irene or Lily. I've known them since they were little girls. They both do what they can't help doing. Julia might have done such a thing but I'm certain it never occurred to her. Besides," she added after a little pause, "she's dead and buried now."

"She came to hate us before she died," persisted Willie.

"Yes . . . that's true enough. I guess she did hate us . . . ever since that affair over the taxes."

Willie clung to his idea. "But don't you see. It's all worked out just the same, just as if they had planned it on purpose. It's the second time they have cost the Mills thousands of dollars."

This, somehow, Mrs. Harrison found herself unable to deny.

"Tell me," she said presently. "How did they appear to take it? . . . Lily and Irene?"

Willie was once more fumbling with the ruby clasp. "I don't know. Irene wasn't even dressed in mourning. She had on the same old gray suit and black hat. She looked like a crow. As for Lily, she was able to smile when she spoke to me. But you can't tell how she feels about anything. She always smiles."

After this little speech Willie rose and began to move about the room, fingering nervously the sparsely placed ornaments—a picture of himself as an anemic child with long, yellow curls, a heavy brass inkwell, a small copy in marble of the tomb of Scipio Africanus, the single memento of a voyage to Rome. He drifted over toward the window and drew aside the curtain to look out into the storm.

XLVI

ALL this time his mother, her vast bulk immovabl[e] beneath the mountainous sheets, followed him with he[r] eyes. She must have recognized the symptoms, fo[r] presently she broke the way.

"Have you anything you want to say?" she asked.

Willie moved back to the bed and for a time stood in silenc[e] fingering the carving of the footboard. He cleared his throa[t] as if to speak but only fell silent again. When at last he wa[s] able to say what was in his mind, he did so without lookin[g] up. He behaved as though the carving held for him the mos[t] profound interest.

"Yes," he said gently, "I want to say that I'm going t[o] get out of the Mills. I hate them. I've always hated them[.] I'm no good at it!" To forestall her interruptions he rushe[d] on with his speech. The sight of his mother lying helples[s] appeared to endow him with a sudden desperate courage. Sh[e] was unable to stop him. He even raised his head and faced he[r] squarely. "I don't like this strike. I don't like the fighting[.] I want to be an ordinary, simple man who could walk throug[h] Halsted street in safety. I want to be left alone."

Mrs. Harrison did not raise her head, but all the violent emotion, pent up and stifled by her helplessness, rose and flashed in her eyes. The scorn was thunderous but somehow it failed to overwhelm the faded, middle-aged man at the foot of the gigantic bed.

"I thank God your father cannot hear those words! H[e] would strike you down!"

Still Willie did not flinch. "My father is dead," he observed quietly. But his smile carried implications and a malice o[f] its own. "My father is dead," said the smile. "And my mother is helpless. Before long I shall be free . . . for the first time in my life . . . free . . . to do as I please . . . the slave of no one."

The smile wavered and clung to his face. Of course he
said none of this. What he said was, "It is a dirty business.
And I want nothing to do with it . . . not even any stock.
If it hadn't been for the Mills, Lily might have married me."

From the bed arose the scornful sound of a hoarse chuckle,
"Oh no, she wouldn't. You don't know her! She wouldn't
marry you because you were such a poor thing."

At this Willie began to tremble. His face became as white
as the spotless coverlet, and he grasped the bed rail with such
intensity that his thin knuckles showed blue against his skin. It
was the old taunt of a mother toward a child whose gentleness
and indecision were to her both incomprehensible and worthy
only of contempt, a child who had never suited her gigantic ideas
of power and wealth.

"And pray tell me what you *do* intend to do," she asked with
rich sarcasm.

A tremulous quality entered Willie's voice as he replied.
"I want to have a farm where I can raise chickens and ducks and
rabbits."

"Great God!" replied his mother in her deep voice. It was
all she said. Moving her head with a terrible effort, she turned
her face to the wall away from her son. But Willie, though
he still trembled a little in the presence of the old woman and
the glowering portrait above his head, had a look of triumph
in his pale eyes. It said, "I have won! I have won! I have
achieved a victory. I am free at last from the monster which
I have always hated. . . . I am through with the Mills. I
am through with Judge Weissman. . . . I can be bullied no
more!"

Outside the wind howled and tore at the eaves and presently
there came a suave knock at the door . . . the knock of the
worldly, white haired butler. "Miss Abercrombie is here to
see Mrs. Harrison," came a suave voice, and before Willie
could answer, his mother's crony, her nose very red from the
cold, had pushed her way like a wriggling ferret into the room.

At the sight of Willie, she halted for a moment winking at
him in a purely involuntary fashion.

"Your mother is so much better," she said bridling. "Aren't
you delighted?"

Willie's answer was an inarticulate grunt.

"I've come to hear all about the funeral," she continued i
her bustling manner. "I would have gone myself except for th
weather. Now sit down like a good boy and tell me all about.'
She too treated him as an anemic child still wearing curls.

Willie shook her hand politely. "My mother will tell you,'
he said. "I have told her everything."

And he slipped from the room leaving the two women, th
ferret and the mountain, to put the finishing touches upon th
obsequies of Julia Shane.

XLVII

I N the house at Cypress Hill the two sisters stayed on to await the settlement of the will proceedings.

The state of siege continued unrelieved, and as the winter advanced, as if Nature herself were hostile to the strikers, there came that year no January thaw at all. There was only more snow and unbroken cold so that Irene, instead of finding freedom with the death of her mother, encountered only more duties among the wretched inhabitants of Halsted Street. The Harrisons and Judge Weissman evicted a score of families from houses owned by the Mills. Bag and baggage, women and children, were thrust out into the frozen street to find refuge in other squalid houses already far too crowded.

Judge Weissman also saw to it that the strikers were unable to secure a hall in which to meet. When the men attempted to congregate in the streets, they were charged and clubbed by the constabulary. When they sought to meet in vacant lots, Judge Weissman saw to it that the owners ordered them off. When there was a fire, the strikers were charged by the Town papers with having set it. When there was a riot, it was always the strikers who caused it. But there was one charge which the Town found, above all others, unforgivable. The editors accused the workmen of obstructing progress. They charged the strikers with menacing prosperity and injuring the "boom spirit." The Rotary Club and the Benevolent Order of Elks, the Chamber of Commerce, even the Episcopal church (very high and much given to incense and genuflexions) espoused the cause of prosperity.

The strikers had no newspapers, no money, no voice. They might starve as slowly as they pleased. Krylenko himself was powerless.

Of what took place in the Town itself the two sisters knew nothing. During the day while Irene was absent Lily, clad

in a peignoir of black silk, wandered aimlessly about the hous
in search of ways to divert herself. She suffered profoundl
from boredom. In the course of her ramblings she discovere
one morning a great wooden box piled high with the yellow
backed French novels "skimmed" and cast away by her mother
These occupied her for a time and when she grew tired of read
ing, she sought to pass the time by writing letters—addresse
always to one of three people, Jean, Madame Gigon or Madam
Gigon's cousin, the Baron. Wrapped in her mother's old
fashioned cloak of sealskin, she made her way to the foot of th
drive and paid a passing boy to post them for her. She wa
careful always that none of them fell in the way of Irene.

She had the mulatto woman lay a fire in the drawing-room
and, opening the grand piano which had fallen sadly out o
tune, she spent hours in playing fragments of Chopin, Bach an
a new composer called Debussy. Mingled with these were od
snatches of music hall waltzes and the bawdy, piquant ballad
of the Cuirassiers. Once at the suggestion of Irene she too
up knitting socks and mufflers for the families of the strikers
but the work progressed so slowly that at last she gave up i
despair and, making a solitary excursion up the hill to th
Town, she purchased an enormous bundle of socks and sweater
which she turned over to her sister to distribute among th
suffering laborers and their families.

She slept a great deal too, until her opulent beauty showe
signs of plumpness and this led her into the habit of walkin
each morning a dozen times around the border of the barren
deserted park. These perambulations wore a deep path in th
snow, and the Mill guards, coming to expect her at a certai
hour each day, took up positions inside the barrier to watch th
beautiful stranger as she passed, wrapped in the antiquated sea
skin coat with leg of mutton sleeves, her eyes cast down mod
estly. As the month advanced, they grew bolder and stare
quite openly. One or two even ventured to whistle at her, bu
their demonstrations aroused not the slightest response, nor di
they interrupt the regular hour of her exercise. They migh
have been owls hooting among the branches of the dead trees

The only visitors were Hattie Tolliver and William Baines
the "old fogy" lawyer, who paid a round half-dozen calls bear

ng a little black bag filled with papers. With Mrs. Tolliver,
e shared an attitude of supreme indifference alike toward the
trikers and the guards. It appeared that he still lived in a
lay when there were no mills and no strikers. He was a tall
withered old man with drooping white mustaches and a thick
mass of vigorous white hair. He went about his business
gruffly, wasting no time over details, and no emotion over
entiment. He treated both sisters in the same cold, legal
manner.

The will was brief and concocted shrewdly by Julia Shane
nd old Mr. Baines. Nor was it complicated. The house and
ll the old woman's jewels were left to her daughter Lily.
There was also a sizable gift for Hattie Tolliver and a strange
equest which came as a surprise to all but old Mr. Baines.
t was added in a codicil, so he said, a short time before her
leath. It provided for a trust fund to support Welcome
House and provide a visiting nurse until Mr. Baines and the
wo daughters deemed these things no longer necessary.

"That," observed the cynical Mr. Baines drily, as he read the
vill, "will be as long as the human race exists. I tried to
ersuade her against it but she would not listen. She always
new what she was doing and just what she wanted, right to
he very end."

Thus Julia Shane placed herself for all time among the
nemies of the Mills.

Otherwise the property was divided evenly with an allowance
nade to Irene for the value of the Cypress Hill holdings.

Then Mr. Baines delivered with considerable ceremony and
dvice two letters, one addressed to Lily and one to Irene,
vhich had been left in his keeping.

The letter addressed to Lily read, "I am leaving the house
o you because Irene hates it. I know that she would only
lispose of it at once and give the money to the church. Like-
vise I am leaving my jewels to you, with the exception of two
ings which I gave Hattie Tolliver years ago—the emerald set
vith diamonds and the single big emerald. No doubt you re-
nember them. There is no use in leaving such things to Irene.
he would only sell them and spend the money to buy candles
or a saint. And that is not the purpose for which God made

jewels. He meant them to adorn beautiful women. Therefor
I give them to you."

And thus the amethysts set in Spanish silver, two emeral
rings, seven rings set with diamonds, a ruby necklace, a festoo
of pearls, a quantity of earrings of onyx, diamonds, emerald
and rubies and a long diamond chain passed into the possessio
of the elder daughter.

"In worldly possessions," the letter continued, "I have le
you both wealthy. There are other possessions over which
had no control. They were left to you by your father and b
me—the possessions which one cannot sell nor throw away, th
possessions which are a part of you, possessions good and evi
bad and indifferent, the possessions which in the end are yo
yourself.

"There are some things which it is difficult to discuss, eve
between a mother and her daughter. I am gone now. I sha
not be forced to look at you and feel shame at what you know
Yet I have always wanted to tell you, to explain to you tha
after all, I was never so hard, so invincible, so hopelessly britt
as I must have seemed. You see, my dear, there are som
things which one cannot control and one of these is the ur
conscious control over self-control—the thing which does no
permit you to speak. Another is pride.

"You see there was never anything in common between you
father and me, unless it was love of horses and that, after al
is not much. Before he ever saw me, he must have know
more of life than I ever knew. But those things were secre
and because of them, perhaps, I fell in love with him—after
fashion. I say 'after a fashion' because that is what it was.
was a country girl, the daughter of a farmer . . . nothing els
you understand. And you cannot know what that meant i
the days when the Town was a village and no one in it eve
went outside the state and seldom outside the county. He wa
fascinating . . . more fascinating than you can ever know.
married him on account of that. It was a great match. H
was a wonderful lover . . . not a lover like the men of th
county who make such good husbands, but a lover out o
another world. But that, my dear, did not make him a goo
husband, and in a little while it became clear that I was littl

ıore to him than a convenience.   Even sending me to France
idn't help matters.

"It was a bad affair, but in my day when one married there
ʋas no thought of anything but staying married. So what
ʋas done was done. There was no unmaking a mistake, even
ıss chance after you and Irene were born. He came of one
ace and I of another. And never once in our life together did
ʋe touch in our sympathies. It was, in short, a marriage
ɔunded upon passion alone—a despicable state of affairs which
 frequently worse than a *marriage de convenance,* for in that
ıere is no desire to burn itself out. . . . You see, I under-
ood the affair of the Governor far better than you ever
ɪagined.

"And so there are things descended to both of you over which
 have no control. I can only ask God to be merciful. Be
entle with Irene and thank God that you are made so that
fe cannot hurt you. She cannot help that which she is. You
ɛe I have known and understood more than any one guessed."
 That was all. The ending was as abrupt as the manner of
ulia Shane while she lived. Indeed to Lily, reading the letter,
 must have seemed that her mother was still alive. She sat
ɪoughtfully for a long time and at last tearing the letter slowly
ɪto bits, she tossed it into the drawing-room fire. Of its
ɔntents she said nothing to Irene.

 The letter to Irene was brief. It read, "I leave you your
ɪoney outright with no string to it, because the dead have no
ghts which the living are bound to respect. You may do with
 as you like. . . . You may give it all to your beloved church,
ɪough it will be without my approval. You may do any-
ɪing with it which will bring you happiness. I have prayed
 God to make you happy. If you can find happiness by bury-
ɪg yourself, do it before you are an hour older, for life is too
ɪort to waste even an hour of happiness. But do not believe
ɪat it is such an easy thing to find.

 "I have loved you, Irene, always, though I have never been
ɔle to understand you. I have suffered for you, silently and
 one. I, who am dead, may tell you these things which in
fe I could not tell you. Only know that I cherished you
 ways even if I did not know how to reach you. There are

some things that one cannot say. At least I—even I, your ow
mother—could not make you understand because I never reall
knew you at all. But remember always that I loved you i
spite of all the wretched walls which separated even a mothe
from her daughter. God be with you and guide you."

Irene, in the stillness of her bare, austere room, wept silently
the tears streaming down her battered, aging face. When sh
had finished reading she thrust the letter inside her dress agains
her thin breasts, and a little later when she descended an
found the drawing-room empty she tore it into tiny bits to b
consumed by the same fire which had secretly destroyed Lily
letter a little while before.

XLVIII

SHE made no mention of this letter to Lily, but before she left the house late the same afternoon she went to Lily's room, a thing which she had never done before. She found her sister lying on the bed in her darkened room. "What is it, Irene?"

Irene standing in the doorway, hesitated for an instant. "Nothing," she said presently. "I just stopped to see if you ere all right." Again there was a little pause. "You aren't raid . . . alone here in the evenings, are you?"

Out of the darkness came the sound of Lily's laughter. "Afraid? Lord, no! What is there to be afraid of? I'm l right." And Irene went away, down the long drive into alsted street which lay in thick blackness because the strikers d cut the wires of the street lights.

On the same evening Lily had dinner on a lacquer table be-re the fire in the drawing-room. She ate languidly, leaning ck in her rosewood armchair, dividing her attention between e food and the pages of Henri Bordeaux. Save for a chair two and the great piano, the room was still in camphor, the rniture swathed in linen coverings, the Aubusson carpet lled up in its corner. Dawdling between the food and the ok, she managed to consume an hour and a half before she ished her coffee and cigarette. Despite the aspect of the om there was something pleasant about it, a certain indefinable armth and sense of space which the library lacked utterly.

The business of the will was virtually settled. She had nounced her intention of leaving within a day or two. Two her bags were already packed. One of them she had not publed herself to unpack because she had not the faintest need clothes unless she wished to dress each night for her lonely nner as if she expected a dozen guests. And being indolent e preferred to lounge about comfortably in the black kimono

embroidered in silver with a design of wistaria. Yet in h
lounging there was nothing of sloppiness. She was too mu
a woman of taste. She was comfortable; but she was trim a
smart, from her bronze hair so well done, to the end of h
neat silver-slippered toe.

When she had finished her cigarette she rose and went to t
piano where she played for a long time, rather sentimenta
and without her usual ecstatic dash. She played as if a year
ing sadness had descended upon her. It may have been t
thought of quitting the old house which had come to the e
of the road. In another week its only occupants would
Sarah and Hennery. The others would have vanished. . .
Irene, Lily, even the black servants. There was no such thi
as age or tradition. The Town had no time for such thin
There was no longer room for Cypress Hill. It stood in t
way of progress. The Town council was eager to buy a
destroy it in order to raise on its site a new railway station, mo
vast and pretentious than any in the state.

It may have been this which made her sad.

Certainly her mood drove her to the depths, for she play
such music as the Liebesträume and a pair of sentimental G
man waltzes. And gradually she played more and more sof
until at length her hands slipped from the keyboard to her l
and she sat with bowed head regarding the pink tips of h
polished finger-nails.

The curtains were drawn across the windows so that
sound penetrated from the outside. In the grate the fire
cannel coal crackled softly and new flames leapt up.

Presently she returned to her chair and novel, but she d
not read. She remained staring into the fire in the sa
distracted fashion.

XLIX

SHE was sitting thus when she turned at the sound of shuffling footsteps and saw Sarah coming softly toward her. The countenance of the mulatto carried a vague, indefinable expression of fear. It was gray with terror.

"What is it, Sarah?" asked Lily. "In the name of Heaven what is the matter?"

The woman trembled. "There's trouble a-brewin', Miss Lily," she said. "The park is full of men. They've been comin' in at the gate and they're all over the place." The woman hesitated again. "Hennery's watching now. He sent me to ask if he was to send for the police?"

Lily stood up and fastened the black and silver kimono higher about her throat.

"Who are they?"

"I don't know, Miss Lily. Hennery thinks mebbe they're strikers. He's put out the light at the back, so he can watch 'em without bein' seen."

For a moment Lily remained silent and thoughtful. Presently she said, "Put out the lights in here, Sarah. I'll go and look myself."

And she went out, leaving the frightened servant to extinguish the lamps.

A moment later, groping her way through the dark hallway to the servants' quarters, she stumbled suddenly upon the terrified figure of Hennery kneeling down by a window, keeping watch.

"It's Miss Lily, Hennery," she said. "Don't be frightened."

The window was a blue rectangle against the wall of the hallway. It was a clear night but moonless, although the bright, cold sky was all powdered with glistening stars. Outside in the park, among the dead trunks of the trees, moved

scores of figures black against the blue gray snow. Some of
them carried lanterns of one sort or another. There were even
women among them, women with shawls over their heads, wearing short heavy skirts which cleared the top of the deep snow.
Behind them, the searchlights from the mill yard fingered the
blue dome of the sky nervously, sweeping now up and down,
now across striking the black chimneys and furnace towers,
cutting them cleanly in two as if the cold rays of light were
knives.

In the hallway the nervous breathing of Hennery became
noisy. It was clear that something about the scene. . .
something which had to do with the silent, cold furnaces, the
dead trees and the blackness of the moving figures aroused all
the superstitious terror of the negro.

Outside the number of men increased. They appeared to be
congregating now, in a spot near the deserted kennels. The
lanterns moved among the trees like dancing lights above a
swamp.

"It's all right, Hennery," said Lily presently. "It's all right.
The police would only make matters worse. I suppose Miss
Irene told them to meet here in the park. The police won't
let them meet anywhere else. It's the last place they have."

"Mebbe," Hennery muttered, doubtfully. "Mebbe."

The figure of the mulatto woman appeared shuffling her way
along the wall of the corridor.

"The best thing to do," said Lily softly, "is for you to go to
bed and forget about it. Nothing will happen. Just don't
interfere. Forget about it. I'll go up to my own room. . . .
You might see that all the doors are locked."

And with that she left the two negroes crouching on the
floor of the corridor gazing with a sort of fascination at the
spectacle in the barren park.

Upstairs in her own room, she drew up the chaise longue and
pulled aside the curtains from the window. The glass ran to
the floor so that she was able, lying down, to watch everything
that took place in the park. The room was in darkness and the
French traveling clock, as if to comfort her, chimed out ten as
she flung herself down, covering her long limbs with a silk
comforter against the chill that crept in everywhere.

Outside the strange pageant continued to grow in size and animation. Sometimes the searchlight, swinging low in its course, flashed swiftly across the park, revealing for an instant a hundred swarthy faces and as many figures wrapped in heavy coats, bits of old blanket, rags . . . anything to shut out the bitter cold. Above each figure hung a little cloud of steaming breath, a soul hovering above a body. There were negroes among them,—the negroes doubtless, whom she had seen working in the choking fumes of the acid vats.

Yet none of the figures held any individuality. They might have been automatons. Figures in a single mob, none of them possessed a distinct personality. All this was welded into one vague mass, which carried a threat of anger and violence. The terror of Hennery was not altogether beyond conception. They kept moving about too in a restless uncertain fashion among the dead trees and deserted borders. In the niches of the dead hedge the figures of the Venus of Cydnos and the Apollo Belvedere gleamed darkly.

And as Lily watched, the light in her dark eyes brightened slowly and steadily. She became like one hypnotized. She began to breathe more quickly as if the old excitement, against which she was so powerless, had entered her blood. The soft white hand holding the back of the chaise longue trembled a little.

Slowly the moving figures gathered into a black throng at the side of the kennels. Somewhere in their midst a light began to glow, increasing slowly in volume until the tongues of red flame showed above the black heads of the mob. They had built a great fire for warmth, and near it some one had set up a barrel for the speakers to stand on. By the light of the flames she was able to see that the first speaker was a little man, rather thin and wiry like a bearded gnome, who danced about a great deal, waving his arms and legs. His manner was explosive. It was impossible to hear above the flames through the heavy glass of the window what he was saying, but clearly it produced an effect. The mob began to churn about and wave its lanterns. Sometimes the sound of shouts and cries vaguely penetrated the darkened room.

At last the little man finished and was lifted down by a score of hands. More wood was thrown on the fire and the red flames hungrily chased a shower of sparks high up among the dead branches of the trees. A moment later a second man climbed to the top of the barrel. He was an enormous fellow, a veritable giant who towered far above the mob. At the sight of him the strikers cheered wildly. Lily, from her point of vantage, must have recognized in him something vaguely familiar . . . the merest suggestion of memory in the sudden, eloquent gestures, the easy powerful grace with which he balanced himself as he spoke, the same grace she had seen one afternoon in the great shed beneath the hill. More wood was thrown upon the fire. The flames leaped higher and in the wild light, doubt was no longer possible. It was Krylenko who harangued, feverishly and desperately, the threatening sullen mob.

L

INSIDE the warm room, Lily raised herself slowly and felt her way to the closet where she took down the old sealskin coat with the leg of mutton sleeves. With this thrown about her shoulders, she went back to the window, cautiously unfastened the clasp and stepped out upon the snow covered roof of the wrought iron piazza. The snow was deep and the silver slippered feet sank to the ankles. But of this she seemed to take no notice. As if fascinated, she leaned close against the bricks, sheltering herself from the wind, and stood listening.

Krylenko addressed the strikers in some foreign tongue which might have been Russian or Polish. He spoke in a clear strong voice that rose and fell with the sincerity of an overpowering emotion. It was impossible to know what he was saying, yet the effect was tremendous. The man was a born leader. In that moment he could have led the mob where he would.

And presently he began to speak Italian . . . rather haltingly and with an air of desperate frustration. This Lily was able to understand in part. He urged them not to yield. He plead with them to fight to the end. The victory, he said, was within. . . .

Above the crackling of the fire and the voice of the speaker the air was ripped suddenly by a solitary rifle shot. Then another and another in quick succession, until the air became alive and vibrant with the sound of guns. From the throng rose a solitary scream, followed by a groan or two and the confused, animal cries of a mob suddenly stricken by a panic. The figure on the barrel disappeared, engulfed by a swarming mass of terrified humanity. Lanterns were flung to the ground and trampled. One or two exploded in bursts of red flame. The little park was alive with running figures, women in shawls, men in rags. On the gray blue snow by the deserted kennels lay a solitary black figure. By the arbor where the wistaria had once flourished was another which stirred faintly.

Lily, leaning against the dead vines on the house, understood what had happened. The Mill guards, from the security of the barrier, had fired upon the helpless mob. The innocent plan of Irene had been, after all, nothing but a trap.

Something struck the bricks above her head with a sharp spatter and bits of mortar fell into her hair. Quickly she slipped through the tall window back into the room and waited.

The little park was empty now, so empty that if it had not been for the embers in the snow and black still figure lying near by, one might have believed that there had been no mob at all, no fire and no savage cries of terror. Lily remained stand-ing inside the window as if she were unable to move. The dying embers appeared to exert an overpowering fascination . . . the dying embers and the still black figure in the snow.

Presently there crept out from the shelter of the kennels a man, bending low to the ground as he moved. Cautiously he made his way to the figure in the snow, halting there for a moment to fumble with the ragged coat for some sign of life, risking his life in full sight of the guards. Another shot rang out and then another, and the man still crouching low to the ground ran toward the shelter of the big house. He came nearer and nearer until, as he crossed the drive, he was no longer a unit in the mob. He became an individual. It was Krylenko.

A second later he disappeared beneath the edge of piazza roof and Lily lay down once more on the chaise longue. She was still trembling. It may have been the cold.

Outside the night once more settled back into a dreadful stillness. The searchlights fingered the sky with a new agitation. The house itself grew still as death. The only sound was the faint, irregular, untraceable creaking which afflicts old houses in the midst of the night. The French traveling clock struck eleven and at the same time a new sound, not at all like the distant unearthly creaking, came faintly through the open door of Lily's room. It was an indistinct scraping sound as if some one were trying a key in a lock.

LI

LILY sat up, listening. The sound was repeated and presently there followed the noise of a door being opened slowly and cautiously. Lily rose and made her way to the dressing table where she pulled the bell. Once she pulled, and then again and again. There was no response. Either the servants were asleep or too terrified to answer. She gave the bell a final pull and when the only answer was silence, she took from the dressing table an electric torch and from the drawer of her carved desk a tiny pistol with a handle of mother of pearl which had been her mother's. Then she made her way quietly into the hall until she reached the top of the stairway where she leaned over the rail and flashed the light.

The glare illuminated all the lower hall, lighting up the familiar carved chest, the straight-backed chair, the crystal chandelier, the mirror. Everything was the same save that on the chest with his head bowed and resting on his hands in an attitude of despair, sat Krylenko, hatless, his coat all torn, the blood streaming down the side of his face.

It appeared that he was weak and dazed, for he remained in this same position for a long time, failing to notice even the bright shower of light which, without warning, drenched the hall. When at last he stirred, it was to lean back wearily against the wall and say in a low voice, "I have used the key, Miss Irene."

At the sound Lily ran down the long stairs, more rapidly than she had descended them in all the years she had lived in the house. She soared above the polished wood, until she stood suddenly by his side. She bent over him and touched his shoulder.

"It is not Miss Irene . . . I am Lily," she said. "Lily . . . Miss Irene's sister."

With one arm Krylenko wiped the blood from his eyes.

"Then you don't know me," he said weakly. "I am not a thief . . . breaking in."

The little revolver Lily placed beside him on the chest. "I know you," she said. "I have seen you . . . you are Krylenko." She placed one arm beneath his. "Come," she said, "this is no place for you. There is a divan in the drawing room. Come and lie down there. I'll fetch some whiskey."

With an air of great weariness the man managed to gain his feet and, leaning upon her, he made his way preceded by the little circle of white light from Lily's torch across the polished floor into the drawing-room. Lily was tall but Krylenko towered above her like a giant.

She made him comfortable, piling the brocade pillows carelessly beneath his bloody head. Then she went out and as she left, there rose behind her the sound of a heart breaking sigh, like the cry of a defeated, sobbing child.

After a little while she returned bearing a white basin filled with water, a pair of linen pillow cases and a small silver flask. Presently he sat up.

It was the first time she had seen him since that afternoon in the Mill shed when Willie Harrison, fumbling with the ruby clasp of his watch chain, proposed to her for the last time. He had changed. He was older. Experience had traced its record in the fine lines about his eyes and mouth. The crudeness of the massive head had likewise undergone a change, giving place to a more certain modeling and a new dignity. Where there had once been a certain shapelessness of feature, there was now a firmness of line, a determination in the fine mouth, the strong nose and the high massive forehead.

Lily, tearing the linen pillow cases into long strips, watched him narrowly.

The wavy blond hair, where it was not stained with blood, clung against the damp forehead. Where the coat was torn and the dark flannel shirt ripped from the throat, the powerful muscles of the arm and shoulder lay exposed. The fair skin was as white as Lily's own soft body. The man's whole figure carried an air of freedom, of a certain fierce desire to burst through the shabby, stained clothing.

All at once he raised his head and looked about him. The color returned a little way into his face.

"The blinds," he said, "are they shut?"

"Yes," said Lily. "You are safe here."

She had thrown off the old sealskin coat and sat by him clad in the black and silver kimono, seductive, beautiful, perfect, save for the tips of her silver slippers all soaked by the melted snow. The kimono had come open at the neck and left her white soft throat exposed. Krylenko was watching her now in a puzzled fashion. He behaved almost as if she terrified him in some new and indefinable way.

"I let myself in with a key," he told her. "A key Miss Irene gave me. She told me to use it if ever I had to hide." He paused for a moment and took a second drink from the flask. "You see, I am safe here because it is the last place they would look for me. They would never look for me in the house of a rich man. They wouldn't expect to find me in the house of an American, a wealthy lady."

He looked up at her in a singularly straightforward fashion. "I suppose," he said, "you too are on our side."

Lily dipping a bit of linen into the basin did not reply for a moment. At last she said, "I'd never thought about it one way or another until now. It doesn't matter, I suppose. But you needn't fear what I'll do. I'd rather have *you* here than the police."

"If they caught me now," he continued weakly, "they'd hang me. I wouldn't have a chance with Judge Weissman and the rest. Any jury in the Town would hang me. You see there were men killed out there in the park . . . men on both sides. That fellow over by the fire . . . he's dead. I stopped to make certain. I didn't kill anybody myself, but that makes no difference. It's me they're after. They've been waiting for a chance like this."

He spoke English with a curious lack of accent, for the chaste Irene as a teacher was thorough. He spoke it deliberately and rather carefully to be sure, but without serious faults. His manner was neither shy nor awkward. It was the manner of a man unused to women's company, of a man who had never before addressed a great lady; for Irene could not properly be called either a woman or a great lady. She was, rather, the embodiment of an idea.

"You're safe," said Lily. "You may depend on it. I, myself, will see to it. I don't love the police or the Harrisons or Judge Weissman . . . I don't love any of them." She drew her chair nearer. "Now lie down and I'll bathe your head."

He lay down and instantly sat up again. "My head!" he protested. "It's all bloody. . . . It'll spoil everything." He picked up one of the pillows. "See, I've done it already. They're covered with blood."

Lily smiled at him in her charming fashion, an imperceptible, secret smile. She behaved as if she were entertaining a great man, an ambassador or a rich banker, as if she were intent only upon making him comfortable, at ease.

"It makes no difference," she said. "In a few days there will be no one to use the pillows. There are times, you know, when such things don't matter. Lie down," she commanded. "One must know when such things are of no account. It is part of knowing how to live."

Protesting, Krylenko laid his great body back gently and she bent over him, first removing the rings from her finger and placing them in a glittering heap upon the lacquer table. He closed his eyes with a sigh and she washed away with great gentleness the blood from his hair, from the side of his face. Her soft white fingers swept across the tanned face, then lower to where the throat became white and across the smooth, hard muscles of the shoulder until at last there was in her touch more of the caress of a woman than the ministering of a nurse.

"It is not serious," she said in a low voice. "The bullet only cut the skin."

She took the strips of linen and bound them with the same gentle, caressing fingers round and round his head. And presently she discovered that he was still watching her in a curious embarrassed fashion. When she had finished the dressing, she bathed the deep cut on his shoulder and bound it carefully.

At length he sat up once more. A sudden change came over him. His blue eyes grew dark, almost clouded.

"You are a good nurse," he said, and took another drink from the silver flask.

Lily moved about, clearing away the blood stained cloths and the bowl of reddish water. The soft glow of the lamp captured the silver of her kimono and fixed it as she moved with a flashing light. And all the time Krylenko regarded her with a strange look of awe, as if he had never before seen a woman.

"Strange," she said presently, "that we should meet like this. You, who have never seen me before."

Krylenko stirred and ran one strong hand awkwardly over the back of the other. "I've seen you before . . . twice . . . No . . . three times. Once on that day you came to the Mills, once in the street in your carriage and once"—he looked up— "once in this room, right here. You were with the boss that time . . . dancing with him."

Lily laughed softly. She must have remembered the shameless gown of chartreuse green. "I'll never be dancing with him again. I doubt if I ever see him."

Krylenko regarded her quizzically. "But he is rich. . . . Don't rich women marry rich men?" And he finished with a puzzled grunt of inquiry.

"Yes," replied Lily. "It's because I'm rich that I wouldn't marry him." It must have occurred to her then how wide was the chasm which separated her world from Krylenko's. Still he failed to understand.

"That's no reason," she continued, "for marrying him . . . a poor thing like that."

She sat down and drew her chair quite close to the rosewood sofa, laughing at the same time. Clearly the whole adventure struck her as bizarre, ridiculous . . . even unreal. Yet she trembled as if she were shivering with cold, and her laugh carried a vague hint of hysteria. She leaned forward and began to stroke his aching head gently.

After a long awkward pause, she said, "Miss Irene will be home any time now."

"Yes." And Krylenko gave a sort of grunt. Unmistakably there was a crudeness about him. He was gauche, awkward; yet there was in his manner a quality of power, of domination which had its origin somewhere in the dim ages, when there were no drawing-rooms and no books of etiquette. He had a manifest self-possession. He did not become obsequious before this great lady as Judge Weissman and other men in stations beneath her had done. He treated her, after all, as his equal. He was even a little arrogant; a trifle scornful of her wealth.

"Miss Irene," he observed presently, "is a noble woman. You understand she gives up her life to my people. Do you know where she is now?" His voice was raised, his manner excited. "She's looking after the fellows that got hurt. There was a woman, too. I saw her . . . shot through the arm . . . Ah, Miss Irene is a saint. You know she could go anywhere in the Flats. No one would touch her."

The whole speech was touched with a tone of simple adoration. The essence of him was a great, a really profound simplicity.

"She works hard," said Lily. "She works hard. She cares for nothing else." By the watch on her white wrist it was midnight. "So that is why she is late," she added.

"There will be much work for her to-night," said Krylenko. He kept watching Lily in the same furtive fashion, his gaze wandering to the lovely line of her bare white throat.

Again there was an awkward pause. "You don't know how much she does," he said presently. "You don't know what life is in the Flats. You sit here in a warm house . . . with silk and pillows and good food. You don't know," he said bitterly. "You don't know!"

Until now their conversation had been broken, disjointed, awkward, as if circumstance compelled them to talk about something. Now for the first time, a certain fire entered the Russian's voice. Lily kept silent, watching him with her great burning eyes. She still trembled.

"Maybe you think I like working twelve hours a day in that hot shed like you saw me. Maybe you think I don't want time to read and think." The man was working himself into a kind of frenzy. "You don't know. . . . You don't know. . . . And then they shoot us down like pigs." He leaned forward and raised at Lily a strong finger. "I come here from Russia. I come here because I could not live in Russia. . . . My father . . . My father . . . He was shot by the Cossacks. I come here because they tell me that in America you are free and have a good life. And what do they give me? They make me work twelve hours in a hot shed. They put me into a filthy house. They say, you must not complain. You must do as we say. We will not pay you more. We will not let you live like a man. You are Hunkies! . . . You are dirt! You did not have to come here. But all the same, they want us. They send men to Russia to tell us great things about America so we will come here because they need men for the Mills . . . men to feed to the furnaces like coal . . . to make a few men rich." He sighed bitterly and buried his face in his hands. "And now they shoot us like the Cossacks shot my father in Russia. . . . I came here full of hope and peace . . . only to be shot like my father in Russia!"

In his excitement he forgot the perfect English Irene had taught him. His blue eyes flashed and his face grew pale once more.

"No. . . . They can take me. . . . They can hang me. . . . Let them! I will not go away. . . . It is not America or Russia that counts. . . . It is all humanity! . . . Christians. . . . Bah!" He spat suddenly upon the polished floor. And all at once he pitched back again among the pillows, weak and fainting. The bandage slipped from his wounded head over one eye.

Quickly Lily bent over him. She poured more whiskey between his lips and refastened the bandage. Then she settled herself to chafing his strong wrists and rubbing his forehead in the old caressing motion with a delicate, white hand that trembled beyond control. A queer light came into her dark eyes.

Presently he sighed and looked up at her. "I am sorry," he said, "to bother a fine lady like you. If it had been Miss Irene." He closed his eyes suddenly. "I have been hungry, you know. We haven't even enough food in the Flats." Then he took her hand and pressed it in a naive, grateful fashion. "I am sorry, you know . . ." he murmured gently.

She did not move. She remained there stroking his head. "I know. . . . I understand. . . . You must lie still. Be quiet," she said softly. For a long time they remained thus, and presently Krylenko, opening his eyes looked up at her with a puzzled expression. "You are not the same as Miss Irene," he said in a low voice. "You are different . . . very different."

To this she made no reply. Gently the motion of her hand ceased. A pool of silence enveloped them. *You are not the same as Miss Irene.*

LII

THE minutes passed and then suddenly, sharply, there arose a loud uproar, the sound of angry knocking and a hand rattling the big outer door. Krylenko sat up white and still. Neither of them moved. The knocking continued, punctuated now by shouts.

"It's the police!" said Lily, and stood up. "Come with me. Bring the bowl . . . the bandages!"

Krylenko stood by helplessly. It was Lily who arranged everything with a sudden clairvoyance which seemed to have overtaken her at the instant of the knocking. She turned the brocade cushions so that the bloody side was concealed and, gathering up the bandages, she led the way through the hall into the corridor where an hour earlier Hennery and the mulatto woman had crouched in fascinated terror. At last she turned into a store room piled high with boxes. Here she led him to a great box in the corner where she halted.

"I'll hide you here," she said. "They'll never find you. It is full of books." And together, with flying hands, they emptied the box. Krylenko climbed in and assumed a crouching position. He was buried beneath the books which Lily hurled into the box in bunches of three or four, in armfuls. At last he lay completely hidden beneath a great heap of yellow backed novels. . . the novels of Paul Marguerite, Marcel Prévost, Paul Bourget, Collette Willy . . . the novels that Julia Shane had "skimmed" and cast aside, the novels which to her covenanting blood *l'amour* made so tiresome.

As Lily ran through the corridor the knocking increased in violence, punctuated by shouts of "Hello, in there!" and "Open the door," uttered in a gruff bass voice. As she ran she wrapped the kimono high about her throat, and as she passed the carved chest she picked up the tiny pearl handled pistol. Then she turned the key quickly and opened the door standing with the pistol in one hand and the yellow backed Les Anges Gardiens in the other.

Outside on the snow covered piazza stood a half dozen men in the uniforms of the constabulary. At the apparition of the beautiful woman in the doorway they remained for an instant silent, startled.

"What is it you want?" she asked.

One of the men, a burly fellow with a brutal jaw stepped forward. "We want to search the house. We're looking for a man."

"What man?" asked Lily.

"Never mind," came the gruff answer. "You wouldn't know him. He's nothing to you. His name is Krylenko."

"There's no one in the house but me and the servants." Her voice trembled a little before the menacing group on the piazza.

"That's all right," said the man. "We're going to see for ourselves. We saw him come in here."

He began to edge his way slowly toward the open door and as he moved the pearl handled pistol raised slowly, menacingly, in an even tempo with his slow insolent advance.

"You cannot come in," said Lily in a slow, firm voice. The pistol was level now with the heart of the intruder. "I've told you there is no one here. You might, it seems to me, take the word of a lady. I've been here all the evening and I would know. . . ." She raised the yellow backed novel in a brief little gesture. "I've been reading. There is no one here but myself."

The man growled. "That's all right but we want to look for ourselves." There was a painful pause. "We're going to have a look," he added with determination.

When Lily spoke again there was a new note in her voice, a sudden timbre of determination, a hint of unreasonable, angry, feminine stubbornness which appeared to awe the intruder.

"Oh, no, you're not," she said. "It is my house. You have no right to enter it. You have no warrant. It is mine. You cannot enter it." And then, as if by an afterthought she added, "Even my sister is not here. I don't know this Krylenko. I never saw him."

The man, it seemed, was baffled. If the woman in the doorway had been the wife of a workman, a simple Italian or Slovak, he undoubtedly would have brushed her aside, shot her if necessary, trampled her under foot the way his comrades had trampled to death the old Polish woman in Halsted street at the foot of the drive. But the woman in the doorway was a lady. She was not a poor foreigner. She was more American than himself. Behind her in the shadows gleamed dully a silver mounted mirror, a chandelier of sparkling crystal. Her fine, beautiful body was clad in a garment of black and silver. On her fingers glittered rings. All these things meant wealth, and wealth meant power. The man, after all, had only the soul of a policeman, a soul at once bullying and servile. For him these symbols might spell ruin. Besides, the woman was hysterically stubborn, strangely unafraid . . . so unafraid that her courage carried a hint of suspicious origin. He did not brush her aside nor did he shoot her.

"It's no use," she said. "If you return with a warrant, all right. I can do nothing. For the present, it is my house."

The man turned away and began a low conversation with his companions. He had a sheepish air, and as he talked the door was closed suddenly and locked, shutting him out in the darkness, leaving him no choice in the matter. For a time the little group of men conversed angrily, and presently they went away in defeat down the long drive.

So Lily had placed herself on the side of the strikers . . . against the Town, against the Mills. She stood now with all her family, with Irene, with the dead Julia Shane, with Hattie Tolliver and her savage umbrella.

LIII

INSIDE the house, she listened until the creak of boots on the snow died away. Then she moved off along the hall toward the corridor. She walked uncertainly and from time to time leaned against the wall for support. The spot of light from the electric torch preceded her slippered feet, a bright moving circle which seemed to devour and destroy the streak of flooring which it crossed on its way to the storeroom. Weakly she opened the door and stepped inside.

"It's all right, now. I've sent them away."

The books in the great box stirred with a heaving motion and out of them presently emerged Krylenko, pale and shaken. He climbed out and as his foot struck the floor, Lily gave a little cry and pitched forward so that he caught her suddenly. The electric torch dropped to the floor. The glass shattered with a faint pop and the room swam in a thick, soft darkness.

She did not faint. In a moment she recovered herself and managed to stand upright, but she did not move away from Krylenko. She stood there, waiting. Slowly his powerful arms closed about her with the vague gesture of a man wakening slowly from a profound sleep.

"It's all right," she whispered faintly. "I've saved you."

He made no other answer than a faint crooning sound. He stroked her hair gently with his strong, calloused hand, and tried to quiet the violent trembling which once more had taken possession of her. Again the house was silent save for the distant, ghostly creaking.

Perhaps he was seized by an overwhelming sense of awe which until that moment he had never experienced . . . an awe for some unknown and terrific force against which he was helpless, like a little child. It may have been that, as Irene believed, he had never known any woman, that he had been pure as a saint. If these things had not been, it is impossible

209

to say what might have happened. He stood holding Lily close to him, kissing with a strange, awed gentleness the white line of her bare throat.

He discovered presently that she was sobbing. . . . Lily, who never wept. It was a terrible heartbreaking sound as if, all at once, she had sensed the tragedy of a whole lifetime, as if she stood in a vast and barren plain surrounded only by loneliness.

Krylenko's hands and arms became unaccountably gentle. His cheek brushed against her white forehead with a comforting, caressing motion. And presently he lifted her as easily and as gently as he had lifted the wounded striker at Mrs. Tolliver's command, and bore her from the room and down the dark corridor. She lay quietly, still sobbing in the same heartbroken fashion.

Thus he carried her into the long drawing-room and placed her among the brocade cushions of the divan, her amber hair all disheveled, her eyes bright with tears. For a moment he stood by her side awkwardly, silent and incoherent, over-whelmed by some new and profound emotion. The fire of cannel coal had died down. In the grate there was nothing now but ashes. Silently he knelt beside the sofa and rested his blond head on her breasts. Neither of them spoke a word, but Lily's hand returned once more to the old gentle caressing motion across his tired eyes.

The minutes slipped away, one by one in a quick stream as if they were no more than the trickle of a clear spring water which is beyond all peril of drought, as if time itself were nothing and eternity even less.

So engulfed were they by the mood that even the sound of a key turning distantly in a clumsy lock and the echo of a light footfall in the hallway failed to disturb them. They were, it seemed oblivious to everything until suddenly there stepped through the doorway the thin figure of Irene in the worn gray suit and battered black hat. At the sight of them she halted, an apparition with a tired white face, drawn and quivering. It was not until she gave a low convulsive cry that Lily and Krylenko discovered she was watching them. Krylenko remained on his knees, only straightening his body to look at her.

Lily turned her head a little, gently, listlessly, almost with indifference.

Irene had become hideous. In her eyes was the light of fury. When she spoke her voice was cold with an insane, unearthly hatred.

"So," she said bitterly, "it has happened!" The worn hat fell from her grasp. Her fingers intertwined with a strangling gesture. "I might have known it. . . . I should have guessed. . . ." And then her voice rose to a suppressed scream. "You are no better than a street walker! You are damned forever! I have prayed. . . . I have prayed but God himself could not save you. . . . He would not want you . . . a vile creature . . . a strumpet! . . . to destroy all that I have spent my life to create." She began to sob wildly. "To destroy in a night what cost me years."

Slowly, silently, Krylenko rose to his feet. He watched Irene with a look of bewilderment, as if he found himself in a wild nightmare. Lily turned away silently and buried her face in the pillows. A Fury had descended upon them unawares.

Irene continued to cry. "I have known always. . . . I have known from the beginning. . . . I knew about the Governor. . . . I saw him go into your room. . . . Only God knows how many men you have had. . . . You are lost, damned, forever!" The terrible sound of her weeping echoed and reëchoed through the silent old house.

Lily raised her body from the cushions and sat with her silver slippers touching the floor. "What are you saying, Irene?" she asked. "You are mad. There has been nothing . . . nothing . . . nothing. You are mad!"

It was true that for the moment Irene was quite insane, yet her madness endowed her with the clairvoyance that is beyond sanity. She rushed toward Lily. She would have strangled her but Krylenko stepped between them and held her as if she had been an angry bad-tempered little child.

"Ah, don't lie to me," she cried. "I'm no fool. I can see. It is written in your eyes. Both of you. . . . I know. I know! . . . It is there! I see it!"

She struggled fiercely in the powerful grasp of Krylenko.

"Let me go. . . . You . . . You are no better than the others
. . . a common beast, a swine like the others . . . a swine
like all men, lying to me all these years. And on a night like
this. May God damn you both in Hell forever and ever!"

She freed herself and sank to the floor at Krylenko's feet.
The tirade gave way to a torrent of wild hysterical sobbing.
Her pale, battered face was all distorted, her thin hair dis-
arrayed. She collapsed suddenly into a barren shattered old
woman, abandoned by life. She had lost in her battle against
something which was far stronger than herself, stronger even
than Lily and Krylenko. She was broken, pitiful.

Lily sat by helplessly, her own tears dried now. She turned
the rings round and round on her fingers and in the gesture
there was a concentrated agony.

"You must not mind her," she said presently. "She is not
well." Then she rose slowly and moved toward her sister.
"Irene," she said softly. "Irene."

But Irene shuddered and drew away from her. "Don't
touch me . . . evil one! Don't touch me!" she cried
monotonously.

"Perhaps if she had rest," said Krylenko. "Perhaps if she
slept."

Irene kept up moaning and rocking. "In the Flats they're
dying. . . . In the Flats they're dying . . . and you two up
here, like beasts all that time . . . like beasts!"

Lily began to walk up and down the long shadowy room in
a wild distracted manner, as if the contagion of her sister's hysteria had touched her too. "There is nothing I can do," she
kept saying. "There is nothing. . . . Perhaps if we left
her . . ."

It was Krylenko who solved the difficulty. He bent over
Irene and picked her up despite her protests. She screamed.
She wept. She would have scratched and bitten him if
his arms had been less powerful and his grip less certain. He
turned to Lily. "Where is her bed?"

He spoke with a curious, intimate understanding. In an
hour he had come nearer to Lily than ten years had brought him
to the chaste fanatic sister.

Silently Lily led the way up the long stairs while he followed bearing Irene who moaned like a wounded animal. At the door of the room with the white bed and the pink-gilt image of the Virgin, he halted as if fearful of desecrating its purity. But Lily led the way boldly and together they laid the sister upon the narrow white bed. When they had gone out, closing the door behind them, the sound of her faint moaning haunted the dark hallway.

At the door of her own room Lily halted. "Wait," she said, and left him, returning in a moment, her arms burdened with blankets.

"Take these," she said. "It will be cold in the drawing-room." In all the confusion, she had not forgotten his wounds, his comfort.

Krylenko smiled vaguely. "It will be hard to sleep anywhere to-night," he said softly.

"But it is spoiled now . . ." replied Lily. "Everything."

And Krylenko turned away and went silently down the stairs.

It is true that no one slept until the dawn. Irene and Lily did not sleep at all. The one lay awake sobbing and praying, the other lay with her head buried in the pillows keeping her body rigid to still its wild trembling. Krylenko was the only one who slept. With the coming of dawn he sank into a deadening thick slumber among the stained brocade pillows of the rosewood sofa.

There he slept undisturbed until midday, for with the curtains tightly drawn there was no light to waken him. When at last he did waken, he found on the lacquer table beside him a note, which read;

"There are some things in this world which are impossible, things fate herself will not permit. This you will understand, I am sure. I have gone away. Irene has gone too. Where she has gone I do not know. Perhaps it does not matter. There is small chance of our ever meeting again. Our paths lie too far apart. . . . I have arranged for you to remain in the house . . . as long as it is necessary. As long even as you desire it. There is no one but yourself and the two black servants. They have been told. It is my house. It would please me to think of you there. It would please me . . . and my mother too . . . to know that you were safe inside it still leading the strike. It is a good place, for you can keep in hiding and still lead the fight. My blessings are with you and your cause."

The note was signed with Lily's name, and underneath it in the same sprawling hand was written, "O God! I love you. Good-by."

She had come in some time between the dawn and the broad daylight to leave the note by his side. She had passed him and gone away without a word, whither he could not possibly know. Nothing remained save a confused memory of her and this short, enigmatic, note which avowed nothing and yet everything.

For a long time Krylenko held the bit of paper between his strong heavy fingers, staring dully all the while at the generous impetuous writing. At last he took out a battered cigarette, put a match to it, and at the same moment set fire to the wisp of paper which he tossed among the cold ashes of the dead fire. . . . *There are some things in this world which are impossible.*

He got up and began pacing the floor angrily, up and down, up and down, scarring the polished floor at each step. It made no difference now. There was no one there any longer to use the floor. Presently he began muttering to himself. "They are no different than the others. They are all alike. When they are tired they run away because they are rich. Damn them and their money!"

And then all at once he went down upon his knees before the sofa and seizing one of the stained cushions in his arms, he kissed it again and again as if it were Lily instead of a feather-stuffed bit of brocade which he held in his arms.

LIV

HE did not quit the old house. He remained there in hiding to direct the strike. He was still there when Hennery packed the glowing Venice of Mr. Turner and the handsome malignant portrait of John Shane to be shipped to Lily in Paris. From the old house he sent out to the strikers message after message of encouragement and exhortation, until, at last, the strike was lost and there was no longer either need or place for him in the Mills or in the Town. No one knew when he went away or whither it was he went.

And the greatest of all the stories of Shane's Castle remained a secret. The Town knew nothing of the greatest sacrifice ever made within its walls.

LV

THE drawing-room of the house in the Rue Raynouard was a long, high-ceilinged room with tall windows opening upon a terrace and a sloping lawn which ran down to the high wall that shut out the dust and the noise of the Rue de Passy. It was curiously like the muffled, shuttered drawing-room in the old house in Cypress Hill, not because the furnishings were the same; they were not. From Shane's Castle Lily brought only two things . . . the glowing Venice and the portrait of her father. Mr. Turner's flamboyant painting hung above the black marble mantelpiece in the Rue Raynouard. The portrait of John Shane hung against the satinwood paneling opposite the row of tall windows. The similarity was not an easy thing to define, for its roots lay in nothing more tangible than the bond between old Julia Shane and her daughter Lily, in a subtle sense of values which the one had passed on to the other.

The cold, impersonal hand of a decorator had nothing to do with either room. There was no striving toward a museum accuracy of period. The effect was much warmer, much more personal than that. The distinction was achieved by the collection, bit by bit, of beautiful things each chosen for some quality which warmed the heart of the purchaser . . . carpets, bits of crystal and carved jade on ebony stands, books, cushions, chairs, pictures, sconces, candelabra, brocades and old Italian damasks, footstools, and mirrors which coldly reflected the warm bodies of beautiful women. Even in a city where taste and beauty were the rule, the drawing-room in the Rue Raynouard was a marvel of these qualities. It was more beautiful than the rooms of Madame Gigon's respectable friends; for these women were French *bourgeoises* and neither wealth nor decorators could endow them with a quality that descends from Heaven only upon the few and the blessed. These women admired

Madame Shane's drawing room and envied it . . . all of them
Madame de Cyon, the Comptesse de Turba, Madame Mar
chand, the mysterious old Madame Blaise, who people said had
been a famous beauty in her youth; Geneviève Malbour, who
wrote novels as dowdy as herself and struck the literary note
even the rich Duchesse de Gand, who frequented the royalist
soirées and the parties given by the *chic* Jews, and only came
occasionally to Madame Gigon to placate her husband whose
title was created by the first Napoleon. They attempted to
imitate the seductive, quiet beauty of Numero Dix but they
failed somehow, perhaps because they could not resist introduc
ing a pillow of just the wrong, violent shade or a pair of rubber
plants, or some monstrous piece of furniture from the period
of the Second Empire.

"This American" had outdone them, quite without striving
or effort. Indeed if the success of Lily's drawing-room had
depended upon either of these things it would have remained
forever as ugly as on the day she moved into it, to succeed a
chocolate manufacturer whose growing prosperity led him to
a small palace in the new German style on the Avenue de Jena
She was incapable of effort. If she had been poor, if she had
been forced to work, she would have become sloven; even her
beauty would have deteriorated and grown sloppy through
neglect. It was money which stood between her and these
disasters . . . money which permitted her to enter a shop and
say, "I will have this and this and this for my drawing-room,"
money which permitted her to enter any *salon* of the Rue de la
Paix and say, "I will have this gown, or this one, or this,"
money which permitted her to go to the hairdresser, Augustine
and say, "I will have my hair waved and my complexion
treated." And having been born with taste, she made no
errors.

Although the friends of Madame Gigon spoke of her as "the
American," it is seldom that they thought of her as a foreigner
Only her indolence and her extravagance could have betrayed
to a stranger the fact that she was not a true Frenchwoman
In the seven years that followed the death of her mother, Lily
abandoned forever all thought of returning to America. She
spoke French to perfection, indolently and gracefully, with a

fine smooth accent. Her son, for all his American parentage and British schooling, was French; or at least, not American. He had a taste for music, for pictures, even for poetry.

"Fancy that," she remarked to Ellen. "Fancy that, and think what his father has become."

And she held up a newspaper photograph of the Governor . . . now the Senator . . . clipped from one of the American newspapers which Ellen brought to Numero Dix. It portrayed him in the act of addressing the Benevolent Order of Camels in Detroit. The pose was in itself flamboyant. Everything about him flowed. His loose black cravat flowed in the breeze. His hair, worn rather long, waved behind him. His alpaca suit ballooned about his heavy figure. His stomach rested upon a flag-draped railing, and his face wore a smile that was old and familiar, the smile of one who patronized his audience. In the background there was a vague suggestion of a square, solid figure in a richly flowered costume, wearing a pince nez and a cloud of flowing veils . . . obviously the figure of the Senatoress.

Though Lily sometimes mocked the Governor, she never mentioned him as the source of Jean's restless vitality and intelligence. But it did not matter, since no one in her world and, least of all Ellen, was interested in the Governor or eager to defend him.

The women who came to her drawing-room were, first of all, "Madame Gigon's friends." Toward Lily, for all her good-nature and her submission to their world, their attitude was never more than that of acquaintances. She saw them many times a month but there remained always an insurmountable barrier. It existed perhaps because she was too indolent to make those overtures necessary to friendship, perhaps because deep down in the heart of their bourgeois respectability they detected in the American traces of the wanton. They came to the "salons" of Madame Gigon and Lily went in turn to theirs. But she never entertained in the evening save at small dinners of four and six, and she never went to balls. Her hunger for gaiety she satisfied in the midst of crowds, at the Opéra, in the music halls, at the races. And always she was accompanied by Jean or Ellen or Madame Gigon so that no one was able to say that she was indiscreet. If she went out frequently with the Baron, he was after all the cousin and protector of the old woman who accompanied them. If the Baron came frequently to her house it was to see Madame Gigon who was flattered by his attentions and his gifts of money.

Yet it could not be said that she was more friendly with men than with women. The men admired her. Indeed men from the world of fashion, from the world of the Duchesse de Guermantes' *soireés,* sometimes mingled with the dowdy Bonapartists of Madame Gigon's salon, brought there by friends who moved in the circle closest to "the American." They were pleasantly received and sent on their way, having accomplished nothing. If they became a trifle ardent she called Madame Gigon or the Baron to her side and the incident ended without difficulty. The visits came to nothing, for Lily appeared to have no ambitions. She was bafflingly content. She might have had great success in a score of ways, for her flamboyant beauty was a sort rarely seen among French women and it attracted notice wherever she appeared. But she had no ambitions; she was both wealthy and content. People remarked her at the Opera but it was seldom that any one was able to identify her, for none knew her. Her circle was small, dowdy and infinitely respectable. She lived quietly with old Madame Gigon, now almost blind, and a charming son. It seemed that she was even content to forego a second marriage. And among those who admired her, because she was so good-natured and lovely to look upon, was the wife of the Baron, a pretty blond woman, rich and stupid, the daughter of a manufacturer from Lyons.

Madame Gigon adored her in two quite distinct fashions. The first because Lily was pleasant, kindly and generous. The second adoration, less commendable perhaps but none the less thorough, was the adoration of a woman pinched all her life by poverty for a fellow creature who secured her declining years with every possible luxury. Madame Gigon could not possibly forget that it was Lily who had set her up in a situation worthy of a woman whose father had been ruined by his loyalty to Napoleon the Little. The widow of the curator of the Cluny Museum had grown very small and dry. Her face resembled a withered pomegranate both in texture and color. Her dog Fifi had long since been laid to rest in the dog's cemetery on a little island in the Seine where Madame Shane had kindly raised a tombstone with Fifi in marble sitting on a bronze cushion, "tout á fait comme dans la vie." Fifi had not one successor but two, both provided by Madame Shane to console "her poor old Louise." One was a black and tan, for all the world like the departed Fifi, and bore the name of Criquette. The other, a perky black Scotty brought back from England as a surprise, bore the name of Michou. They slept in Madame Gigon's room overlooking the garden and had their own corner in the Louis Seize dining room, where they ate when the rest of the household sat down at an enormous table lighted by tall candles. Like Fifi they had gone the way of gateaux and were stout and short of breath.

LVI

THESE four . . . Lily, Madame Gigon, Criquette and Michou . . . were the permanent tenants of Numero Dix. There were two others who came and went, spending now a week's holiday, now a whole month or more. They even paid visits frequently to the lodge at Germigny l'Evec in the park of the Baron, where Lily spent the spring and the autumn of every year, taking a house during the summer at Houlgate where she lived as a Frenchwoman in the very heart of the small American colony. The transients in the establishment of Madame Shane were her son Jean and her cousin Ellen Tolliver. They flitted in and out like birds of passage, less regular in their arrival and departure, though no less spirited and noisy.

The Ellen Tolliver of the pompadour and starched shirt waists had become the Lilli Barr whom crowds packed concert halls to see and hear, whom music critics found themselves bound to commend—the same Lilli Barr whose photograph seated beside a great composer appeared in the Sunday supplements of American newspapers. This of course, the public never knew. It knew only that she was a fine pianist with a sensational presence and a vitality which reached out and engulfed them through the medium of surging music. It knew nothing of her past. Indeed there were few who knew she was an American. Her name might have been Russian or Austrian, Hungarian or German. It carried with it the glamor sought by the public which will receive the most sublime artist with indifference if her name happened to be Mary Smith and her origin Evanston, Indiana. This she realized. She shrewdly explained to Lily the evolution of her name.

"Barr," she said, "is the name of my grandfather. I have a perfect right to it. Alone and unadorned it is not thrilling. Therefore I have chosen Lilli. That, my dear, is a tribute

212

to you, because if it had not been for you I should probably be
an old maid giving music lessons at fifty cents an hour to the
daughters of mill clerks." She laughed noisily. "Lilli
Barr. . . . A great name, don't you think? It will suit everybody. It will suit those who believe American musicians should
be encouraged and it will suit those who must have a little
exotic European sauce with their fowl. Lilli Barr. . . . It
might be anything at all."

"Lilli Barr" was a name which betrayed nothing of a rather
materialistic elopement with a traveling salesman called
Clarence Murdock. It betrayed nothing of Clarence's quiet
passing out of this life from a weakened heart too greatly tried
by life with a robust and ambitious wife. It had nothing to do
with a father, ruined by honesty, who wore away his middle
age as clerk in an industrial bank. It gave no hint of a mother
who, in an effort to follow her ambitious, migratory offspring,
had kept a Manhattan rooming house for five years past. Decidedly, emphatically, it was an exotic name. There were even
people who believed that she was the protégée of a German
Baron named Unschaff (they had his name and the history of
his amours) whom she repaid in the usual way. And this story
Ellen would have been the last to deny, for she knew its value.
She understood that the people who paid money for concerts
must have something beside music. And she understood the
value of money in a fashion never imagined by Lily. The
critics might call her playing sensational, bordering even upon
charlatanism, she would not deny it. The public liked an
artist who understood the value of a gesture, who came upon
the concert stage with air of a queen, who played with gusto
and the sweep of a hurricane. She understood all that. It
was not that she was insincere. There were those for whom
she played exquisitely and with all the distilled beauty of a sensitive artist, with the same curious passion which had engulfed
her music on that last night in the drawing-room at Cypress
Hill. She was a clever woman, far more intelligent than Lily,
and having been nourished in the midst of poverty and failure,
her one God was success, a sort of embittered success which
played upon the silliness and affectation of the world.

Certainly she had kept the promise made to Lily. She fitted

no pattern, least of all the pattern of the Town. She had he
own ruthless law, founded upon consideration for friends alone
She had her own thoughts and beliefs. Indeed she hated th
pattern bitterly, so bitterly that she made a vow never to play i
the Town no matter what the fee offered her. In appearance
she resembled curiously her grandaunt, Lily's mother. Abou
her features there was the same bold carving. Her face was too
long and her eyes a shade too green. Her figure held none o
the voluptuous curves that softened her cousin's beauty; on th
contrary it was slim and strong. She walked with a fine fre
swing that carried in it a hint of masculinity. Beside Lily sh
was not beautiful at all; yet on the concert stage under the glov
of the lights her beauty was infinitely more effective tha
Lily's would have been. . . . Her energy was the energy de
scended directly from Hattie Tolliver. It crackled throug
her whole being. She was not like Lily, a woman of the world
there was a quality of directness and naivete, a breezines
springing from her background and her ancestry, which all th
courts of Europe might never overcome. She was, above al
else, herself, incapable of affectation or pretense. And this
she also understood, was a thing of great value because one ex
pected it of the artistic temperament. An artist made no
compromises.

LVII

ONE late afternoon in April, nineteen thirteen, when
the trees in the garden were all feathery and soft with
the first green of the Gallic springtime, Madame
Gigon sat in her chair by the door of the long
drawing-room bidding her guests good-by, one by one, as they
left her usual Thursday *salon*. The drawing-room, owing to
the sharp slope of the ground upon which the house was built,
lay below the surface of the Rue Raynouard on the garden side
of the house so that the guests leaving were forced to climb a
long flight of stairs that led up to the street door. The stairway, opening directly into the drawing-room, provided a long,
high vista leading up to a door, itself noticeable by its very
insignificance. It was one of the charming features of the
house that on the street side it was but one story high with
a single door and a row of high windows which betrayed
no hint of the beauty and space within its walls. On the
garden side, however, the house presented a beautiful façade
some three stories high, constructed of Caen stone and designed in the best manner of the eighteenth century. Lenôtre
himself was said to have had a hand in the planning of the
terraces and the pavilion that stood at a little distance completely embowered by shrubs and covered by a canopy made of
the broad green leaves of plane trees. The house, after a fashion, turned its back upon the world, concealing its beauties from
the eye of the random passerby, preserving them for the few who
were admitted by the humble and unpretentious door that
swung open upon the cobble stones of the Rue Raynouard. To
the world it showed the face of a *petite bourgeoise*. To its
friends it revealed the countenance of an eighteenth century
marquise. And this fact had influenced for more than a century
and a half the character of its tenants. The prosperous chocolate manufacturer abandoned it for the German palace in the
Avenue de Jena for the very reason that Lily Shane seized it

215

the moment it fell vacant. It was no sort of a house for one who desired the world to recognize his success and the character of his life, but it was an excellent house in which to live quietly, even secretly. It stood isolated in the very midst of Paris.

Madame Gigon sat in a high-backed chair, her small, withered body propped among cushions, her feet resting on a footstool. Since her eyes had grown dim she used her ears as a means of watching her guests; and these, after the fashion of such organs, had become sharper and sharper with the failure of her sight.

A fat and dowdy woman dressed all in white and wearing an extravagant white veil moved up to her.

"Good-by, Madame Gigon," she said. "You come to me on Friday. Don't forget. The Prince himself will be there."

Madame Gigon, instead of peering at the white lady, leaned back. "Ah, it's you, Héloise. . . . Yes, I will be there on Friday. But you are leaving early."

"No," replied the white lady, who was a countess and possessed a fine collection of armor. "No. Others have gone before me. I am dining out in the Boulevard St. Germain."

Madame Gigon smiled. "With your Jewish friends?"

"Yes. It is a long way."

"They say her eldest daughter is to marry a rich American . . . millions. He is called Blumenthal."

"Oui . . . a very nice gentleman and the Good God alone knows how rich."

"Well, money is a great thing . . . the foundation of everything, Héloise."

"Yes . . . Good-by . . . On Friday then. And fetch Madame Shane if she cares to come."

And the plump white lady made her way with effort up the long polished stairway to the unpretentious doorway.

Madame Gigon, holding Michou on her lap, began fondling the dog's ears. She leaned back and listened. Most of the guests had gone. Her sharp ears constructed the scene for her. A shrill and peevish voice in the far corner betrayed Madame de Cyon. The old woman saw her, fat, with dyed black hair and a round face well made up to conceal the ravages of time. A Russian woman, married to a French diplomat

. . . Bonapartist of course. She translated American novels into French to amuse herself and to help keep up the household in Neuilly. Yet she was rich, for her fat pig's hands were covered with rings and the sable of her cloak was the best.

A man's voice, ill-tempered and gruff, rose through the shadowy room. Captain Marchand, who did not get on with his wife. Tactless of Madame de Cyon to have led them to the bridge table to play with each other. Bridge-mad . . . was Madame de Cyon . . . bridge-mad, and she hated like the Devil to lose. To lose five francs was like losing one of her fat legs. Strange game . . . this bridge. It put every one into a bad temper. Not at all like piquet.

"Deux pique!" announced Madame de Cyon.

"Passe!" . . . "Passe!" . . . "Passe!"

From the dining-room issued the sound of two voices in dispute, the one high-pitched, old and somewhat shrill, and the other rather deep and gentle, almost conciliatory. They drifted to Madame Gigon across the murmurous spaces of the drawing-room. Madame Blaise and "Mees Ellen's" friend, Schneiderman. Madame Blaise was a Gasconne, old, shrill and vituperatory, yet somehow amusing and stimulating . . . a little cracked perhaps but still full of spirit, and mysterious in the fashion of those whose existence has its foundations in a world of fanciful, half-mad unreality. She was tall and thin, with a mass of dyed red hair (it must have gone gray ten years earlier) under an old-fashioned purple bonnet trimmed with purple plumes and perched high on her head in the fashion of the eighties. Madame Gigon knew she was by the gateaux . . . eating . . . eating . . . eating . . . as if she starved herself at home. Yet she too was rich.

"Ah, you don't know the Germans as I do!" came the high-pitched voice. "My fine young fellow! I tell you I have lived with them. I have been on business for the government. They are capable of anything. You will see . . ."

And then the voice of Schneidermann, mild and a little amused by the old lady. "Ah . . . ," gently. "Perhaps . . . perhaps. But I do not think that war is any longer possible."

"Nevertheless," persisted the voice. "One fine day you will go marching away like the rest."

LVIII

SCHNEIDERMANN was Alsatian, and Jew on his father's side, rich, for his family owned steel mills at Toul and Nancy and in the very environs of Paris, as well as coal mines in the neighborhood of St. Quentin and La Bassée. Schneidermann, tall, handsome, swarthy . . . was beautiful in an austere, sensual fashion as only Jews can be beautiful. He came sometimes to play the 'cello with "Mees Ellen," choosing queer music they called "modern" that had none of the beauty and melody of Offenbach and Gounod.

The voice of "Mees Ellen" joining the pair in the dining-room. . . . "War! . . . War! . . . Nonsense! There can't be any war. I must play in Berlin and Munich next season." Her voice rang with genuine conviction, as if she really believed that war itself dared not interfere with still more amazing successes. Madame Blaise' cynical laugh answered her.

"Ah, you young people . . . you young people. What do you know of war and politics? I have been through wars, through revolutions, you understand. I know about these things. I am as old as time."

The old woman was talking in her most fantastic vein. It was her habit to talk thus as if she were wise beyond all people. She was, as Madame Gigon said, a little cracked on this side of her.

"I know . . . I know," she continued to mutter in the most sinister fashion until an unusually large madeleine put an end to her talk.

"How much did you say . . . eight francs?" It was the peevish voice of Madame de Cyon settling her bridge debts.

"Eight francs," came the gruff reply of Captain Marchand. "Eight francs, I tell you." And then the tinkling of the Russian's woman's innumerable gold bangles as she thrust her fat bejeweled hand into a small purse to wrench loose from it the precious eight francs. "I had no luck to-day . . . no luck at all," she observed in the same irritable voice. "No cards at all. What can one do without cards? Now last week I won. . . ." And she fell to recounting past victories while Captain Marchand's chair scraped the floor savagely.

And then the voice of Madame Blaise quite close at hand, bidding Madame Gigon good-by.

"On Tuesday, then, Louise. I shall expect you."

"On Tuesday," repeated Madame Gigon.

"And bring Madame Shane if she wishes to come. But not 'Mees Tolliver.' I can't bear her and her American ways." The old harridan bent lower, her reticule shaking with the aged trembling of her thin body. "That Schneidermann!" she observed scornfully. "He is a fool! The men I knew when I was young were interested in revolutions and politics . . . not music. Music! Bah!" And to show her disgust she spat on the bare floor. . . . Then she made a hissing noise and swept up the long dim stairway, her boots squeaking as she walked.

Then the confusion of farewells as the last guests departed, Madame de Cyon passing by, still in bad humor over her losses.

"On Friday, Madame Gigon," she said. "My husband will be there. He is home from the Balkans and full of news."

"Of the wars I suppose. . . . On Friday, Madame."

"And tell Madame Shane she is expected also."

Then Captain Marchand and Madame Marchand, also in a bad humor because they got on badly. Madame Marchand's day fell on Monday and she too asked the old woman to bring Madame Shane. Her invitation was made in the same oblique fashion as the other. "Bring Madame Shane if she cares to come."

At last there remained no one save those whom Lily, in her vague, lazy fashion called "the family." These were old Madame Gigon, Ellen Tolliver, Jean, herself and the Baron.

As the blond little Captain Marchand, pompously clanking his spurs as he walked, disappeared up the darkening reaches of the long stairway, Jean, who had been reading in a corner reserved for himself, sprang up with the bound of a young animal and ran across to Ellen and Schneidermann.

"Alors! Viens donc . . . la musique!" he cried, seizing her by the hand while she struggled against his youthful strength, and Schneiderman laughed at his exuberance. She resisted, bracing her strong slim body and indulging in a mock struggle.

"Not a sound from me,"she replied. "Unless we talk English. I can make no more effort with this waiter's chatter."

It was a price which she exacted frequently, for she spoke French badly, though with great vigor, and with an accent so atrocious that it seemed quite beyond hope of improvement. Her English carried the drawling tang of the middle west. She called "dog" *dawg* and "water" *watter*.

Jean resembled his mother. His hair, like hers, was red though less soft and more carroty. His nose was short, straight, and conveyed an impression of good humor and high spirits. He was tall for his age and strongly built with a slim figure which gave every promise of one day growing into the bulky strength of the Governor. He possessed a restless, noisy, energy quite incomprehensible to Lily. To-day he wore the uniform of a cadet at the cavalry school at St. Cyr. It was the idea of the Baron, himself a cuirassier, that Jean should be trained for the cavalry. "If he does not like it, he may quit," he told Lily. As for Jean, he appeared to like it well enough. He was as eager for a war as Madame Blaise had been certain of one.

"Come along, Nell," he cried. "Be a good cousin, and play that four-handed stuff with me."

Madame Gigon, with Michou and Criquette waddling amiably after her, stole quietly away to her room to lock her door against the hideous sounds which Ellen, Schneidermann and Jean made when they played what they called modern "music."

From the shelter of a divan placed between two of the tall windows, Lily and the Baron watched the three noisy musicians. On the verge of middle-age, her beauty appeared to have reached its height. There are those who would have preferred her as a young girl, fresher, more gentle and more naive. But likewise there are those who find the greatest beauty in the opulent women of Titian, and it was this beauty which Lily now possessed. She wore a black tea-gown, loosely and curiously made with a collar which came high about her throat and emphasized the ivory green tint of her skin and the copper red of her hair. She lay back among the cushions watching Jean with the triumphant, possessive look which strayed into her dark eyes whenever her son was with her. It was an expression so intense as to be almost tragic.

The Baron smiled too, but his smile was concealed somewhat by the fierce black military mustaches that adorned his face. They were the mustaches of the French army, very long, very luxurious, and purposely rather ill-kempt. There was nothing silky about them. On the contrary they were the mustaches of an *homme de guerre*—stiff, bristling and full of vitality. He was a dark, wiry Frenchman, with strong, nervous hands and very bright black eyes which clouded easily with anger. He was perhaps four or five years older than Lily and did not look his age. Indeed his figure was youthful and muscular with the hard, fierce masculinity which belongs to some men of the Latin race.

Whenever he regarded Ellen, it was with a stern glance that was almost hostile. They did not get on well. Even Lily, indifferent and unobservant, must have seen the hidden clash of their two strong natures. It appeared that he resented Ellen's wilfulness and even the masculine simplicity of her clothes. On this evening she was at her best. Her dark hair she no longer wore in the manner of Lily. It was drawn straight back from her high forehead with an uncompromising severity and done in a knot low on the back of her strong, well-shaped neck. Jean dragged her by sheer force of strength to the piano where the two sat down noisily, the boy searching through the music while Ellen played the most amazing, delicate and agile roulades and cascades of notes on the polished ivory keyboard. Schneidermann, thrown a little into the background by the wild exuberance of the pair, drew up a chair and waited quietly until it was time for him to turn the pages.

And during these preliminaries Lily and the Baron rose and made their way silently through one of the tall windows on to the terrace and thence into the garden. Lily herself confessed that she could not abide the new music.

"I do not understand it," she told her cousin. "And I do not find it beautiful. It is beyond me, I confess. I cannot see what you and Jean find in it. I suppose it is because I am growing old. You and Jean belong to the same generation. I am too old for new ideas." And for the first time her laugh was not all geniality and warmth. It carried a fine edge of bitterness, scarcely to be discerned but none the less unmistakable.

And now in the soft spring twilight of the garden she and the Baron walked along the neat gravel paths until they reached the wall shutting out the Rue de Passy. Here they sat for a time on a stone bench saying nothing, remaining quite still and silent. And at last as the darkness grew more heavy they rose and wandered off again, aimlessly and slowly, until in the shadow of a laburnum tree, the man seized her suddenly and kissed her, long and passionately. And after a little while when it was quite dark they entered the pavilion hidden by shrubbery where Jean lived when he was home on a holiday.

The garden lay breathless and silent. Even the rumbling noises from the street beyond the wall had died away with the coming of darkness. From the distant Seine arose the faint whistle of the St. Cloud steamer, and through the tall window drifted in wild fragments the savage, barbaric chords of Stravinsky's music.

LIX

D AY in and day out Lily's life followed its easy, happy course. Always there were diversions, always gaiety, always people. Yet there were times now—indeed they seemed to have begun upon her return from America following her mother's death—when a cloud of sadness descended upon her, times when she would withdraw suddenly to her own room as if some tiny thing, a word, a gesture, an intonation, had set fire to a train of secret memories. Frequently she kept her room for the rest of the day, seeing no one, lunching and dining alone on a gilt table placed before her chaise longue by the window.

These sudden fits of melancholy disturbed Ellen who remarked on them gravely to old Madame Gigon.

"She was never like that before. I can't see what it is that disturbs her."

Madame Gigon saw no cause for alarm. "It's true," she said. "She was never like that before. But it may be that she grows tired. You see she is growing older, my dear Mees Ellen. All of us, as we grow older, like moments of solitude and quiet. It gives one time to reflect on life. You don't understand that yet. You're too young. But some day you will understand. As you get older you begin to wonder what it's all about . . . (*pourquoi le combat*)."

"Perhaps," replied Ellen with a vigorous shrug. "I'm sure it can't be her mother. It might, of course, be Irene."

And they fell to discussing for the hundredth time the case of Irene, whom Madame Gigon had not seen since she was a little girl. They talked of her strange behavior, Madame Gigon wagging her old head, staring before her with sightless eyes.

"It is tragic . . . a life like that," she would say. "A life wasted. You know she was a pretty little girl. . . . She could have married."

223

They spoke of her as if she were dead. It was true that to them . . . to Ellen, to Madame Gigon, she was forever lost. Perhaps they were right, with that instinctive knowledge which underlies the consciousness of women chattering together over the strangeness of human behavior. Perhaps Irene *was* dead. . . . Perhaps she had been dead since a certain night when the last traces of her faith in humanity were throttled. It was true that she had left the world and turned her faith toward God alone, as if she were already dead and in purgatory.

"She was always queer," Ellen would say.

And then Madame Gigon, as if she were conscious of toying with thoughts of blasphemy, would say piously:

"But she is a good woman, who has given her life to good work and prayer."

But she spoke as if trying to convince herself, as if she did not quite believe what she said.

And Lily, all the while, kept her secret. Undoubtedly she was no longer in her first youth. This may have depressed her, for she was a woman to whom beauty and youth were the beginning and the end. Yet the fits of melancholy had something to do with a more definite and tangible thing. They were associated in some way with a little enameled box in which she kept a growing bundle of clippings from the American newspapers which Ellen brought into the house at Numero Dix.

In the solitude of her room, she opened the box and reread them many times, over and over again until the edges became frayed and the print blurred from much fingering. They had to do with the career of a certain labor leader, a man named Krylenko who seemed a strange person to excite the interest of a woman like Madame Shane. The clippings marked the progress of the man. Whenever there was a strike, Krylenko appeared to take a hand in it. Slowly, clipping by clipping, the battle he fought was being won. The unions penetrated now this steel town, now that one. There were battles, brutalities, deaths, fires in his trail, but the trail led steadily upward toward a goal. He was winning slowly. That he was strong there could be no doubt. He was so strong that great newspapers printed editorials against him and his cause. They called him an "anarchist," "an alien disturber," "a peril to the great American nation" and, most frequently of all, "a menace to prosperity and the inalienable rights of property."

Lily kept the enameled box locked in a drawer of her writing desk. No one had ever seen it. No one would see it until she died. It had been there for seven years.

It was on the morning after one of these attacks of melancholy, a few days after Jean's visit, that the Town suddenly intruded once more upon the house in the Rue Raynouard.

Lily sat on the sunlit terrace of the garden before a late breakfast of chocolate and buttered rolls, opposite Ellen whose habit it was to arise early and pursue some form of violent exercise while her cousin still slept. This morning she had been riding in the Bois de Bologne. As a little girl she learned to ride under the instruction of her grandfather, old Jacob Barr, and she rode well and easily with the air and the skill of one who has grown up with horses. The languid Schneidermann accompanied her on these early morning jaunts. She owned her horse because in the long run it was more economical and, as she said, "No pennies slip through my fingers."

She wore a tight black riding habit with a white stock and a low derby hat. The riding crop lay across her strong, slim knees as she smoked and watched Lily devour too many rolls and a too large bowl of rich chocolate.

Between them on the table lay the morning's letters. In Ellen's little heap there were three or four notes from struggling music students, begging help or advice from her, one from a manager proposing an interview with regard to an American tour, a bill from Durand the publisher. Lily's pile was altogether different. It consisted almost entirely of bills, from Coty, from Worth, from Henri the florist, from Augustin the hairdresser, from Lanvin . . . from . . . on and on endlessly and at the bottom a letter from the lawyers who succeeded on the death of William Baines, "the old fogy," to the management of Lily's holdings in the Town.

The last letter she read through twice with so deep an interest that the chocolate grew cold and she was forced to send for a hot cup and more hot rolls. When she had finished she leaned back in the wicker chair, buried beneath the silk, the lace ruffles and the pale tiny bows of her peignoir.

"D'you know, Ellen," she remarked, "I am growing too rich. I've no idea what to do with all my money."

Ellen put down her letter abruptly and knocked the ash from her cigarette.

"There are plenty of places for it." She slapped the envelope against her slim thigh. "I've had two letters this morning asking me for money . . . from two music students. Heaven knows I've got nothing to spare. All that's left over I send to Ma. What is it now? A gold mine or an oil well?"

"Neither," said Lily. "It's just the Town making me richer and richer. It's from Folsom and Jones . . . I guess they're since your time. They're lawyers and they handle Irene's and my estate. They want me to sell the rest of the property we own."

Ellen pursed her lips reflectively. "How much are they offered?"

"Something over five hundred thousand. They say they can get six in a pinch."

She whistled softly. "Take it . . . take it. Those old shacks can't be worth that."

"It isn't the shacks," said Lily. "It's the land itself they want. The shacks aren't even worth repair. Why, they were built, most of them, while father was still living. The lawyers hint that the Town is ashamed of them, that they are a disgrace to the Town."

"I suppose it has changed," remarked Ellen.

"The population has doubled," said her cousin. "There aren't enough houses for the people. Why, last summer people who came to work at the Mills had to live in tents for a time. Even the people on Park avenue let out rooms. The Chamber of Commerce asked them to. They appealed to their pride not to stop the tremendous growth. There's been a tremendous . . ."

Ellen interrupted her. "I know . . . I know. . . . 'Watch us grow. The biggest city in the state in ten years. Well, it's money in your pocket. You've no kick coming."

The chocolate and rolls arrived and Lily began once more to eat.

"I don't see how you can eat all that and keep your figure," observed Ellen.

"Massage," said Lily. "Massage . . . and luckily the time is coming when I can eat all I want and be as fat as I like. In another fifteen years I'll be an old woman and it won't matter what I do." The faint bitterness again drifted through the speech, evasive and imperceptible.

"What does Irene say to your selling?" inquired Ellen.

"The lawyers say she wants to sell. You know I haven't had a line from her in years. She's in France now, you know."

"In France!" said Ellen, her eyebrows rising in surprise.

"Yes, at Lisieux."

"I should think you'd go and see her."

"She wouldn't see me if I went. What good would it do?"

LX

THERE was a sudden silence while Ellen beat her riding crop against her leg. "I must say she's very queer. I never understood her. You know when I was a girl, she gave me the creeps . . . the way she had of looking at you with those pale eyes."

"I know," replied Lily. And then after a pause. "You know they want to buy Cypress Hill too. The Lord alone knows how many times they tried. They began before Mama died. Irene hasn't any share in it. It belongs outright to me."

"I suppose it's the Mills."

"No, not this time. The Town wants it now." She paused while she buttered another roll. "They want it for a new railway station . . . a union station, you know, for all three roads. It's perfect for that. And each time they increase the offer. Now they write me that they've made a last offer. If I won't sell, they'll undertake proceedings to condemn it."

During this speech the countenance of Ellen Tolliver underwent a complete metamorphosis. The devil-may-care look vanished slowly, replaced by a certain hardness, a squaring of the handsome jaw, a slight hardening of the firm lips. It may have been that while Lily talked her cousin was swept by a torrent of memories—memories of hurt pride, of poverty and indignities endured because she was helpless, memories of patronizing women and young girls who spoke of "poor Ellen Tolliver," memories of her father's defeats and disappointments, of Judge Weissman's dishonesty and corruption, of her mother's agonizing and endless struggle to keep up appearances. As sometimes occurs with individuals of strong personality, a whole life, a complete philosophy stood revealed for an instant in her intelligent face. She had run off with Clarence Murdoch "to show the Town." She had become famous and successful because, deep down in her heart, she was resolved always to

228

show the Town how little it counted in her life, how great was the contempt she felt for it. It was always this thought—this more than everything else—which had driven her forward. And now came this new opportunity, perhaps the best of all, to block the Town, to thwart its most cherished desire. It was a chance to prevent a new and flamboyant effort to advertise its wealth, its prosperity, its bigness.

"As if," she said aloud, " 'bigness' was something to be proud of. Let them try and condemn it, Lily. I doubt if they can. Anyway I'd keep it just to spite them. It's a chance to show your power." She leaned earnestly across the table, striking it with her riding crop to emphasize her words. "You hate the place as much as I do. Why, it isn't even the same Town we grew up in. It's another place built upon filth and soot. It's not that we're fouling our own nest. Why, Lily, the Town your mother and my grandfather loved wasn't that sort of place at all. It was a pleasant place where people lived quietly and peacefully, where they had horses and dogs and were decent to each other. And now that's all buried under those damned filthy Mills, under a pile of muck and corruption with Judge Weissman and his crowd enthroned on the very top." She stood up, her blue eyes flashing. "It's changed the very people in it. It's made them noisy, common, cheap. Damn it! I hate them all!" She struck the table a violent blow with her riding crop. "Don't sell it. You don't need the money. It's nothing to you . . . not even if they offered you a million!" And then she laughed savagely. "That's the best part of it. The longer you hold it, the more they'll have to pay you. The more prosperous they are, the more it will cost them to have a new railway station. You're the one who has the power now. Don't you see what power there is in money? . . . the power that grows out of just owning a thing?"

Lily, it appeared, was amazed by the passion of the sudden outburst. For a time she lay back in the wicker chair, regarding her cousin with a thoughtful look. At last, she said, "I had no idea that you felt that way about it. It's the way Mama used to feel. I suppose I never had enough of the place to really hate it."

Ellen again interrupted her passionately. "If you'd had as much as I had, you'd have hated it all right."

"I just ran away from it as soon as I could," continued Lily. "Besides," she added after a pause, "Mama left a letter asking me to keep Cypress Hill. She always felt that way about the Town."

Ellen, persistent, bent over the table toward her cousin. The riding crop fell to the gravel terrace. "Promise me you won't sell it, Lily. . . . Promise me you'll keep it. It's a chance to hit back. . . . Promise!"

And Lily, who after all was indifferent in matters of business, promised, perhaps because the violent revelations made by her cousin astounded her so completely that she was unable to think of any argument. Doubtless she had reasons of her own . . . secret reasons which had to do with the worn clippings in the enameled box.

"I'll keep it," she replied. "They can wait until Hell freezes over. And besides you put the idea so that it amuses me. I'll sell the other stuff and invest the money."

Ellen interrupted her with a bitter laugh. "It's funny, you know, that all this time they've been pouring money into your pocket. That's the joke of it. In a way, it was all this booming and prosperity that helped me too. If you hadn't been so rich, I suppose I'd never have made a success of it."

Lily languidly finished the last of her chocolate. "I'd never thought of it in that way. It's an amusing idea."

Ellen was satisfied. Gathering up her letters she went into the house, changed her clothes, and in a little while, seated under the flaming Venice of Mr. Turner, she was working stormily at her music, filling the house with glorious sound until it overflowed and spilled its rhapsodies over the terrace into the garden where the first bright irises were abloom.

LXI

UPSTAIRS Lily made her way, after a toilette which occupied two hours, to the room of Madame Gigon. It was, amid the elegance of the house, a black-sheep of a room, its walls covered with books, its corners cluttered with broken fragments of Gothic saints and virgins, the sole legacy of the distant and obscure M. Gigon, curator at the Cluny Museum. In the center stood a table covered with dark red rep, heavily embroidered and cluttered with inkpots, pens and all the paraphernalia of writing. Bits of faded brocade ornamented the wall save for a space opposite the door where hung an immense engraving of the First Napoleon, dominating a smaller portrait of Napoleon the Little in all the glory of his mustaches and imperial. An engraving of the Eugènie by Winterhalter stood over the washstand, a convenience to which Madame Gigon clung even after Lily's installation of the most elaborate American plumbing.

Madame Gigon huddled like a benevolent old witch among the bedclothes of her diminutive bed. At the foot, in a bright patch of sunlight, lay Criquette and Michou amiably close to each other and both quite stuffed with toasted rolls and hot chocolate.

Lily came in looking fresh and radiant in a severe suit and smart hat. They exchanged greetings.

"How are you this morning, Tante Louise?" she inquired of the old woman.

"Not so well . . . not so well. I slept badly. The pain in my hip."

Lily went and sat on the bed, taking the old woman's hand which she caressed as she felt her pulse.

"You have everything you want?" she inquired.

"Oui . . . everything." There was a little pause and

Madame Gigon peered at her with dim eyes. "I've been thinking how lucky I am."

Lily smiled.

"I mean that I'm not left poor and alone. You've been good to me."

Lily's smile expanded into a laugh. "Nonsense. . . . Nonsense. It's given me enough pleasure. . . ."

"It seems like the hand of God," said the old woman very piously.

"It may be," said Lily. "Mees Ellen has been telling me it's the hand of man."

And Madame Gigon, not having heard the talk on the terrace, was puzzled. Secretly she disapproved Mees Ellen's lack of piety.

"Mees Ellen plays well this morning . . . beautifully," said Madame Gigon. "She is an artist . . . a true artist. Will you ask her a favor?"

Lily nodded.

"Will you ask her to play something of Offenbach? I've been hungry for it." She looked feeble and appealing somewhat confused by violence of the life with which she found herself surrounded since the advent of Mees Ellen and the grown-up Jean.

"Of course," said Lily.

"And one more thing," said Madame Gigon. "This I must ask of you. . . . I'm too ill to go to Madame Blaise this afternoon. I want you to go and explain why I have not come. Tell her I am too ill." A slight frown crossed Lily's brow. Madame Gigon, with her dim eyes could not possibly have seen it, yet she said, "Madame Blaise admires you. . . . She thinks you are all that a woman should be . . . a perfect woman."

If Lily had felt any genuine hesitation, the faint flattery destroyed it, for she replied. "I'll go, certainly. I'm lunching out and I'll go there late and tell her."

"Not too late. . . . She is easily offended," said Madame Gigon. "You know she is a little . . ." She made a comic gesture indicating that Madame Blaise was a little cracked.

Then Lily read to her for a time out of Faure's History of

Art which undoubtedly bored her but gave Madame Gigon the greatest pleasure; and at last she left for her mysterious lunch. A little while later there arose from below stairs the tinkling melodies of the overture to Orpheus in the Underworld. Somewhere among the piles of old music in the drawing-room closet, Ellen had discovered the whole score and she played it now in a wild good humor. Sometimes the music became actually noisy in its triumphant violence. It was the playing of a woman who had achieved a victory.

LXII

I T is possible that Madame Blaise felt for Lily the admiration which Madame Gigon attributed to her, but she was such a queer old thing that it was impossible ever to know for a certainty. It could not be said that she revealed these sentiments by any open demonstration, or even by an occasional word of approval. There are women whose manner of showing their devotion assumes an inverted character; it takes to displaying itself in sharp criticisms of the object they love or admire. There are women who nag their lovers, who deprecate the charms of their own children, who sharply denounce the behavior of their dearest friends. And if there be any truth in this theory of inverted demonstration, it could be said that Madame Blaise admired Lily. Indeed judging from her behavior it could be said that she experienced a profound affection for the younger woman.

The old woman seldom addressed Lily, yet when Lily politely assumed the initiative and inquired after the health of Madame Blaise or her plans for the summer, Madame Blaise was flattered and smiled with all the warmth of an August sun. To Madame Gigon she criticized Lily unmercifully. She called her indolent, without ambition. She accused her of having wasted her life and permitted her beauty to fade without using its power. It was not true that Lily had faded, yet Madame Blaise was convinced of it. To have heard her talk, one would have thought Lily was a withered old harridan.

"I understand these things," she told Madame Gigon confidentially, "because I was a beauty myself . . . a famous beauty." And the memory of her triumphs led her to bridle and cast a glance at the nearest mirror. Yet she never spoke of these things to Lily, whose greater youth, already turning into middle-age, seemed to inspire the old woman with an awe tinged by actual worship.

234

"Why does she bury herself among these old women?" she would say. "Has she no energy . . . no zest for life? If only she could capture some of Mees Tolliver's *élan*. Mees Tolliver could spare her a great deal and be the more charming for it."

And to all this, Madame Gigon had one answer which it was her habit to repeat over and over again. "Madame Shane is content. Is not that enough? What more can any of us wish upon this earth?"

So it ran, this perpetual and carping interest of Madame Blaise. Although she avoided Lily, she could not resist discussing her. And Madame Gigon, believing firmly that Madame Blaise was a little cracked, never mentioned these things to Lily.

There hung about Madame Blaise something of the mystery which envelopes people suffering from delusions. Not only was it impossible to know when she was lying and when she was speaking the truth . . . it was impossible even to say, "Madame Blaise is thus and so. She is mean or she is benevolent. She is hostile or she is friendly." It was impossible to reach any sensible opinion concerning her. She was subject to the most absurd whims which rendered impossible any anticipation of her actions. Besides, she lived in a world of her own which resembled in no way the world of her friends, so bound up in shopkeepers, food, laundry, housekeeping, etc. Her world was inhabited by all sorts of fantastic and imaginary creatures. She believed passionately that she was still a fine figure of a woman. Not even a mirror could persuade her otherwise. She asserted with a challenging pugnacity that she had once played a prominent part in European politics, and hinted that she was the last of the women who would go down in history as creatures who ruled kings; but what it was she had done or when she had done it, no one could discover. The tragedy was that no one took her seriously. When one spoke of her, there was always a suspicion in the speech of that comic gesture which Madame Gigon used to indicate that her friend was a little cracked. Yet they were kind to her. No one allowed her to suspect that she was accepted generally as a mere pack of highly animated hallucinations. Indeed her *faiblesse* gave her the whip hand over her friends. People humored her. They submitted to her insults with a calm good-nature.

When she began one of her long tales, people smiled and feigned interest and remarked, "How wonderful! Who would have thought it?" Or with mock protests, they would say, "But my dear Madame Blaise, you are still a fine figure of a woman." And she would go off home delighted that she had managed to preserve her figure and her youthful complexion, even if a bit of rouge was at times necessary. Her delight was always apparent. It was visible in every line of her seamed old face.

There were all sorts of stories concerning Madame Blaise, stories of the most fantastic and incredible nature, stories that she was well known in the generation which she had outlived, stories even that she had been the mistress of this or that politician. Indeed some of the most fantastic tales were contributed slyly by Madame Blaise herself. But no one really knew anything of her youth; and although every one repeated the stories with a certain relish, there was no one who really believed them.

The old women who came to Madame Gigon's salon knew that she had come to Paris some twenty years earlier as the widow of a merchant from Marseilles. She was rich, respected, and at that time seemed wholly in her right mind, save for an overfondness to surround herself with mystery. A respectable Bonapartist, the uncle of Captain Marchand, acted as her sponsor. She settled herself presently into the respectable circle. She had her *salon* and all went well. By now she had been accepted for so long a time that she seemed always to have been a part of that neat little society, so neat, so compact and so circumspect. She was a figure. Madame Blaise? Why, of course, every one knew Madame Blaise . . . always. What had gone before became quickly veiled in the mists of the past, and Madame Blaise, whose life may have been after all one of the most romantic and exciting, found herself a part of a singularly dull and prosaic society.

Lily could have known no more than this concerning the old woman. Indeed it is probable that she knew even less, for her good nature and her tolerant indifference had long since stifled all her curiosity concerning people. She went to Madame Blaise on that Tuesday afternoon to please Madame Gigon, because she had no other engagement, and because she was accustomed to obliging her friends. She may even have suspected that the visit would give pleasure to Madame Blaise herself. She arrived very late as usual (it was impossible for Lily to be punctual) having lingered a long time over lunch and made an expensive tour of the shops in the Rue de la Paix.

In a little enclosure shaded by old trees and high, neglected shrubbery in Passy five minutes walk from the Trocadero, Madame Blaise had her house. The enclosure was shared by two other houses, less pretentious, which stood respectfully apart at a little distance. The dwelling was built of wood in imitation of a Swiss chalet, and ornamented with little carved balconies and fantastic ornaments in bizarre exaggeration of some cowherd's house on the mountains above Lucerne. A wall ran about the enclosure with an opening which was barred at night by a massive iron gate. Here Lily stepped down from the fiacre, passing, on her way through the gate, Madame de Cyon and the Marchands, who were leaving.

"You are late," observed Madame de Cyon, taking in Lily's costume with her small green eyes.

"I have been hurrying all the way," replied Lily. "I was kept by business."

Captain Marchand and his wife bowed gravely.

"Every one has gone," observed Madame de Cyon, waiting as though curious to see what Lily would do.

"Well, I must go in. . . . Madame Gigon was too ill to come. She asked me to convey her compliments."

Madame de Cyon brightened. "Nothing serious, I hope."

"No," said Lily. "Madame is an old woman. . . ." And then politely, "She tells me Monsieur de Cyon is back from the Balkans."

"Yes. He is full of wars and intrigues. You must come to me on Thursday. He has asked for you."

Lily smiled. "Please remember me to him. I find him very interesting." She turned suddenly. "But I must hurry in. It is disgusting to be so late. Good-by until Thursday."

Madame de Cyon laid a hand on her arm. "Madame Blaise

was eager that you should come. She has been asking for you."

"It is good of her," said Lily politely, at the same time moving away.

"Good-by until Thursday," said Madame de Cyon, and as Lily hurried into the shadows of the enclosure the Russian woman turned and looked after her, her small green eyes alight with an interest in which there was a shade of malice and envy. It was well known that de Cyon admired Madame Shane.

When Lily had disappeared in the thick shrubbery surrounding the house, Madame de Cyon made a clucking noise and passed through the gate into the street on her way to the Metro. She had lost money again to the Marchands. She was planning to economize.

LXIII

A T the door Lily was admitted by a fat Bretonne maidservant who ushered her through a dark hall and up a
dark stairway where the light was so bad that she
was unable to distinguish any of the furnishings. It
might have been a tunnel for all the impression it made upon a
visitor. At a turn of the stairs she was forced to press her
body against the wall in order to allow pass two strangers
whom she had never seen at Madame Gigon's salon. At the
top she was led through another hall lighted by a sort of chalice,
with a gas flame burning inside a red globe suspended by
Moorish chains from the low ceiling. Here it was possible to
discern the most enormous quantity of furniture and decorations, bronze ornaments, bits of chinoiserie, pictures of all sizes
in enormous gilt frames, umbrellas, cloaks, chairs, pillows and
what not. At the end of the hall the maidservant opened the
door of a large square room and silently indicated Madame
Blaise who was seated before a gentle charcoal fire. Lily
entered and the servant closed the door behind her.

Madame Blaise, dressed in old-fashioned gown of some thick
black stuff, sat on the edge of her chair like a crow upon a
wall. Her cheeks and lips were rouged and this, together with
the red glow from the fire and the thick mass of dyed red hair,
gave her an appearance completely bizarre and inhuman. She
could not have heard Lily enter, for she did not look up until
the younger woman came quite close to her and said, "Madame
Blaise!"

"Ah!" said the old woman suddenly, as if waking from a
dream. "It's you."

Lily was smiling and apologetic. She lied about being de-
tained on business. She explained Madame Gigon's indispo-
sition. Altogether she made herself charming, agreeable and
insincere.

239

"Yes," said Madame Blaise. "Madame Gigon is old," in a tone which implied "much older than I shall ever be."

"I shan't stay but a moment," said Lily, sitting in a chair on the opposite side of the fire.

"No, I suppose not."

And then a silence fell during which it seemed that Madame Blaise returned again to her dream. Lily took off her gloves, straightened her hat and fell to regarding the room. It was an amazing room, full of shadows and indefinable and shapeless objects which danced in the dim gaslight. Gradually these things began to take shape. There were all sorts of chairs and tables and cushions of every fashion and period. The room fairly crawled with furniture. Near the fire stood a red lacquer table, exquisitely made, laden with the remnants of tea—a chocolate pot, a tea urn with the lamp extinguished and the tea growing cold, plates with sandwiches and gateaux. The windows were covered by thick curtains of some brocaded stuff which were drawn now to shut out the twilight. But the most remarkable feature of the room was the number of pictures. They hung in every conceivable nook and corner, standing upright in little frames of gilt bronze, tortoiseshell or ebony, leaning against the walls and against the mirror over the fireplace. Some, judging from the flamboyance and heroic note of the poses, were pictures of actresses and opera singers. Others from the pomposity of the subject were undoubtedly politicians. There were pictures of ladies in crinolines and gentlemen with beards or flowing mustaches. Some were photographs, faded and worn; others were sketches or prints clipped out of journals. There were at least a half dozen portraits in oil of varying degrees of excellence.

Lily occupied herself for a time in studying the room. At last Madame Blaise. "I am glad the others have gone. They weary me—inexpressibly." She leaned forward a little in her chair. "You understand I have had an interesting life. These others . . ." She made a stiff gesture of contempt. "What have they known of life? They go round and round like squirrels in a cage . . . always the same little circle. Always the same dull people."

Lily smiled agreeably. She was remarkably beautiful in the

soft light. "I understand," she said, with the air of humoring the old woman.

Madame Blaise rose suddenly. "But I forgot. . . . You must forgive me for not asking you sooner. Will you have some tea or some chocolate?"

"Nothing," said Lily. "I must think of my figure."

Madame Blaise sat down again. "I am glad you have come. . ." And after a little pause, she added, "Alone." A frown contracted her brow beneath a neatly clipped bang. "You understand. . . . I think we have some things in common . . . you and I."

Lily still sat complacently. "I'm sure we have!" she said, purely to oblige her companion.

"But not what you suppose," said Madame Blaise looking at her sharply. "Not at all what you suppose. I am not speaking of the youth which we share . . . you and I. I am speaking rather of the qualities which have nothing to do with youth. I mean the capacity to love." This sentiment she uttered with a look of profound mystery. In spite of her eccentricity, there gleamed now and then through the cloud of mystery traces of a grand manner, a certain elusive distinction. It showed in a turn of the head, a gesture, an intonation . . . nothing very tangible, indeed, little more than a fleeting illusion.

Lily's eye began to wander once more, round and round the room to this picture and that, hesitating for a moment on one or another of the amazing collection which caught her fancy. When Madame Blaise fell silent once more for a long interval, she remarked,

"But have you no picture of yourself among all these?"

"No," replied the old woman. "I am coming to that later." And without pausing, she added, "You have had lovers of course." And when Lily, astounded by this sudden observation, stirred nervously in her chair, Madame Blaise raised her hand. "Oh, I know. I am not going to reproach you. I approve, you understand. It is what beautiful women are made for." Her eyes took on an uncanny look of shrewdness. "Don't fancy that I am ignorant. Some people of course say that I am crazy. I am not. It's the others who are crazy, so they think that I am. But I understand. You have a lover now. . . . He is Madame Gigon's cousin." She looked fiercely into Lily's face which had grown deathly pale at the crazy outburst of the old woman. She appeared frightened now. She did not even protest.

"I have watched," continued Madame Blaise, in the most intimate manner possible. "I understand these things. I know what a glance can mean . . . a gesture, a sudden unguarded word. You, my dear, have not always been as cautious, as discreet, as you might have been. You needn't fear. I shall say nothing. I shall not betray you." She reached over and touched Lily's hand with an air of great confidence. "You see, we are alike. We are as one. It is necessary for us to fight these other women . . . like de Cyon. She is a cat, you understand."

Lily, all her complacency vanished now, glanced at the watch on her wrist. She stood up and walked to the fireplace in an effort to break the way toward escape. She was, it appeared, unable to collect her wits so that she might deal with Madame Blaise.

"You must not go yet," continued the harridan. "I have so much to tell you." She pursed her withered lips reflectively and put her head a little on one side. "When I was a young girl, I was very like you. You can see that my hair is still the same. People notice and remark how beautifully it has kept its color. Oh yes, many have spoken to me of it. There is nothing like preserving your beauty." And at this she chuckled a little wildly with an air of savage triumph.

LXIV

SO she talked for what must have seemed to Lily hour upon hour. When the younger woman betrayed any sign of leaving, Madame Blaise thrust her tall thin body between her and the door. Even if Lily had desired to speak she would have found small opportunity, for Madame Blaise never once stopped talking. It was as if all the talk of years, repressed and hidden, was suddenly rushing forth in a torrent. The room became intolerably stuffy from the burning gas. Lily's head began to ache and her face to grow more and more pale. If she had been less pleasant by nature she would have made her way by force past the old woman and out into the open air. As it was, she kept hoping, no doubt, that Madame Blaise would come to an end of her talk, that some one would come in and interrupt her . . . the maid perhaps . . . any one. She no longer heard what Madame Blaise was saying. The talk came to her in fragments, the inexpressibly boring chatter of a cracked old woman. To break the monotony she took up the pictures on the mantelpiece and began to examine them. During a brief pause, she observed. "Your pictures are interesting, Madame Blaise. I should like to call again when I have more time, in order to see them all."

"Ah, yes," said the old woman. "So they are . . . so they are. The men . . . they were not all lovers you understand. But I might have had them for lovers by the raising of my finger."

"This one," said Lily, holding up the portrait of a heavily built man wearing the mustachios of a dragoon. "He is interesting."

"Yes . . . yes. He was a Spaniard . . . a nobleman, very aristocratic. Dead now. . . . Extraordinary how many of them are dead!"

Then all at once the attention of Madame Blaise was

arrested by the most extraordinary change in her companion. So remarkable was the change that the old woman actually stopped talking and fell to observing the face of Madame Shane.

Lily held in her hand a small photograph, very faded and soiled, of a man in a black coat with sharp eyes, a high brow and a full black beard. It bore in one corner the stamp of a well-known photographer of the seventies, a gentleman with an establishment in the Galerie des Panoramas. It was a handsome face, fascinating, fanatic, which at once arrested the attention. Beyond all doubt it was the mate of a photograph which Julia Shane, dying, had left to her daughter. Across the face of the one Lily held in her hand was written, *"Á la Reine de la Nuit de son Cavalier Irlandais."* The ink was faded, almost illegible.

"You find that gentleman especially interesting?" asked Madame Blaise in a tone of unbearable curiosity.

For a moment Lily did not reply. She regarded the photograph closely, turning it this way and that under the gaslight. "Yes," she said at last in a low, hushed voice. "Who is he?"

Madame Blaise bridled. "He was a gentleman . . . very interesting," she said. "He admired me . . . greatly. The inscription? It was a joke between us. He was full of deviltry and fun (*un vrai diable . . . tout gamin*). I have forgotten what the joke was. . . . He was forced to leave the country by some unpleasantness. . . . I too went away for a time." And again her eyes narrowed in a mysterious look, invoking romantic, glamorous things. Lily, the picture still clasped in her hand, sat down weakly.

Above all else, old photographs have the power of calling up dead memories. It is so perhaps because they are so terribly, so cruelly, realistic. Those things which the memory, desiring to forget, succeeds in losing among the shadows of time, remain in a photograph so long as it exists . . . the posture of a head, the betraying affected gesture of a hand, the manner of carrying oneself, the arrogance of countenance, the habit of dress . . . all these things survive on a bit of paper no larger perhaps than the palm of one's hand.

The photograph with *"A la Reine de la Nuit"* written across it must have invoked forgotten things . . . memories of John Shane's savage temper and whimsical kindnesses, of terrible scenes between him and his proud wife, of his contempt for the anemic Irene and his admiration for the glowing Lily, of a thousand things distant yet appallingly vivid.

While Lily sat thoughtful and silent, Madame Blaise kept up a stream of hysterical chatter, turning crazily from one subject to another, from personalities to anecdotes, from advice to warning. Lily heard none of it. When she had recovered a little, she said, "This gentleman interests me. I wish you could tell me more of him."

But Madame Blaise shook her head ruefully. "I have forgotten so much," she said. "It is terrible how one forgets. Do you know?" And again the look of mad confidence came into her face. "I have forgotten his name. What is it he calls himself in the inscription?"

She took the photograph from Lily's hand and thrust it under the circle of light, holding it at arm's length and squinting in order to discern it properly. "Ah, yes," she said. *"Cavalier Irlandais.* . . . That was his name. I don't remember his other name, though I believe he had one." She paused, thoughtful, as if trying by a tremendous force of will to recapture the thing which had escaped her. "His father was Irish, you understand. . . . Strange I can't remember his name." So she talked on crazily, answering Lily's questions madly, tangling the answers hopelessly in a flood of insane philosophy and distorted observation. The look of mystery and the remnants of a grand manner persisted. Lily watched her with a look of intense curiosity as if she believed that, after all, the queer old creature might once have been young,—young, mysterious and lovely. But she learned little of the gentleman in the portrait. It was impossible for Madame Blaise to concentrate upon her subject. Lily learned only that the gentleman had been forced to leave the country following some unpleasantness arising out of a duel in which he had killed a relative . . . a cousin perhaps. She did not remember. He had been in politics too. That played a part in his flight. He returned once, Madame Blaise believed, but she did not remember why he had come back.

Altogether it was hopeless. Lily replaced the photograph on the high mantel, powdered her nose and drew on her gloves. Presently there came an opening in the flood of Madame Blaise' talk and Lily seized it sharply.

"I must really go, Madame Blaise. I have stayed much too long. It has been so interesting."

She rose and began to move slowly backward in the direction of the door, as if she feared to rouse the old woman to fresh outbursts. She made her departure gently, vanishing noiselessly; but she got no further than the inlaid music box when Madame Blaise, detecting her plan, sprang up and seized her arm fiercely with her thin old hands.

"Wait!" she cried. "There is one more thing I must show you . . . only one. It will take but a second."

The patient Lily acquiesced, though she kept up a mild protest. Madame Blaise scurried away, rather sidewise as a crab moves, into a dark corner of the room where she disappeared for an instant through a door. When she returned, she bore two dusty paintings in oil. Each was surrounded by a heavy gilt frame and together the pair burdened the strength of the old woman. Her whole manner reeked of secrecy. With an air of triumph she smiled to herself as she took from the chair where she had been sitting a red silk handkerchief with which she dusted the faces of the two paintings. All this time she kept them turned from Lily. At last she stiffened her thin body suddenly and said sharply, "Now, look!"

Lily, bending low, discerned in the light from the fire the character of the two pictures. Each was the portrait of a woman, painted in the smooth, skilful, slightly hard manner of Ingres. Yet there was a difference, which the connoisseur's eye of Lily must have detected. They were cleverly done with a too great facility. But for that one might almost have said they were the work of a genius. Clearly the same woman had posed for both. In one she wore an enormous drooping hat, tilted a little over one eye. In the other she wore a barbaric crown and robes of Byzantine splendor.

Madame Blaise stood by with the air of a great art collector displaying his treasures. "They are beautiful, aren't they?" she said. "Superb! You know I understand these things

I have never shown them to any one in years. I am showing them to you because I know you understand these things. I have seen your house. I have seen your beautiful things. You see it is the same woman who posed for both. . . . The one is called 'The Girl in the Hat' the other is 'The Byzantine Empress.' Theodora, you know, who was born a slave girl."

LXV

LILY, it seemed, had scarcely heard her. She had taken one of the pictures on her lap and was examining it minutely. She held it close to her and then at a little distance. Madame Blaise stood surveying her treasures proudly, her face lighted by a look of satisfaction at Lily's profound interest.

"I wonder," said the old woman presently, "if you see what I see."

For a moment Lily did not answer. She was still fascinated by the pictures. At last she looked up. "Do you mean the woman is like me? Did you see it too?"

Madame Blaise assumed a secretive expression. "Yes," she said. "I have known it all along . . . ever since I saw you. But I never told any one. I kept it as a secret for you." And she spread her skinny hands in an exhibitive gesture, full of satisfaction, of pride, even of triumph.

The likeness was unmistakable. Indeed, upon closer examination it was nothing short of extraordinary. It might have been the Lily of ten years earlier, when she was less heavy and opulent. The Byzantine Empress had the same soft bronze hair, the same green-white skin, the same sensuous red lips.

"It is like me when I was younger."

"Very much," observed Madame Blaise, and then with the air of an empress bestowing a dazzling favor, she added, "I am going to give them to you."

"But they are valuable," protested Lily. "I can see that. They are no ordinary paintings." She spoke without raising her eyes, continuing all the while to examine the pictures, first one and then the other as she frequently examined with infinite care the reflection in her mirror in the Rue Raynouard.

"I realize that you could not carry them home alone," continued Madame Blaise, ignoring her protests. "You might

248

appear ridiculous. You might even be arrested on suspicion. But I shall have them sent round. I must give them to you. What would you have me do? When I die they will be sold. I have no relatives . . . no one. My sister is dead these ten years. I have no child . . . nothing. I am alone, you understand, absolutely alone. Would you have my pictures knocking about some art dealer's place?"

She shook her head savagely. "No, you must have them. You cannot refuse. It is the hand of God in the matter. I understand these things because there is in me something of the woman of all time. The pictures are for you. Nothing can dissuade me."

Again the good-natured Lily was forced to yield, simply by the force of the old woman's crazy will. She must have sensed the fantastic, uncanny quality of the entire affair, for she stirred uneasily and put the Byzantine Empress on the floor, face down. The Girl in the Hat lay across her knees, forgotten for the moment.

Madame Blaise had begun to walk up and down the room in a crazy fashion, muttering to herself. All at once she halted again before Lily.

"It was a famous woman who sat for those pictures," she said. "You could never imagine who she really was."

Vaguely, as if she had been absent from the room for a long time, Lily replied. "No. I'm sure I have no idea. How could I? She was evidently a great beauty."

A look of delight swept the countenance of the old woman. "Wait!" she cried. "Wait! I will make it easy for you. In one moment you will understand!" And she scurried away once more into the dusty closet from which she had brought the pictures. While she was absent Lily leaned back in her chair closing her eyes and pressing a hand against her forehead. For some time she remained thus and when, at last, she opened her eyes at the sharp command of Madame Blaise she found the old woman standing before her with the big hat of the girl in the picture drooped over one eye.

The effect was grotesque, even horrible. Madame Blaise had arranged the dress of black stuff so that her breasts and shoulders were exposed in the fashion of the Girl in the Hat;

but the ripe full breasts of the girl in the picture were in the old woman sunken and withered, the color of dusty paper; the gentle soft curve of the throat was shrunken and flabby, and the soft glow of the face and the fresh carmine of the caressing, sensuous lips were grotesquely simulated with hard rouge, and powder which had caked in little channels on the wrinkled face of the old woman. Even the bit of hair which showed beneath the big hat was travestied horribly by dye. Madame Blaise simpered weakly in imitation of the mysterious, youthful smile which curved the lips of the girl in the picture.

There could be no mistake. The features were there, the same modeling, the same indefinable spirit. Madame Blaise was the Byzantine Empress and the Girl in the Hat. The caricature was cruel, relentless, bitter beyond the power of imagination. Lily's eyes widened with the horror of one who has seen an unspeakable ghost. She trembled and the Girl in the Hat slipped from her knee and fell with a clatter face downward upon the Byzantine Empress.

Madame Blaise had begun to walk up and down the room with the languid air of a mannequin. The big hat flopped as she moved. Turning her head coyly, she said, "I have not changed. You see, I am almost the same."

And then she fell to talking rapidly to herself, holding unearthly conversations with men and women who stood in the dark corners of the room among the innumerable pictures and bits of decaying bric-a-brac. Crossing the room she passed near Lily's chair where, halting for a second, she bent down until her painted cheek touched Lily's soft hair. "You see," she cried, pointing toward the dusty closet, "that one over there. . . . He would give his life to have me." She laughed a crazy laugh. "But no . . . not I. Never yield too easily and yield only for love. Live only for love." And she moved off again on her mad promenade, gibbering, bowing and smiling into the dusty corners.

In the midst of a tête-á-tête which the old woman held with an invisible beau whom she addressed as "Your Highness," Lily sprang up and ran toward the door. Opening it, she rushed through the upper hall down the stairway into the dark tunnel below. As the outer door slammed behind her, it shut in the sound of Madame Blaise' cracked singing, punctuated by peals of crazy laughter.

Lily did not stop running until she passed the gate of the little enclosure and stood, breathless and fainting with terror, beneath the lights of the Rue de l'Assomption.

LXVI

THEY passed the summer at Germigny-l'Evec in the lodge on the terrace above the winding Marne. The little house at Houlgate kept its shutters up all through the hot months. It is true that the health of Madame Gigon was none too good. It is true too that she might have benefited by the sea air. Although Lily mentioned the migration once or twice as the summer advanced she did not insist upon it. Madame Gigon, it appeared, preferred the house where she had always passed her summers, and Lily was content to remain there as the weeks passed through June and into a hot and breathless July. It seemed that, for the first time, she was tired. Indolent by nature, she had reserves of energy which could be roused when the occasion arose. But it appeared that this occasion was not one of sufficient importance; so she remained quietly, reading, walking by the Marne; sometimes in the early morning when the weather was not too hot, she even rode one of the Baron's horses along the paths of the wood on the opposite side of the river near Trilport.

For diversion the pair were visited by Jean who came romping down from St. Cyr for a brief holiday now and then, always looking handsome and behaving with the ferocity appropriate to a budding cavalryman. Ellen came too, but her visits tired her cousin, especially during the hot months. While she was there Lily pretended that she did not ride because Ellen made riding impossible for her. Ellen insisted upon riding at top speed. She searched for stone walls to jump. She even swam her horse through the Marne on one hot morning in July. Unlike Lily she made no effort to preserve her complexion. She became as tanned as an Indian and as hard as an athlete. Jean admired her enormously, and together they careered wildly across country; for Ellen sat her saddle lightly and as well as any man. Indeed she was as good as a boy for a companion.

She even enjoyed the risqué barracks jokes which Jean told her. She listened to the ballads he sang, the bawdy ballads of the cavalry, old songs filled with the traditions of Napoleon's army . . . the same ballads which Lily sang to herself as she dressed for the last ball ever given at Cypress Hill.

Ellen could swear too, in English or in bad French. They became great friends. Lily saw them off in the mornings from her window, looking after them with an expression of mingled envy and regret in her dusky blue eyes. She must have envied the pair their youth. She was jealous of Ellen as she was always jealous of any one for whom Jean showed affection.

But an end came to the early morning excursions when Ellen in August sailed for New York to spend a month with her mother and father. They lived in a little house on Long Island; for Hattie Tolliver, since her children had become successful, no longer kept a rooming house in Manhattan.

"Pa is content now," Ellen said. "He's got a horse and a garden and chickens. That's what he always wanted. Ma is too. But it's different with her. She ought to have another complete family of children. She's never gotten over being a mother. She wants us to stay with her always. She can't bear having us grown up."

It was true. The more successful her children became, the less Hattie Tolliver saw of them.

"It is a warning," said Ellen, "never to be too fond of your children." She laughed ironically. "And yet, if it hadn't been for Ma, I don't suppose I'd be where I am . . . or Fergus or Robert either. She brought us up well. She made us ambitious." And she concluded the speech with the remark that "it was a damned funny world anyway." She had never seen any one who was content.

There had been a time, even a little while before, when she might have said that Lily was the supreme example of contentment, but that time seemed to have passed. Lily was clearly unhappy during that summer. She became more grave and quiet. She was content only when the Baron came down to stay for a week or two and rode with her through the mists of the early summer mornings. When he had gone again, the vague restlessness returned.

Madame Gigon grew to be more and more of a care; and added to the calamities, Criquette on short notice gave birth to a family of puppies of which it appeared the black and tan at the farm was the father. Somehow Madame Gigon took this as a betrayal on the part of the hitherto virginal Criquette. She complained of it as if Criquette had been her own daughter, as indeed she might well have been for the affection and care lavished upon her by the blind old woman. She succumbed completely to her arthritis and lay most of the day in a chair under the clipped linden trees, wearing an injured, fretful air when Lily was not by her side to talk or read to her. Indeed it appeared that between the riotous visits of Jean and Nellie a grayness had descended upon the lodge.

LXVII

IT may have been that Madame Blaise played her part in the depression. After the night that Lily ran out of her house, she never saw the crazy old woman again, for a day or two later Madame Blaise, in a purple hat and a bright Venetian shawl, was led away on the promise of a wonderful adventure to a house in Versailles where well-to-do lunatics were cared for and allowed to indulge to the utmost their idiosyncrasies. Her guardian was none other than the handsome and distinguished M. de Cyon, who with his brother, a lawyer, looked after the old woman's property. She seemed completely happy in the new establishment, so M. de Cyon reported, because she found there an elderly wine merchant who believed himself descended from Henri Quatre and Diane de Poitiers, and therefore the rightful heir to the French throne. Together they spent their days plotting intrigues and revolutions by which he was to be set upon the throne with Madame Blaise as his consort. So there was no opportunity for Lily to wring from the old woman any further information regarding the photograph of the handsome gentleman in the black beard. The photograph together with the hundreds of other pictures, was packed away in a cavernous storehouse in Montparnasse when the furniture was cleared out of the chalet in the enclosure near the Trocadero and it was let to an Englishwoman interested in art. Life, as old Julia Shane said, was after all no story book in which everything was revealed. Every man had secrets which he carried into the grave.

But before Madame Blaise was led away, she kept her threat and sent round to the house in the Rue Raynouard The Byzantine Empress and The Girl in the Hat. The pictures were left there by the driver of a battered fiacre who went off immediately. To Lily, the pictures had become objects of horror. She would not see them. She bade the housekeeper put them away in the top room of the house where she could not possibly find them. When they arrived she was still in bed, suffering from a wild headache that did not leave her for days after the experience with Madame Blaise.

"It was horrible," she told Ellen. "More horrible than you can imagine, to see that old devil dancing before me like an omen . . . a warning of old age. If you had seen her . . . so like me in the pictures . . . so like me even in the reality, like me as I might easily be some day. It was horrible . . . horrible!" And she buried her face in her hands.

Ellen, as usual, consulted Madame Gigon.

"She is really ill, this time," she said. "It isn't that she's just tired. She's frightened by something. She's much worse than she's ever been before."

And they sent for a physician, a great bearded man, recommended by Madame de Cyon, who diagnosed the case as a *crise de nerfs* and bade her go at once to the lodge in the country. The servants remarked that Madame seemed ill and tired for the first time in her life.

After a time she appeared to forget the mysterious photograph. It was clear that her father was destined to remain, as he had always been, a solitary, fascinating, malevolent figure translated by some turn of circumstance from the intrigues of the old world into the frontier life of the new. What lay in the past—murder, disgrace, conspiracy—must remain hidden, the secret of the dead and of a mad old woman who in her youth and beauty had been his mistress at the very moment that his bride struggled in the school at St. Cloud to learn the tricks of a great lady. Out of all the mystery only one thing seemed clear—that Lily was his favorite child; and now the reason seemed clear enough. By some whim of Fate she was like The Girl in the Hat, the lovely creature who was now Madame Blaise.

So the *crise de nerfs* persisted throughout the summer. Indeed there were times when it appeared that Lily was on the verge of a settled melancholia, times when she would walk in solitude for hours along the towpaths beneath the mottled limbs of the plane trees. Yet her beauty persisted. She might have been a goddess . . . Ceres . . . as she walked along the green path, bordered on one side by the Marne and on the other by waving fields of yellow grain.

As the weeks passed she suffered increasing annoyance through the persistent efforts of the Town to acquire the property at Cypress Hill. A dozen times a month letters arrived from Folsom and Jones, pressing letters that carried threats which Folsom and Jones passed along smoothly with all the suavity of true lawyers playing both ends against the middle. Indeed, from the tone of certain of the communications it appeared that they too, although they were Lily's agents and paid by her, believed that the interests of the Town surmounted those of their client. Its growth, they wrote, was stupendous. It was rapidly becoming one of the greatest steel centers in the world. If she could only be induced to return for a visit, she would understand the anxiety of the Town council to acquire the holdings at Cypress Hill. Surely she could understand that while sentiment was a commendable thing, it had its place. One could be too sentimental about a situation. The price offered was excellent. ("But not so excellent as it will be in another five years," thought Lily with a certain malice.) The house brought her no return. She only paid taxes on it. And so on, for page after page, letter after letter.

All this, no doubt, sounded reasonable enough, but Lily reading those letters aloud to Madame Gigon, who desired to be read aloud to no matter what the material, would murmur irritably, "Why the devil can't they leave me in peace? Go back and visit that place? My God! What for?" And then sarcastically, "To see Eva Barr, I suppose. I'm sure I'm not interested in their prosperity."

And she would write again that she had no intention of selling and that the more they annoyed her the less she was likely to alter her decision.

It may have been that she enjoyed the sense of power with which the possession of Cypress Hill endowed her . . . a feature she had not realized until it was shown her by Ellen. It may have been that she was simply tired and a little perverse and ill-natured. And it was true that she had not the slightest interest in the money involved. Indeed she had no idea how rich she was. Each year she spent what she desired to spend, and never did she come to the end of her income. What more could she desire? What could she do with more money?

But it is also more than probable that somewhere far back in the dark recesses of her consciousness, there were memories which kindled as she grew older, new fires of resentment against the Mills and the Town and all the things they stood for . . . memories of her mother's open hatred for the Harrisons and Judge Weissman, memories of a terrible night when men and women were shot down under the dead trees of the park, memories of an heroic, unattainable figure, wounded and bloody, but undefeated . . . a figure which doubtless grew in fascination as it receded into the past. It is true, too, that there is sometimes greater peace, even greater happiness, in renunciation than in fulfilment. What has never been a reality, may remain a fine dream. Krylenko had never been more than this.

And so the affair ran on until one evening in September Eustache, the farmer's boy, brought back from Meaux a small envelope bearing the post mark of the Town and addressed in the scrawled, illiterate handwriting of old Hennery. It recounted briefly the end of the house of Cypress Hill. It had caught fire mysteriously in the night and before dawn nothing remained save a hole in the ground filled with the scorched and blackened fragments of fine old carpets, mirrors, jade, crystals, carved chests and old chairs, all the beautiful things which encumbered the site of the proposed railroad station.

The mulatto woman, Hennery wrote with difficulty and the most atrocious spelling, swore that she saw two men running away from the house after the fire began. The police, he added, had been able to find no trace of them.

And the following day Lily received a polite letter from Folsom and Jones giving her a brief account of the catastrophe. They also mentioned the story told by the mulatto woman. They believed, however, that it was simply the crazy imagining of a demented old woman.

"Perhaps now," the letter concluded, "Miss Shane would desire to rid herself of a property that could no longer hold her even by ties of sentiment."

LXVIII

LILY did not sell and for a time the letters of Folsom and Jones ceased to arrive regularly. Since all her property in the Town was sold save the site of the house at Cypress Hill, there remained no cause for correspondence. Her money she invested through the American banks in Paris. She heard nothing more of the Town until November when she returned to the city. The prospect of a winter in Paris appeared to revive her spirits, and she went, as usual, to hear Ellen play her first concert of the season. That year Lilli Barr played a new Poem with the Colonne Orchestra under the bâton of the elegant Gabriel Pierné. The performance was not a great success. There was too little sympathy between the scholarly soul of the conductor and the vigorous, barbaric temperament of the pianist. Yet it was Ellen who came off best, bearing all the laurels, with all the simpering critics trotting attendance. "Mlle. Barr," they said, "has the perfect temperament for it . . . the superb adjustment of soul and intellect indispensable to the interpretation of such febrile music. It is music which requires a certain coldness of brain, a perception delicate and piercing . . . a thing of the nerves." And so they ran on, wallowing in their delight for the *mot juste,* praising more extravagantly than was either honest or in good taste. One or two saw an opportunity in the praise of hitting a back handed slap at the conductor and his orchestra.

It was M. Galivant, critic of the Journal des Arts Modernes, who hit upon the phrases "febrile music" and "delicate perception." He showed Lilli Barr the article in the salon after the concert, with the keys of the great piano barely cool from her hot fingers.

"Pish! Tosh!" she remarked to Lily who waited for her in the dressing room. "Did you see what Galivant has written?

It's too exquisite for me. To hear them talk, you'd think I took the veil for months at a time just to meditate what my music is all about. I know what it's about and I don't want praise that's written before they hear me play, just because I help their modern music along. Nerves! Nerves! I haven't got such things!"

Yet she was, as always after a concert, tense and nervous, filled with a terrible energy which would not let her sleep until dawn. To-night she wore a long tight gown of cloth of silver, without sleeves and girdled by a single chain of rhinestones. With her dark hair drawn tightly back, she resembled a fine greyhound—lean, muscular, quivering.

"At least they liked it," said Lily, "judging from the applause." She sat waiting in a long cloak of black velvet, held together with silver clasps.

There was a sudden knock at the door and Lily murmured "Come in." It was the porter, a lean, sallow, man with a stoop and enormous black mustaches.

"There is a gentleman to see Madame l'artiste," he said.

Ellen turned. "Who it it?"

The man grimaced. "How should I know? He says he knows you."

A shadow of irritation crossed Ellen's smooth brow. "If he wants to see me, tell him to send in his name." And then to Lily as the porter withdrew, "You see what fame is. The porter doesn't even know my name. He calls me Madame l'artiste . . . Madame indeed! He hasn't even bothered to read the bills."

The fellow returned again, this time opening the door without the courtesy of a knock.

"His name, Madame, is 'arrisong."

Ellen pursed her lips thoughtfully and struck a match on the sole of her slipper, holding the flame to the cigarette in her strong slim fingers.

"Harrison? . . . Harrison?" she repeated, holding the cigarette between her lips and the lighted match poised. "I don't know any Harrison. . . . Tell him to come in."

The stranger must have been waiting just outside the door, for at the word he stepped timidly inside. He was dressed in black and wore a derby hat set well on the back of his head. Over one arm hung an umbrella. He was rather sallow and macabre despite his plumpness. There was the faint air of an undertaker about him. He might have been any age.

As he advanced he smiled and, observing Lily, his countenance assumed an expression of surprise. Ellen gave no sign of recognition. It was Lily who stirred suddenly and stood up, her face glowing with a genuine spontaneous pleasure.

"Willie Harrison!" she cried. "Where have *you* come from?"

At the sound of his name Ellen's smooth brow wrinkled in a slight frown. "Willie Harrison," she murmured, and then joined Lily in welcoming him.

For a moment he stood awkwardly regarding the two women. Then he said, "I came to your concert, Ellen. . . . I saw it advertised in the Herald. I knew you were Lilli Barr." He chortled nervously. "Funny how famous you are now! Nobody ever would have thought it!"

The sight of Willie appeared suddenly to loosen all Ellen's taut nerves. She sat down, leaned back in the chair, and laughed. "Yes. I fooled them, didn't I?" she said. "I fooled them." And a sort of grim satisfaction entered her voice.

Lily was smiling now, out of sheer pleasure at the sight of Willie. It amused her probably more than anything that could have happened to her at that moment.

"But what on earth are you doing in Paris?"

From the tone of her voice, it was clear that she regarded his presence as a sort of miracle. . . . That Willie Harrison should have had the energy to cross the Atlantic and wander about alone in Paris.

Willie sat down, rather stiffly, and told his story. He was with a Cook's party. His tour included London, Paris, the château country and Switzerland. He was leaving shortly.

"It's been a wonderful trip," he remarked, his plump face all aglow. "I'd no idea how much country there was over here."

"Yes," said Ellen, "there's a good deal, taking it all in all." She said this with an undisguised air of patronizing him. It was she who was great now, she who held the whip hand. She was no longer an awkward girl in a home-made ball gown so unpretentious that men like Willie Harrison failed to notice her.

But Willie failed to understand. He was childishly excited over Paris. "It's a great city!" he observed, fingering nervously the ruby clasp of his watch chain. "A great city!"

Lily stood up suddenly.

"Willie," she said, "come home and have supper with us." And turning to Ellen she added, "Paul will be waiting for us. He must be there already." And to Willie, "Paul is Monsieur Schneidermann, a friend of Ellen's and mine."

Willie rose. "I don't know," he said timidly. "Maybe you aren't prepared for me. Maybe I'd be in the way. I didn't mean to force my way in on anything when I called. It was just for the sake of old times."

Lily, moved toward the door trailing the magnificent cloak of black and silver. She thrust her arm through his. "Come along, Willie," she said. "No nonsense. Why, we grew up together."

And they went out, Ellen following them in her plum-colored wrap, to the motor which bore on its polished door the crest of the Baron.

Throughout the journey Willie kept poking his head in and out of the closed motor, drinking in the sights along the way . . . the hushed, shadowy mass of the Madeleine, the warm glow before Maxims', the ghostly spaces of the Place de la Concorde, the white palaces of the Champs Elysées. Ellen in her corner remained sulky and taciturn, smoking savagely. Lily talked merrily, pointing out from time to time sights which she deemed worthy of Willie's appreciation. He seemed not to be listening.

"It's a wonderful place," he kept saying over and over again. "It's a wonderful place." And a kind of pathetic and beautiful awe crept into his thin voice. It seemed that he had no other words than "wonderful." He kept repeating it again and again like a drunken man holding a conversation with himself.

At Numero Dix, Rue Raynouard, Willie underwent the experience of every stranger. He entered by the unpretentious door and found himself suddenly at the top of a long, amazing stairway which led down to a drawing-room all rosy with the glow of warm light. Half-way down the stairs candles burned in sconces against the dull paneling. From below drifted the faint sound of music . . . a Debussy nocturne being played with caressing fingers in the shadowy, dim-lit spaces of the drawing-room.

"Paul is here," observed Ellen and led the way down the long stairs.

Lily followed and close at her silver heels Willie Harrison, divested now of his derby and umbrella. Half-way down, he paused for a moment and Lily, conscious that he had ceased to follow her, waited too. As she turned she saw that he was listening. There was a strange blurred look in his pale eyes . . . the look of one awaking from a long sleep.

"It's beautiful," he said reverently. "My God! It's beautiful!" A kind of dignity seized him. He was no longer gauche and timid. He stared at Lily who stood with her back to a mirror, the black and silver cloak thrown carelessly back from her voluptuous white shoulders, her handsome head crowned with gold bronze hair. And then all at once the tears shone in his eyes. He leaned against the paneling.

"I understand now," he said softly. "I understand . . . everything. I know now how little I must have counted. . . . me and all the Mills together."

And in Lily's eyes there was mirrored another picture . . . that of a vast resounding shed bright with flames and thick with the odor of soot and half-naked bodies . . . Willie, eternally fingering the ruby clasp of his watch chain, herself turning the rings round and round on her slim fingers, and in the distance the white, stalwart body of a young Ukrainian steel worker . . . a mere boy . . . but beautiful. Krylenko was his name . . . Krylenko . . . Krylenko . . . It was a long time ago. more than fourteen years. How time flew!

Lily's dusky blue eyes darkened suddenly and the tears brimmed over. Perhaps it came to her then for the first time . . . a sense of life, of a beautiful yet tragic unity, of a force which swept both of them along helplessly.

All at once she held her handkerchief, quite shamelessly, to her eyes. "We are beginning to be old, Willie," she said softly. "Do you feel it too?"

And she turned and led the way downwards. The music had ceased and the voices of Ellen and Paul Schneidermann rose in dispute. They were arguing with a youthful fire over the merits of the new concerto.

"Here," came Ellen's voice. "This part. It is superb!" And then the sound of a wild, ecstatic sweep of music, terrifying and beautiful. "You understand the strings help a great deal. Part of it lies in the accompaniment." And she began singing the accompaniment as she played.

But Lily with her companion trooping along behind her, did not interrupt the discussion. They made their way, enveloped in a peaceful silence, into the dining-room where supper waited them—some sort of hot stuff in a silver dish with an alcohol flame burning beneath it, an urn steaming with hot chocolate, a bowl of whipped cream, a few sandwiches—superlatively French sandwiches, very thin and crustless with the faintest edge of buff colored paté showing between the transparent slices of white bread. It was all exquisite, perfect, flawless.

"Sit down," said Lily, as she flung off the black and silver cloak. "Sit down and tell me all about yourself."

Willie drew up a chair. "I shan't be able to stay very late," he said. "You see, I'm leaving early in the morning." He watched Lily fumbling with the lamp beneath the urn. She was plumper than he had expected. Indeed she was almost fat. There was a faint air of middle-age about her, indiscernable but unmistakably present.

"What about yourself?" he asked politely. "What has your life been?"

Lily kept on turning and pushing at the silver burner. "My life?" she said. "Well, you see it all about you, Willie." She made a little gesture to include the long, softly glittering rooms, Ellen, the piano, Paul Schneidermann. "It's just been this," she said. "Nothing more . . . nothing less. Not much has happened." For a moment she stopped her fumbling and sat thoughtful. "Not much has happened," and then after another pause, "No, scarcely anything."

There was a sudden, sharp silence, filled by the sound of

Ellen's music. She had become absorbed in it, utterly. It was impossible to say when she would come in to supper.

Then Willie, in an attempt at courtliness, strained the truth somewhat. "You don't look a day older, Lily . . . not a day. . . . Just the same. It's remarkable."

His companion lifted the lid of the chafing dish. "Some hot chicken, Willie?" she asked, and when he nodded, "I must say you look younger . . . ten years younger than the last time I saw you. Why, you look as though you'd forgotten the Mills . . . completely."

Willie laughed. It was a curious elated laugh, a little wild for all its softness.

"I have," he said. "You see I'm out of the Mills for good. I've been out of them for almost seven years."

Lily looked at him. "Seven years," she said, "seven years! Why that's since the strike. You must have gotten out at the same time."

"I did," he replied, "I own some stock. That's all. Judge Weissman is dead, you know. When mother died, the old crowd went out of it for good. All the Mills are now a part of the Amalgamated."

LXIX

THUS in a few words, he sketched the passing of one epoch and its succession by another. The day of the small private enterprise in the Town had passed, succeeded by the day of the great corporation. Everything was owned now by capitalists, by stockholders who never saw the Mills, to whom the workers of the Flats were little more than mythical creatures, animated engines without minds or souls, whose only symbol of existence was the dividend twice a year. Machines they were . . . machines . . . dim machines . . . not in the least real or human.

Most of the tale Willie omitted. He did not tell of the monkey-faced little man who came to the Town representing the Amalgamated. Nor did he tell of the monkey-faced man's address to the Chamber of Commerce in which he talked a great deal of Jesus and declared that religion was what the world most needed, religion and a sense of fellowship between men. He did not tell of how the Amalgamated broke the strike by buying all the wretched houses and turning out the strikers, men, women and children. He omitted the blacklisting, the means by which the strikers were prevented from obtaining work elsewhere. He did not observe that the power which money gave Judge Weissman, himself and his mother, was as nothing compared to the power of the Amalgamated—a vast incalculable power founded upon gold and the possession of property. Nor did he say that the passing of the Mills had killed Mrs. Julis Harrison . . . a thing which was as true as truth. These things were to him of no importance. He was now simply "an average citizen" minding his own business.

All Willie said was, "When mother died, the old crowd went out of it for good."

In the drawing-room Ellen had been completely captured by the concerto. She was playing it all over again, from beginning to end, rapturously, savagely. Schneidermann lay among

266

the cushions of the divan, his lean figure sprawled languidly, his dark eyes closed.

"And what do you do now?" asked Lily. "You must do something to occupy yourself."

Willie's plump face brightened. "I have a farm," he said. "I raise ducks and chickens." A slow smile crept over Lily's face. "It's a success too," he continued. "You needn't laugh at it. I make it pay. Why, I made this trip on last year's profits. And I have a great deal of fun out of it." He smiled again with an air of supreme contentment. "It's the first time I've ever done what I wanted to do."

Lily regarded him with a faint air of surprise. It may have been that she guessed then for the first time, that he was not after all a complete fool. He, too, like Ellen, like herself, even like Irene, had escaped in spite of everything.

They had been talking thus for half an hour when Ellen, followed by Paul Schneidermann, joined them. Willie stood up nervously.

"Paul," said Lily, "Mr. Harrison—Mr. Harrison, Monsieur Schneidermann." They bowed. "You are both steel manufacturers," she added with a touch of irony, "You will find much in common."

Willie protested. "No longer," he said. "Now I am a farmer."

"And I," said Schneidermann, "have never been. I am a musician. . . ." Ellen laughed scornfully and he turned to her with a curious blushing look of self-effacement, "Perhaps," he said, "dilettante is a better word."

For a time they talked—the stupid, polite conversation that occurs between strangers; and then, the proprieties satisfied, Ellen and Paul drifted quickly back into the realm of music. Lily devoted herself to Willie Harrison.

"It was too bad," he remarked, "about the house at Cypress Hill."

Lily leaned forward on the table holding up one white wrist to shield her eyes from the light of the candles. "Yes," she said. "I'm sorry . . . sentimentally, I suppose. I should never have gone back to it. It was perfectly useless to me. But I'm sorry it's gone. I suppose it, too, was changed."

"You would never have known it," said Willie. "It was completely black . . . even the white trimmings." He leaned forward confidentially. "Do you know what they say? They say in the Town that some one was hired to burn it, so that you would be willing to sell."

For a moment Lily remained silent. Her hand trembled a little. She looked across at Ellen to see whether she had been listening. Her cousin was plainly absorbed in her argument.

"They can have it now," said Lily, with an intense bitterness. "I begrudge them even the taxes I have to pay on it. But they'll have to pay a good price," she added quietly. "I'll squeeze the last cent out of them."

It was the end of their conversation, for Willie glancing at his watch, announced that he must leave. Lily accompanied him up the long stairs to the unpretentious door. There he hesitated for a moment on bidding her good night.

"You have changed," he said. "I can see it now."

Lily smiled vaguely, "How?"

He fell to fumbling with the ruby clasp. "I don't know. More calm, I think. . . . You're not so impatient. And you're like a Frenchwoman. . . . Why, you even speak English with an accent."

"Oh, no, Willie . . . I'm not like a Frenchwoman. I'm still American. There's a good deal of my mother in me. I've realized it lately. It's that desire to run things. You understand what I mean. . . . Perhaps it's because I'm getting to the age where one can't live upon the food of youth." She laughed suddenly. "We Americans don't change. What I mean is that I'm growing old."

Willie shook hands politely and went out, leaving Lily in the doorway to watch his neat figure, silhouetted against the glow of light from the Café des Tourelles, until he reached the corner and disappeared.

It was the last time she ever saw him so it was impossible for her to have known the vagaries of his progress after he left the door of Numero Dix. Yet this progress held a certain interest. At the corner of the Rue Franklin, Willie hailed with his umbrella a passing taxicab and bade the driver take him to an address in the Rue du Bac. It was not the address of the American Hotel; on the contrary it designated a three story house with a café on the first floor and lodgings above. In one of these lived a discreet lady who frequented the Louvre by day and employed Art as a means of making the acquaintance of quiet gentlemen hanging about the fringes of tourist parties. Indeed, she could have written an interesting compendium on the effect of art and Paris upon the behavior of soberly dressed, mousy gentlemen.

For Willie, with the death of his mother and the passing of the Mills, had begun to live . . . in his own awkward timid fashion, to be sure . . . but none the less he had begun to live.

As he sped on his way in the crazy taxicab, it became more and more evident that his mood was changed by the encounter with Lily. He sat well back in the cab, quietly, immersed in the thought. The dim white squares, empty and deserted now; the flamboyant houses of the section near the Étoile, the light-bordered Seine, the tall black skeleton of the Eiffel Tower . . . all these things now left him, for some strange reason, unmoved. They swept by the windows of the cab unnoticed. Willie was thinking of something else.

As the taxi turned into the ghostly spaces of the Place de la Concord, Willie stirred himself suddenly and thrust his head out of the window.

"Cocher! Cocher! Chauffeur!" he cried suddenly in atrocious French. "Allez a l'hotel Americain."

The mustachioed driver grunted, turned his cab, and sped away once more as if pursued by the devil; and presently he pulled up before the American Hotel, a respectable hostelry frequented by school teachers and temperance workers.

An hour later he lay chastely in his own bed, awake and restless in the dark, but still innocent. And in the Rue du Bac the sophisticated lady waited until long after midnight. At length, after cursing all Americans, she took her lamp from the window and went angrily to bed.

LXX

A T two o'clock in the house in the Rue Raynouard,
Ellen came in to sit on the edge of her cousin's bed
and discuss the happenings of the day.

"I guess," she observed, "Willie will be able to tell
them a good story when he gets back to the Town. His mouth
fairly hung open all the time when he was here."

Lily smiled. "I don't know," she replied, braiding her heavy
bronze hair. "From what he tells me, he's in the backwater
now. There are a lot of people there who have never heard of
us. I suppose Willie and you and I are just back numbers so
far as the Town is concerned."

After Ellen had gone to her own room, Lily settled herself
on the chaise longue and, wrapped in a peignoir of pale blue
chiffon all frothy with old lace the color of ivory, she took
from her desk the enameled box, opened it and read the worn
clippings. The pile had grown mightily. There were a score
of new clippings. The headlines had increased in size and the
editorials were an inch or two longer. The man was progressing. He was denounced with a steadily increasing hatred and
bitterness. It was clear that he had become a national figure,
that he was a leader in the battle against the roaring furnaces.

For a long time she lay with her eyes closed . . . thinking.
And at last, hours after the rest of the house had grown still
and dark, she sighed, replaced the clippings in the box and
locked them once more into her desk. Then she settled herself
to writing a letter over which she spent a long time, biting the
end of the silver penholder from time to time with her firm
white teeth. When at last the effort satisfied her, she placed
it in an envelope and addressed it to Sister Monica in the
Carmelite Convent at Lisieux. It was the hundredth letter
she had written, letters in which she abased herself and begged
forgiveness, letters to which there was never any reply save an

unforgiving and relentless silence. It was like dropping the
pale gray envelopes into a bottomless crevasse.

In the following May, Ellen went to Munich. It was the
first step in a grand tour of the German cities. She would visit
Salzburg, Cologne, Vienna, Leipsic. She would call upon
Schönberg, Busoni, Richard Strauss, Pfitzner, von Schilling.
. . . If the spirit moved her, she might even penetrate Russia.
And certainly she would go to the festival at Weimar. All this
was included in the plan she set forth to Lily. There was no
schedule. She would simply progress from one place to another as her fancy dictated. She knew no German but she
would learn it, as she had learned French, by living among the
people. She went alone. Therefore she would have to learn
the language.

The expedition was singularly characteristic of all her life.
When she found that the Town was unendurable she had re-
versed the plan of her pioneer ancestors and turned east instead
of west, to seek a new world which to her was far more strange
than the rolling prairies of the west had been to her great-
grandfather. When the traveling salesman, whom she used as
a stepping stone, fell by the wayside and departed this life she
was free to go unhindered on her own roving way, fortified by
the experience of a few years of married life. She owned no
fixed home. On the contrary, she moved about restlessly . . .
exploring, conquering, exhausting now this city, now that one.
She was, it seemed, possessed of a veritable demon of restlessness, of energy, of a sharp inquiring intelligence. It was this
quality, stimulated constantly by an overpowering curiosity,
which sent her pioneering into the world of new music which
Lily disliked so intensely. She explored those regions which
musicians of a more contemplative and less restless nature dared
not enter. It was as if she were possessed by a Gargantuan
desire to devour all the world within a single lifetime.

Once in Paris she said to Lily, "You know, I am obsessed by
a terrible sense of the shortness of life. It is impossible to know
and experience all that I wish to know."

But this was as near as she came to a contemplative philosophy. She had no time for reflection. The hours she spent
with the indolent Lily inevitably fired her with a fierce and

resentful unrest. It was then that she grew impatient, bad-tempered, unendurable. It was the descent of one of these black moods which drove her from the peaceful solitude of the house at Germigny upon a new voyage of exploration.

And so it happened that Lily and Madame Gigon were alone on the peaceful summer evening when Eustache, the red-cheeked farmer's boy, returning on his bicycle through the rain from Meaux, brought the final edition of the Figaro containing a short paragraph of the most enormous importance to all the world.

Madame Gigon had been installed days before on the first floor of the lodge, because she was no longer able to leave her bed and insisted upon being placed where her ears would serve her to the greatest advantage. The door of her room opened outward upon the terrace above the Marne and here, just inside the door, sat Lily when Eustache arrived.

She opened the Figaro and spread it across her knees.

Madame Gigon, hearing the rustle of the paper, stirred and said peevishly, "What is new to-day?"

"Not much of importance," said Lily, and after a pause. "The archduke of Austria has been assassinated. Shall I read you that?"

"Certainly," replied the old woman with a fierce impatience. "Certainly!"

It was only part of a daily game . . . this asking Madame Gigon what she would have read to her; because in the end the entire journal was read aloud by Lily—the daily progress of the celebrated case of Madame Caillaux, the signed articles by this or that politician, the news of the watering places . . . Deauville, Vichy, Aix, Biarritz, the accounts of the summer charity fêtes, the annual ball at the Opéra, the military news . . . everything was read to the old woman. For Madame Gigon found a keen delight in the recognition of a name among those who had been present at this fête or were stopping at that watering-place. After her own fashion, the blind old woman reduced all France to the proportions of a village. To her, the Caillaux trial became simply an old wives' tale, a village scandal.

So Lily read of the Archduke's assassination and Madame

Gigon listened, thoughtfully, interrupting her occasionally with a clucking sound to indicate how terrible the affair really was. She understood these things, being a Bonapartist. It was as if the Prince himself had been shot down. It was the natural result of the Republican movement, of Socialism, which was, after all, the same thing. Just another example of what these wild ideas might lead to.

"These are sad times," remarked Madame Gigon when Lily had finished reading. "There is no such thing as law and order . . . no such thing as respect and regard for rank. A wild confusion (*une melée sauvage*) to see who can gain the most wealth and make the greatest display. Money!" the old woman muttered. "That's it. Money! If you make a fortune out of chocolate or soap, that is enough to put you into the government. Good God! What times are ahead!"

To this harangue, Lily listened absently. It was all monotonously familiar to her. Madame Gigon had said it a thousand times. Every evil she attributed to "these dirty times." She concluded by saying, "Crazy Madame Blaise is right after all. There will be a war . . . She was right. . . . There will be."

While she was speaking, Lily tore open the only interesting letter among the dozen. Quietly she read it to herself. When she had finished she interrupted Madame Gigon.

"I have a letter from M. de Cyon," she said, "about some furniture I was selling. He writes that Madame is ill again with indigestion . . . quite seriously this time."

Madame Gigon made a little grunting noise. "Nadine eats too much . . . I have told her so a dozen times but she will not listen. A woman as fat as that . . ."

And from the superior pinnacle of her great age, Madame allowed the sentence to trail off into unspeakable vistas of Madame de Cyon's folly. At the end of a long time during which they both sat silently in the dripping quiet of the summer evening Madame Gigon said explosively, "She will go off suddenly one of these days . . . like that," and she snapped her finger weakly.

At the sound Criquette and Michou got up lazily, stretched themselves, and waddled close to her chair. For a moment she scratched their heads with groping fingers and then turning to Lily said, "It is time for their milk. . . . And see to it, my child, that they have a little cream in it."

Lily rose and called the dogs inside the lodge. Across the river in the tiny church, the old curé, M. Dupont, rang the vesper bell. Behind the cropped willows along the Marne the last glow faded above the rolling fields of wheat. Inside the house Lily was singing softly, "O, le coeur de ma mie est petit, tous p'tit, p'tit." There was no other sound.

Presently, Madame Gigon leaned back in her bed and called to Lily. "To-morrow," she said, "you might ask M. Dupont to call on me. It has been two days since he was here."

LXXI

UPON Germigny l'Evec, removed from the highroad and the railway, the war descended at first slowly, with the unreality of a vague dream, and then with a gathering, ponderous ferocity of an appalling nightmare. In the beginning even the farmer and his men, familiar with the army and with military service, could not believe it. Still there was the memory of 1870, said the pessimists. It was not impossible.

"Ah, but war is unthinkable," said Lily to Madame Gigon. "The days of war are over. It could not happen. They would not dare to permit it."

But Madame Gigon, again from the pinnacle of her superior age, replied, "My child. You have never seen a war. You know nothing of it. It is not at all impossible. You see, I can remember well 1870."

All the talk, it seemed, turned back at once to 1870. Sooner or later every one returned to it—M. Dupont, the curé, who had served at Metz with MacMahon, the farmer and his wife, even Eustache. 1870 was no longer a half-century away. It became only yesterday, an event which was just finished the evening before at sunset. And slowly it became clear that war was not at all an impossibility. The order for mobilization made it a reality so hideous, so monstrous, as to be utterly lacking in reality. In the château and at the farm, there were no longer any barriers. The cook and the farmer's wife, came and sat on the terrace, red-faced and weeping. In the quiet of the evening there drifted across the wheatfields the ominous whistling of trains which followed no schedule, and from the distant high-road the faint sound of an unceasing procession of taxicabs and omnibuses rushing east and north through Pantin, through Meaux, on to La Ferté-sous-Jouarre.

From Paris came three letters, two by messenger, an orderly

of the Baron, the other by post. One was from the Baron himself and one was from M. de Cyon.

"It is all more grave than any of us suspect," wrote the Baron. "Unhappily, Dear Lily, it is impossible for me to see you. I cannot leave my regiment. You cannot come to Vincennes. We must try to endure all this in the fashion of philosophers. It is not, you understand, as if it had been unexpected. It has been slow—more slow than any one hoped —in arriving.

"As for what may come of it, to me or to Jean. What is there to do? We are all helpless as if caught in a web. May God be with us all! Jean will be with me. Your heart can be assured that I shall do all it is possible to do for him. The rest remains with the good God. I would give . . . What would I give? Ten years or more of my life to have seen you before going away. But that, it seems, is impossible. So we must wait until it is possible.

"We are leaving to-night. I have sent old Pierre to see to it that you and Madame Gigon are brought safely back to Paris. Germigny is safe from the Germans, but there is always a chance. Who can say what will happen? Good God! The suddenness of it!

"Au revoir, dear Lily, in haste. A thousand kisses from thy Césaire."

It was the first time that there had been in all their correspondence even the faintest note of anything more compromising than a proper friendship between the Baron and the woman who had made his old cousin, Madame Gigon, comfortable for life. It was this which somehow gave the letter a gravity more terrible than any hint of foreboding contained in its crisp white pages. It was as if the barriers of convention had suddenly been destroyed, as if they had gone down in ruin to reveal life in all the primitive directness of unfettered nature. It seemed to say, "Nothing matters any longer save those things which have to do with life, death and love."

The letter from M. de Cyon was more calm and dignified, the proper letter of a diplomat. It was the letter of a distinguished, white-haired gentleman.

"You must leave Germigny as soon as it is possible. I write

you this in confidence and beg you not to arouse a panic among the peasants and the citizens of Meaux. It is war, Madame, and no one can say what will happen. Your security is of the deepest concern to me. I beg you to waste no time. Go on foot, by ox-cart, by train—however it is possible, but go. A battle is no place for so beautiful a woman."

That was all, yet it contained hints and innuendoes of things too terrible for the imagination. M. de Cyon undoubtedly knew more than he chose to reveal in his circumspect note. He was, to be sure, near to the Ministry of War.

There was a letter too from Jean, breathless and full of spirit, the letter of a young warrior eager for battle, forgetful of all else, of God, of his mother, of everything save the prospect of fighting.

"Dear Mama," he wrote, "we are leaving to-night for the front. I shall return perhaps a captain. Think of it! Thy Jean a captain! Do not worry. Our troops are in excellent condition. I fancy the war will be over in a fortnight. I am in Césaire's company. I think of you, of course.

"THY JEAN."

With the three letters in her hand Lily left Madame Gigon and set out to walk the white tow-path at the edge of the river. On the far side the farm appeared deserted as if suddenly its occupants had been overcome by a sleep of enchantment. The oxen were nowhere to be seen. The fowls were gone. The house lay shuttered and empty as a house of the dead. Above the tow-path, the château likewise stood silent and empty. In all the landscape there was no sign of life, no dogs, no chickens, no crying children. And as she walked she turned her head presently and saw, leaving the far side of the farm, a lumbering two-wheeled cart piled high with furniture,—mattresses, a sewing machine, a few chairs, and swinging underneath, little cages of osier in which were crowded the barnyard fowls. Tied to the wheels, three goats followed the gentle motion of the cart. Fat Madame Borgue, the farmer's wife, trudged by the side guiding the slow-gaited oxen with a long wand, and high up, perched on a truss of straw, sat her mother, an immensely old and wrinkled woman, with Madame Borgue's baby in her arms. They were deserting, driven before the straggling columns of refugees which had appeared like magic during the early morning along the high-roads from La Ferté to Meaux. There could be no doubt. The farm and the château were empty. At Germigny only Lily and Madame Gigon remained behind.

LXXII

IT appeared that the discovery made no impression upon
Lily, for she continued on her way along the deserted
river path without stopping, without even checking the
mad speed at which she walked. Her manner was that of
one fleeing before a terror from which there is no escape.
When she had reached a spot opposite the little island that
divided the waters of the river, she halted suddenly by a clump
of hazel bushes and flung herself down upon the thick grass in
the shadow of the plane trees. She began to weep, soundlessly
with long, racking, silent sobs which shook her whole body as if
she had been stricken by some frightful pain.

Far off a train whistled distantly. The bright red kepis of
the soldiers showed in rows like poppies at the windows of the
coaches. On the white solid bridge at Trilport there appeared
a double procession; one column hot, dusty, bedraggled, full of
crying, exhausted, women and children, moved toward Paris.
The other was gay and bright. The men wore bright red
trousers and bright red caps. It moved briskly forward. The
guns were like a field of wheat come suddenly to life, moving
gallantly to throw itself upon the reaper.

After a time, Lily sat up, her hair all blown and disheveled,
her dark eyes bright from weeping. She read the letters over
and over absorbing the same phrases . . . May God be with us
all! . . . It is all more grave than any of us suspect . . . A
thousand kisses from thy Césaire . . . It is war, Madame, and
no one can say what will happen . . . A battle is no place for
a beautiful woman . . . Perhaps I shall return . . . Perhaps
I shall return a captain . . . Think of it! Thy Jean a
captain! . . . Thy Jean! . . . Thy Jean . . . Thy Césaire!
. . . Thy Jean! Thy precious Jean!

Slowly she refolded the letters and thrust them into the
bosom of her dress and then, as if her emotion were too strong

for silence, she said aloud. . . . "Me . . . myself . . . Why
do they worry about me? . . . Do they think that I am
afraid?" She laughed suddenly. "Afraid of what?"

Besides it was impossible to flee with a sick old woman and
no means of conveyance. She laughed again and said bitterly,
"What do they think . . . that I am a magician?"

Lying there in the deep grass, it must have occurred to her all
at once that her whole life had been pillaged and destroyed
because an Austrian archduke was shot in a little hole called
Serajevo. Madame Gigon dying. Césaire and Jean on their
way to destruction. Who remained? What remained? De
Cyon, perhaps. No one else. No one in all the world. The
years of her life come to an end like this . . . that everything
she loved, everything she cherished, might be swept away overnight like so much rubbish into a dustbin. As if she were no
more than a poor forsaken flower vender or charwoman!
What was money now? What were beautiful things? What
was all her life?

And she flung herself down once more, sobbing wildly as she
had sobbed another time in the old house at Cypress Hill, when
all at once, she had sensed the tragedy of a whole lifetime, as if
she stood in a vast plain surrounded only by loneliness.

At dusk she arose slowly and, from long habit put her hair
in order, smoothed her dress, and set out upon her homeward
journey, walking slowly, with feet from which all youth had
gone. When she arrived at the lodge, the traces of her weeping
had disappeared and she entered proudly and in silence. For
a moment there came into her pale lovely face a fleeting likeness
to her mother, a certain determination that was inseparable
from the rugged countenance of the stoic Julia Shane.

The house was still because old Madame Gigon had slipped
out of her bed and was lying asleep on the floor. When Lily
attempted to rouse the old woman, she discovered that she was
not sleeping at all but unconscious, and suddenly Lily too
slipped to the floor, buried her face in her hands and wept
noisily and without restraint. The sound of her sobbing penetrated the breathless garden and the distant empty rooms of
the château, but there was no one to answer it. The only
sound was the triumphant, ironic whistle of a steel locomotive,

its belly hot with red flames, its nostrils breathing fire and smoke.

At last she lifted Madame Gigon into the bed by the window and, lying by the side of the unconscious old woman, she fell into a profound sleep.

LXXIII

IT was dark when she awoke and rose wearily to light a
lamp. The first flame of the match illuminated the room.
It revealed all the familiar furniture . . . the chintz
covered chairs, the bright curtains of *toile de Juouy,* the
bowl of ghostly white phloxes by the window. Everything
was the same save that Madame Gigon . . . old Tante Louise
. . . lay unconscious upon the bed, and the house was so still
that the silence was suffocating.

She went into the kitchen and prepared a mixture of egg,
milk and brandy which she fed the old woman through a tube.
She understood the care of Madame Gigon. The old woman
had been like this before. Lily, herself, ate nothing, but took
from the cupboard by the window a bottle of port and drank a
brimming glass. And after a time she went outside to listen
to the silence.

With her black cloak wrapped about her she sat there for a
long time. The farm, the tiny inn, the houses of the village
were black and silent. There hung in the atmosphere the
ghostly feeling of a house suddenly deserted by its inhabitants,
standing empty and alone. The mournfulness was overwhelming. After a time she lighted a cigarette and smoked it, holding the ember away from her and regarding it at a little distance as if the faint light in some way dissipated the loneliness.

For a time she regarded the distant horizon and the queer
flashes of color like heat lightning which appeared at intervals.
Sometimes the rising night wind bore toward her a faint sound
like that of distant thunder. And then all at once, there appeared in the house by the village church a bright light. It was
a lamp placed close to the open window so that the rays piercing
the darkness traversed the river, penetrated the low branches of
the plane trees and enveloped Lily herself in a faint glow.

She watched it for a time with a breathless curiosity. The

cigarette, untouched, burned low and dropped from her fingers, and then behind the light appeared the figure of the curé in his rusty black clothes. He had stayed behind to guard his church. He was there, moving about his little house, as if nothing had happened. Presently he took down from a shelf above the table a heavy book, laid it before him, took out his steel rimmed spectacles, and began to read.

After an hour of silence during which she lay motionless in her chair, Lily rose and went inside to look at Madame Gigon. The old woman lay on her back, snoring peacefully. She felt her pulse. It was weak and irregular. Then she brought more brandy and milk, fed it to Madame Gigon, and wrapping the black cloak about herself, set off down the terrace to the iron bridge that led across the Marne to the house of the curé.

Away to the north the flashes in the sky became more frequent and the distant thunder less broken and more distinct. On the way to the bridge the alder branches stirring softly in the breeze, whispered together in a vague, ghostly fashion. She walked slowly in the same tired fashion until she reached the little white house by the church.

LXXIV

INSIDE, the old priest at the sound of her knock looked up from his reading and took off his spectacles.

"Come in," he said, and Lily stepped uncertainly through the door, her eyes blinded by the bright flame of the petrol light. M. Dupont, regarding her with an expression of amazement, rose from his chair.

"It is I, Madame Shane," said Lily. "The friend of Madame Gigon."

"Ah, yes, I remember you well."

Before this night there had passed between them occasional greetings when he came to the lodge to play piquet with Madame Gigon, when he passed Lily riding through the wood in the early morning.

"Won't you sit down?" and then, "Why are you here? You know the Germans may come any time now. Surely before morning."

"As soon as that?" asked Lily indifferently. She had not thought of the Germans. Perhaps they would come. It did not matter greatly.

The old man bent his head over the table and began to turn the pages of the book. "Our soldiers are brave, Madame," he said. "But there is too much against them. They were not ready. In the end we will win. . . . For the present . . ." He finished with a gesture implying that the matter lay in the hands of the good God. He was a simple man, a peasant trained for the priesthood by devout and adoring parents.

"It would be better if you would go away," he said after a sudden pause. "I imagine it will not be pleasant."

Lily laughed softly. For a moment something of her old gay indifference appeared to return, even a shade of the spirit with which she had met another adventure years before in the park at Cypress Hill.

"There is Madame Gigon," she said. M. Dupont again bent over the table silently. It was a gesture of assent, of resignation, of agreement.

"Besides," continued Lily, "I am not afraid. I think I may even enjoy the experience. . . . I should like to know what war is like." And then, as if she feared that he did not understand her, she added, "Not, of course, because I like war. Oh! not at all! But you understand what it means for the men. . . . I have men in it." She shivered a little and drew the black cape more closely about her. "I think it might be easier for the women if they could go into battle as well. It would be easier than waiting . . . at home . . . alone."

The man closed his book. "Madame is a beautiful woman," he said, softly.

Again Lily smiled faintly. "Oh, I understand what you mean . . . perfectly." A thoughtful expression entered her dark eyes. She seemed suddenly to be listening to the faint and distant thunder. "Yes," she said with a sigh, "I understand. Fortunately I have no temptation to run away. I could not go if I chose. Madame Gigon, you understand, has given up her life to me. . . . It would be impossible to desert her now."

She sat now with her back to the whitewashed wall of the little room; her black cape and her red hair carried the quality of a beautiful painting. All the color was gone from her face and beneath her eyes hung dark circles which somehow increased the brilliance of her eyes and the whiteness of her skin. She looked old but it was the oldness of beauty, possessing a clear refinement and delicacy.

"She is a good woman . . . Madame Gigon," said the priest.

M. Dupont spoke in a low voice, respectful, scarcely audible, but the words exerted upon his visitor an extraordinary effect. All at once she leaned forward resting her elbows on the table. The cloak slipped to the floor. She began to talk passionately with a kind of fierce melancholy in her voice.

"Ah, she *is* a good woman," she said. "She has given her life to me. She has lived with me for twenty years. She has been everything to me. You understand . . . a friend . . . a companion . . . even a mother."

And then, without warning, she poured out the whole story of her life, incident by incident, chapter by chapter, reserving nothing, disguising nothing. Before the eyes of the astonished old priest she recreated the house at Cypress Hill, the Mills, the Town, the figures of her bizarre father, her cynical mother, the hysterical Irene, all the kaleidoscopic picture of a wandering, aimless life. She told him of Jean. She even related bit by bit the long tale of her love for the Baron. She told him that in her heart she had even sinned for the sake of a common laborer . . . Krylenko.

"And yet," she said, "he was not exactly that. He was a great deal more. He was, you understand, something of a martyr. He gave up everything for his people. He would have given his life had it been necessary. . . . It hurts me, even now, to think of him. He was a powerful man . . . a good man . . . a noble man."

It was of him that she talked for a long time, wildly, passionately invoking him in her enthusiasm before the stricken eyes of the old priest. He stood there for a long time in the bare, whitewashed room, powerful, austere, suffering, as he had been on the night of the slaughter in the park at Cypress Hill.

"He was a good man. . . . He still is," she said. She talked breathlessly with a bright exalted light in her eyes. "I have never told this to any one. . . . There was no sin between us . . . nothing unless to love deeply is a sin."

As if turned to stone, M. Dupont sat listening quietly. Only once did he speak and that was when she mentioned the Baron. Then he stirred uneasily and peered at her closely as if he suspected her of lying.

"Incredible!" he murmured to himself. "Incredible!" And after a little pause. "Only God can know what lies in the darkness of men's hearts. Only God. . . . It is impossible to know. . . . It is impossible to know!"

But Lily swept past the interruption. The torrent of her revelations flowed on. She talked eagerly, with a kind of wild delight; yet what she said lacked the quality of a confession. She seemed to have no profound consciousness of sin. She was even unrepentant. She told the story breathlessly with a kind of wonder at herself, at the tragedy of her own soul, that she loved so easily. Instead of confessing, she appeared to be pouring out to the trembling old man secrets, too long confined, which she found herself driven to reveal.

At last she drew to a conclusion. "You understand now," she said, "why to me the war is inexpressibly tragic. You understand what Madame Gigon has been to me."

She picked up the fallen cloak and, shivering, wrapped it about her and sank back in the stiff little chair with a weary air of finality and resignation. "You see, it is not only the war . . . Madame Gigon is dying. The war has taken everything. You understand I shall be alone . . . completely alone."

M. Dupont made no reply. He kept his head bowed. He was repeating a prayer as Irene had done in the old days. They prayed for Lily, who had not been inside a church in more than seven years.

"I came to fetch you to her," continued Lily, "She is dying now. . . . I am certain she cannot live much longer."

When the priest at last raised his head, it was to say, "Come. If she is dying we must waste no time," in so gentle a voice that the tears welled in Lily's eyes. She took out her handkerchief, already wet.

"I thought," she said, "that I was through with weeping. I must have a great many tears." (Lily who never wept.)

LXXV

M DUPONT, after collecting those things which are necessary in the administration of the last rites, put on his shovel hat and took up a lantern.

"Come," he said, "we must hurry." And together they set out along the white road, between the whispering alders and over the iron bridge. The lantern swung feebly in his grasp. They walked in complete silence until they reached the terrace when Lily, looking up suddenly, saw that the sky behind the lodge was filled with a cloudy whiteness as if gray smoke were drifting across the sky.

"There is a fire somewhere," she said placing a hand on the arm of her companion.

M. Dupont halted and regarded the sky for a moment, holding his lantern high so that the rays might penetrate the darkness beyond the vine covered lodge.

"It is not smoke," he said suddenly. "It is dust. The cavalry is passing along the road."

And then for the first time the small revealing noises reached Lily's ear . . . the clanking of spurs, the creaking of girths, the muffled sound of hoofs striking the white road, and then the solitary whicker of a horse.

LXXVI

INSIDE the lodge, Lily left Madame Gigon to the curé. He assured her that she was right. It was impossible for the old woman to live much longer. It would have been useless to have secured a physician even if one had been available.

"She has been dying a long while," said the old man. "I fancy she would prefer not to be hindered in her going."

As Lily closed the door upon the two old friends, she saw M. Dupont kneel down in the lamplight and begin to pray.

Wearily she climbed the narrow winding stairway which led to the upper floor and, finding herself unable to sleep, she went to the window above the gateway and sat down to watch the column of cavalry on its way into battle. The men had been riding for hours and now they rode silently, white with dust, the black plumes of horsehair swaying as the horses moved. It was impossible to distinguish one from another. They were simply black figures, units of a body, mysterious and without personality. There was not even the sound of a voice, nothing but the faint rattle of sabers and the ghostly breathing of the horses. Jean might have been among them . . . even Césaire himself. It was impossible to say. They were each like the other, no longer individuals, now only units, cogs in a vast machine. No one of them counted any longer for anything.

Presently the column came to an end and a battery of artillery, caissons rattling, men upright upon the cartridge boxes, followed in its place. And at last it too passed, swallowed up by the questioning darkness. The silence became unreal, terrifying. From below stairs arose the droning sound of M. Dupont's voice conducting the service that would lead Madame Gigon safely into the world beyond . . . the world beyond. To-night in all the lonely breathless quiet, the world beyond was very near. One might almost enter it simply by closing one's eyes, by stepping through a doorway into the night.

Lily sat motionless and upright, watching. A second column passed and then a third; and at last, a man riding a black horse whose chest was white with froth turned in at the gateway. He was a man like the others . . . a unit, a being without individuality save that he rode alone a little in the rear of the other horsemen. Under the archway he dismounted from his horse, and in the next moment he performed an act which at once restored to him his identity. He walked directly to the iron ring which hung concealed among the ivy leaves and there fastened the black horse. Thus he betrayed himself. Only one person could have known the exact place where the ring lay hidden among the leaves. There could be no longer any doubt.

When he had fastened the black horse, he stepped out a little way from the house and called softly, "Lily . . . Lily."

LXXVII

THERE was no answer, but before he called again a tall figure in a black cloak ran from the doorway and hurried toward him.

"Césaire! . . . Césaire!" were the only words she spoke. She clung against him, the metal of his bright cuirass pressing her lovely, soft body. For a time Césaire kissed her passionately and at length, without a word, she led him away from the house to the pleached walk that led from the château garden down to the river. They walked sadly with arms encircling each other's waists.

"I have but a moment," said the Baron. "At most, ten minutes. I have no right even to that."

She told him that Madame Gigon was dying. She explained that old Pierre had not appeared to help them to escape and that he would have been of no use since it was impossible to move her companion. And when she had wasted three precious minutes in these explanations, she said, "You need not worry for me . . . I shall be quite safe. . . . If only I could be as certain of you."

At this he laughed softly, reassuring her and pulling his fierce mustachios in warlike fashion.

"You need not fear for me," he said. "I have had such great luck . . . always." And he looked at her closely with shining eyes.

Then they sat for a time in silence, clinging closely to each other. Presently he took off his helmet and rested it in her lap allowing her to twist her fingers in and out among the long black hair of the plume.

"And Jean," she said, after a time. "He is with you?"

"He is with me. He passed with the others beneath your window. He sent you his love. He would have come too, but he knew it was unsoldierly to break the ranks. . . . He is a good soldier," he added softly. "A valiant fellow. With me it is different. I am an old fellow. I have learned that there are times when one must break the ranks. There are times when even breaking ranks does not matter."

In the darkness Lily's eyes closed as if she felt a sharp, sudden pain. "Ellen advised me," she said, "never to be too fond of my child."

Her lover kissed her and answered, "Come, you must not think of it like that. You must understand he is a boy . . . an ardent boy."

And then he fell again to talking of her danger. He urged her not to remain.

"I have the curé here . . . M. Dupont," she said.

"Leave him with Madame Gigon."

"No. That I will not do. . . . Besides the Germans may never arrive here after all."

"No," he said, gravely. "Perhaps not. We shall try to prevent them."

Then they walked back again to the gateway. The house was silent now and the voice of M. Dupont no longer to be heard. The Baron replaced his helmet, untied his horse and swung himself on the back of the animal. Leaning down, he kissed her again and then turned through the gateway into the road. She listened to the sound of the black horse's hoofs as he galloped past the moving columns, and at last when the echo was no longer audible she reentered the house and flung herself down upon the bed. Throughout the brief visit, she had restrained herself. Now she wept quietly, almost in peace, as if she were enveloped already by a great resignation.

LXXVIII

MADAME GIGON lived through the night, sleeping peacefully in her high bed near the door that opened upon the terrace. But Lily did not sleep at all. She kept watch, sometimes sitting at the bedside, sometimes lying wrapped in her cloak in the long chair beneath the plane trees. She watched the flashes on the horizon beyond the wood, until the dawn rising slowly absorbed them and rendered them invisible in a faint glow which grew and grew until it enveloped all the dome of the sky and transformed, suddenly and without warning, the dark wood from a low black wall extending across the sky into a grove of slender trunks silhouetted against the rising light.

At dawn the troops no longer passed the house. The dusty white road lay deserted between the rows of chestnut trees. But in the dust were the prints of a thousand hoofs and the tracks of the wide wheeled caissons. The little procession on the distant bridge at Trilport had vanished. There were no soldiers going forward; and coming back, there was now only an occasional, straggling cart or the figure of a shopkeeper pushing before him in a wooden wheelbarrow all that he had salvaged of his little shop.

At noon there appeared out of the wood a rolling kitchen drawn by tired horses and driven by weary soldiers all white with dust. It came nearer and nearer until it arrived at the farm where, in the shadow of the big gray barns, it halted and the men ate. A little while later soldiers began to appear among the trees, tiny figures in red trousers and red caps, no longer bright like the poppies, but all stained and dust covered. The red marked them against the wall of greenery as if it had been planned that they should serve as targets.

Singly and in little groups of two or three the soldiers straggled across the fields toward the kitchen set up against the gray wall of the barn. The sun shone brilliantly, and in the clear white light the red tiles, the white walls, and the green of the trees appeared gay and bright. Some of the men carried arms suspended in slings. One or two wore about their close-cropped heads bandages that were stained with spots of red as if the color had come loose from their tragic little caps and stained their skins. There was one dandified young officer, with fine waxed mustaches, who dragged a shattered leg and still wore the bedraggled remnants of the spotless white gloves he had carried into the battle.

When they had eaten and drunk, the soldiers made their way across the iron bridge and turning along the tow path at the foot of the garden kept on their way, moving in a thin, trickling stream in the direction of Paris.

At length Lily, rousing herself, went to the foot of the garden, opened the gate and stood on the path. She carried wine which she gave them to drink as they passed.

"And how does it go?" she asked now and then.

The respectful answer was always the same. "Badly, Madame. . . . Badly. It would be better if you did not remain."

Or a shrug and "What can we do, Madame? They have better guns . . . better shells. One cannot see them. They are dressed so that they look like the trees themselves. And we . . . we." A gesture indicating the fatal red trousers and kepi.

Early in the afternoon the sound of the guns became audible again, not distant this time and indistinct like thunder, but sharp and clear . . . the barking "ping" of the seventy-fives.

When the wine was all gone, Lily returned again to the terrace to wait. She had not been sitting there long when there arose all at once the sound of a terrific explosion. Turning her head she saw above the river at Trilport a great cloud of white dust and black smoke. They had destroyed the solid white bridge. It was the French themselves who had destroyed it. The Germans must be very near.

Madame Gigon slept peacefully just inside the doorway, all undisturbed by the explosion.

As for Lily, lying in the low chair, the explosion appeared to have worked a miracle. The color had begun to return to her white face. It showed itself in bright spots as if she had been seized by a fever. And presently she arose and began to walk about, up and down the garden, going at last into the château itself from which she returned in a little while carrying a pair of the Baron's binoculars. With these she climbed to the little turret which rose above the vine covered dove-cote. There she settled herself to watching.

In a little while the men about the kitchen gathered themselves into a group, put the horses once more into the harness and drove away, carrying with them a boy of the last class whose strength had given out. M. Dupont followed them until he reached the edge of the iron bridge where he halted and stood looking after them, his hands shading his old eyes against the long rays of the setting sun, until they disappeared around a turn of the river. Then he went quietly indoors.

A little while later a battery of guns appeared among the trees, halted on the edge of the wood, and began firing in the direction of La Ferté where a cloud of smoke from the burning houses hung low upon the horizon. It was a pretty picture. The men worked the guns rapidly. The cannon spat forth little curls of white smoke followed by sudden angry barks, not in the least deafening. In the clear evening light it was all like one of Meissonier's battle pictures, rather clear and pretty and bright-colored.

But in a little while the battery stopped firing, the horses leaned forward once more into the harness and the guns drew away down the lane, past the white farm and across the iron bridge. The planks reverberated with a thunderous sound under the hoofs of the galloping horses. The little cavalcade turned along the tow-path and vanished. Out of the wood there appeared suddenly three gray-green figures on horseback who halted and surveyed the landscape. They were the first of the Uhlans.

LXXIX

WITH the falling of night, the Germans were in possession of the château and the gardens. In bands of twenty or thirty they pushed beyond across the field and through the copses in the direction of Meaux. A few remained behind, and these occupied the château, using the best linen of the Baroness, taking down from the wall of the kitchen the cook's great battery of spotless copper kettles in which to cook their beans and soup.

Lily, sitting quietly inside the darkened lodge by the side of Madame Gigon, heard their shouts and the stamping of their horses in the stables. Dark figures moved above among the trees of the garden, the figures of her enemies, the men who would kill if it were possible Césaire and Jean. In the excitement, no one ventured as far from the château as the lodge, and for a time she remained safe and in peace.

The cannon were no longer to be heard. For a little while there arose the distant crackling of rifles like the sound of brush fires made by the foresters in August; but this too died away after a time.

She bathed her head, fed Madame Gigon once more and sat down again to wait, and at last, overcome by exhaustion she sank quietly into sleep.

In the château the weary Germans slept and in the stables the horses ceased their stamping. A deep unbroken stillness settled again over the garden and the wheatfields beyond, so peaceful that the firing and the shouting of a little while before might have been wholly an illusion, a nightmare which had nothing to do with reality.

Thus passed three hours.

It was the sound of knocking which aroused Lily, a violent imperious sort of knocking which wakened her sharply and brought her quickly to her feet. As if by force of habit, she

opened the door and said in French, "Gently . . . please. . . .
Gently. It is not necessary to break down the door. There is
a sick woman here."

As it swung open she was enveloped by the sudden bright
glare of an electric torch. At the same moment a voice speaking the most excellent French said, "I am sorry, Madame. I
ask your pardon. I did not know the lodge was occupied."

The voice was not gruff. It was rather cold and smooth and
carried a hint of weariness. "I found the door locked. I
always knock upon locked doors," continued the voice. "May I
come in?"

All this time Lily, blinded by the sudden light, stood leaning
against the door, emerging slowly from the effects of her deep
slumber. For a moment she was silent.

"I prefer to come outside," she replied. "There is a sick
woman here. . . . If you will turn your light inside, you will
see that I am not lying. She is there."

The light flashed across the high bed of Madame Gigon. "I
believe you, Madame."

Lily closed the door and stood leaning against it. From the
one of the lower windows of the château streamed a path of
light which illuminated faintly the terrace, the front of the
lodge and the Uhlan officer. He was not tall and was not in
the least savage in appearance. On the contrary his face was
smooth shaven and narrow, rather the face of a scholar than
a soldier. Yet he carried himself very erect. There was something about him that was cold, stiff, almost brittle.

"What do you want of me?" asked Lily in a voice expression-
less and free of all emotion.

For a moment her companion hesitated. He switched off the
electric torch which until now he had kept turned full upon her.
"Were you sleeping?" he asked.

"Yes." Again in the same dead tone.

"Extraordinary. You must be a woman of great nerve."

"No . . . not at all. I had not slept in thirty-six hours."

Again he hesitated. "I . . . I have been riding for that
length of time . . . and still I cannot sleep. I have tried. . . .
My nerves are too much on edge."

She waited silently.

"Tell me . . . why did you remain behind?" he began presently.

She made a gesture indicating the window behind which lay Madame Gigon. "You have seen the reason," she said. "It was impossible to go away."

The man whistled softly. "Aren't you in the least afraid?"

For a time there was no sound except a deep sigh. "There was nothing to be done," she answered presently in the same dead voice. "When there is nothing to be done, it is foolish to fret. It is best to make the most of it. What would you have me do?" For a moment a trace of life, almost of humor entered her voice. "Would you have me lie down and scream?" Again she sighed. "What good would it do? What would come of it? I do not believe in scenes."

The Uhlan laughed. "Unlike most women," he said. "But you are right. Afterwards, scenes are ridiculous. Nothing really matters much. . . . I've learned that in two days," he added with a sort of pride.

To this she made no reply but her very silence carried its own gesture of assent. She did not deny his statement.

"I suppose you hate me," he began, "like a good French-woman."

For the first time she raised her head and looked squarely at the stranger. "What do you want?" she asked. "Why are you talking in this fashion? You understand I am helpless. I must talk with you if you choose." In the darkness she frowned. "I suppose that is war." And then, "Besides, I am not a Frenchwoman at all. I am an American."

At this the stranger gave a sudden start, in the darkness more audible than visible by the sudden click of metal on some part of his uniform.

"Then you must hate me even more. . . . I have lived in Paris. The Americans there are more French than the French."

This remark, it appeared, angered her for she answered quickly. "I know no Americans in Paris. I know nothing about them."

The Uhlan laughed. "Madame, I have no intention of injuring you . . . in any way."

To this she replied, "I suppose you do not mind if I sit down. I am a little weary."

The stranger's manner changed abruptly. He became courteous, almost courtly.

"I am sorry. I did not know there were chairs. You see I am a stranger here. Sit down if you prefer it, by all means. . . . I am not one to work hardships for a woman." She moved toward the long chair under the lindens and lay down, wrapping the cloak about her and closing her eyes.

"Perhaps," said the stranger, "you would prefer to sleep."

"No," she replied quietly, "I could not sleep now." And as if the idea amused her she added, "I might as well talk with you . . . since you too suffer from insomnia."

"As you will . . . if you do not hate me too much."

He sat in the chair by her side and slipped from his waist the belt in which hung his black lugar pistol. Thus they remained for some time, silently and peacefully, as if they were old friends between whom there was no necessity for speech. The German sat with his elbows resting on his knees, his head buried in his hands. There was a smoothness and angularity about his thin figure so trimly clad in a uniform that now carried the stains of battle.

At last he took out a cigarette and said, "I suppose you smoke, Madame?"

To which Lily replied without opening her eyes, "No."

He was so polite, so scrupulously polite. And presently he sighed, "Ah, this civilization . . . this world of monkeys. (*Monde de singes.*)" And once more the night stillness descended, for Lily made no effort at speech now. She lay motionless, so still that she might have been dead. Her silence appeared to reproach him for he turned suddenly and said, "Do you fancy I like this . . . this living like a burglar in a château . . . your château?"

"It is not mine," Lily murmured.

"Do you fancy I like this war. . . . I am not pleased with killing men. Why should I? I do not hate them. How is it possible? How can you even hate me?"

She stirred impatiently. "No. It is impossible to hate genuinely . . . without a reason one can put one's finger on. All the same you are my enemy," she added stubbornly.

The Uhlan laughed. "Who has made me so, Madame? Not myself, surely." And then after a little pause, he added with a kind of desperation, "No, I am like all the others. I have nothing to do with it. We are all caught, Madame, . . . hopelessly caught in one great web spun by a monster. Ah, what a monster!"

In the distant stable arose suddenly the sound of two horses quarreling. There was a violent kicking . . . a squealing that was savage and implacable.

"We are not even like that," he said. "It is not even that we bite and kick. . . . We shoot each other at a distance. You, Madame, perhaps have friends among the men I am fighting. I kill them and they me only because the first who shoots is the safest. You know the artillerymen kill men they never even see." He spat suddenly. "Bah! It is mechanics . . . all mechanics . . . machinery, you understand, which they make in great roaring factories. They kill men in factories in order to kill more men on the battlefield. What is there in that?"

Again she made no answer to his question. The quarreling horses had been separated and their squealing silenced. There was only the overpowering stillness once more, a stillness unearthly in quality which lifted all that it enveloped upon a new plane, determined by new values. Life, death, reality, dreams—all these things were confused and yet amazingly clear, as if the whole had been pierced by a single beam of cold white light.

LXXX

IT must have occurred to Lily that the man was talking in an hysterical fashion with all the frenzy of a neurasthenic. "Madame, you should see one of our towns where there are great furnaces . . . Essen, Madame, or Saarbrucken , . . black, incredibly vile, a wallow of roaring fire and white hot steel . . . I know them, Madame, I have lived in them."

Then for the first time Lily stirred. She even laughed, faintly yet with unmistakable bitterness. "Know them? I know them. We have them in America."

The stranger paid no heed to her interruption. "Look, Madame," he commanded, pointing to the north where the horizon was lighted by the glow of a burning town. "Look, Madame. You see that fire in the sky. The ladles have overflowed. The white hot steel has spread across Europe. There is gold in it too . . . red hot gold. . . . Melted Gods . . . idols which we worship to-day."

His voice rose until he was shouting. When he finished, he leaned back in his chair, the fine uniform suddenly crumpled and limp. And after a time he began to speak again, softly as if the torrent of emotion had exhausted him.

"And where have we to go? If we sought to escape where have we to go? There is no place. Because the monkeys . . . the fools have civilized all the world, so that they might sell their cheap cotton and tin trays. They have created a monster which is destroying them. There is no longer any peace . . . any solitude. They have even wrenched the peasant from his plow . . . the shepherd from his hillside." Again he pointed toward the burning horizon. "They have driven them out upon the plains where the cauldrons have overflowed across all Europe. It is the monsters, Madame, who are at the bottom of all this. Ah, commerce, industry, wealth, power." He tossed away his cigarette and lighted another. "When this is over,

301

who do you think will have gained? Not the peasant, Madame. Not the shepherd, not the poet. Ah, no! They will be shoveled under the earth . . . whole bodies and pieces of bodies because they are no longer of any use. Not the worker, Madame, whom the monster devours. Ah, no." His voice rose suddenly. "It is the monster who will have gained . . . the monster and the men whose pockets he fills with gold . . . the monster of material, of industry. He will destroy us. He will devour us. What can we do? You see, I know. I have lived in France. I have lived in England. . . . My grandmother, you understand, was English. I would prefer to live in England. But No! I was in England three weeks ago. And suddenly I must go home to join my regiment, to set out upon the expedition that has brought me here into this trampled garden. What for? Who can say? Why? Who knows? Not surely because it gives me pleasure. Not surely because I care a fig whether the German empire lives or dies. That is merely an excuse to drag us into battle." His head dropped wearily again. "You see, this is why I have not been able to sleep. I have been thinking of these things. They are not the sort that lull a man to sleep. There is blood on my hands. I killed to-day . . . by shooting and stabbing. I assure you it gave me no pleasure. I should doubtless have loved the men I killed. I am helpless. I cannot fight against it. No, there is only one thing to be done. I must kill as many men as possible. I must destroy all that it is possible to destroy because if we destroy enough the monster will have nothing to feed upon. He, too, will die . . . and with him this civilization . . . banal, ugly, materialistic, unchristian . . . this greed-ridden world."

The Uhlan fell forward upon the table, burying his face in his arms. At the sight Lily raised herself gently and watched her strange companion in a wondering silence. At last she said softly, "Why do you tell me this? Is it because you are afraid?"

The man made a chuckling, confused, sound and sat up once more. "Ah, no! Madame. You fancy I am hysterical. Well, so I am. I don't deny it. You see it is not easy for me to be a warrior. I am a little mad. No, I talk like this because . . ." For a moment he hesitated as if groping for some explanation of an emotional crisis which in a soldier was not logical at all. His manner seemed to imply that he should have accepted the affair without question. "Because . . . Well, there is a time when fear does not matter, when terror does not exist, when one is enveloped by a despair so great that what happens to one's body is of no concern. You understand that. You have answered it yourself a little time before, when you said there came a time when it was useless to be afraid." He leaned back and made a little gesture of negation. "It does not matter," he concluded. In the faint light from the lower windows of the château it was plain that he was smiling in a bitter, despairing fashion. "No, I shall go on killing until I am killed. It will not be a long affair. It is absurd to hope that I shall live many more days." He whistled softly. "I might even be killed to-night . . . after I have left you. I shall kill as many men as possible. I can only submit. There is nothing I can do. I am not a boy full of playing soldier."

At this Lily winced suddenly as if he had struck her. Then she raised herself slowly. The black cloak fell from her shoulders.

"I have in the war a son and a lover," she said. "If you met them, you would kill them. Is it not so?"

The Uhlan bowed his head in silent assent.

"And yet you do not believe in it?"

"No, Madame."

"Then that is wrong. It is sinful."

The stranger leaned toward her. "It is not I who would kill them. I am only a chance, a little dagger in the hand of fate . . . one of a billion chances that have to do with their deaths. I myself would not be killing them. . . . It would be a strange . . . even an impossible accident, if I killed one of them with my own hands. You understand, we are talking facts now . . . hard facts. There is no room for sentimentality at a time like this. . . ." He smiled ironically. "I can understand that it is difficult for a woman to talk facts. It is simply a matter of chances . . . like roulette shall we say?"

For a time Lily remained thoughtful and silent. At last she said, "They are in the cavalry like yourself. You would kill them. You are one of the chances." The calmness of her manner stood in terrible contrast to the hysterical outburst of the soldier.

"I can see you are a philosopher . . . a *femme savant,*" mocked the stranger.

"You might choose a better time to jeer."

The man coughed. "Forgive me. . . . I am sorry. . . . I was wrong. If you were a *femme savant,* I would not be talking to you like this. . . . You are a woman . . . a beautiful woman. One cannot help talking to you."

"I am only a woman living by what she believes. That is simple enough."

"It requires courage, Madame . . . and indifference, far more of both than I have." He coughed again, nervously. "Perhaps I am too rational. . . . Perhaps I do not think resistance worth the trouble . . . especially now, at a time when the mob . . . the politicians rule absolutely."

"You are one of the chances," Lily repeated stubbornly.

LXXXI

THE German laughed softly. "You are a primitive woman, Madame. It refreshes me to find a woman so charmingly direct, so completely feminine. There are not many left. It is a quality which should always accompany beauty. If a woman is not beautiful, it does not matter." He paused waiting for her to speak and when she said nothing, he continued. "I envy your lover. He is a fortunate man."

At this Lily stirred once more. It was a faint movement, yet it carried a warning of anger.

"Of course, you may say and do what you please," she said. "I am completely helpless."

The Uhlan rattled his spurs in the darkness. "Come . . . come, now. I have no intention of harming you. I told you that before. It seems to me that this once . . . on a night such as this . . . we might talk honestly . . . as if there was no nonsense in the world. I do not know your name and you do not know mine. We shall never meet again, for I, no doubt, will be dead before many days. You have admitted that you have a lover." He leaned across the table with a curious pleading gesture. "You see, I am tired. I mean to say that I am wearied of keeping up deceits. Has it ever occurred to you how many barriers surround us all . . . even those friends whom we know very well. The countless secrets which lie behind them . . . the things which we never know, even about our dearest friends. For once . . . just once, it would be a delight to talk without pretense . . . to speak as if each one of us were free, quite free, to do as he pleased . . . to answer to no one, to fear no one. There is no more freedom in the world. There are too many people in the world. And the life of no one is any longer his own." He paused and passed a thin, nervous hand across his brow as if he would clear away some entanglement which had entrapped his thoughts. "I cannot say what I mean. I, like all the others, have kept my secrets hidden for too long a time. You see, if it were possible for us to talk thus with freedom . . . we might separate, you knowing me and I knowing you, better than any one else in the world." He laughed and his mood changed quickly from a resigned weariness back to the old mocking flippancy. "It is an interesting idea, but impossible of course . . . because we no longer know even ourselves. We have sacrificed ourselves to those who crowd in upon us, who dare not share our secrets . . . because the crowd is too stupid . . . too cowardly . . . too weak . . . too bereft of understanding. The crowd is like sheep. They must be protected by little shepherd laws . . . against themselves. And so the strong are sacrificed to the weak. That will put an end to us all some day . . . an end to all this blessed civilization. Ah, if you knew how stupid sheep can be. I have a farm in Silesia, Madame. I can tell you all about sheep." For an instant he paused, considering the imbecility of sheep. "And socialism! It's no better, Madame. It simply buries the individual deeper under layers of muck. No, it is all wrong from the bottom up. We must kill . . . kill . . . you understand . . . until there is room to breathe! Until the earth is freed of the sheep! Then we can be free! Then we can find solitude!"

Again his voice rang with subdued frenzy. Inside the house the frivolous gilt traveling clock struck midnight, and far away in the direction of Trilport there arose again the faint crackling sound like the brush fires. It rose and fell, tossed about at the caprice of the night wind.

"They have begun again," said the Uhlan. "In a little while I shall be forced to leave. You see, we cannot remain here. We have pushed in too far." He leaned forward and drew with his lighted cigarette upon the top of the table between them a V shaped line. "You see," he said, indicating the point of the V. "We have been pushed in here. . . . We cannot possibly remain. It is as far as we shall advance. We have come too far already. Any fool could see it. Any fool but Von Kluck. . . . Why, my boot boy would know it." He laughed again. "But my boot boy is not a general. He is not stupid enough."

He kept wriggling, wriggling helplessly, like a butterfly impaled by a pin . . . an individualist, a lonely man, caught by the savage rush of the mob.

LXXXII

WHAT he said appeared to pass ignored by Lily, for when he had finished she began to talk once more. "I can understand the bravery of fighting for that which you believe," she said. "I cannot understand yielding without a fight to the monster you despise. I knew a man. . . ." For a second she hesitated. "He fought for what he believed. He gave up everything for the fight . . . his health, his friends, his work, his money. He was beaten and bloody and wounded. He would have given his life if it had been necessary. He was a poor, ignorant Ukrainian peasant . . . a Russian who could barely read. Yet he fought. He fought and learned . . . up from nothing." Again she paused and the distant crackling sound filled in the silence, this time more distinct and sharp, nearer at hand. "You see, I am telling you this because it is the very monster that you hate which he too fought. He is still fighting it. In the end he will win. . . . If one could not believe such things, one could not live. He will go on fighting because there is inside him something which will not let him stop. But there are not many like him. There are too many like you."

Her voice carried the ring of supreme scorn. There was a quality of iciness in it, penetrating, contemptuous, acid.

Suddenly she covered her face with her hands. "In times like this," she said, "I think of him. It helps one to live." And after a moment, she added bitterly. "He would not have gone off to kill!"

"I can see, Madame," said the stranger, "that you despise me."

"It is more than that," answered Lily, her face still covered by her white hands. "I am certain now that I hate you."

The Uhlan frowned. "I am sorry," he said, "I thought you were sympathetic."

The only answer was a laugh, incredibly cold and savage from so beautiful a woman.

Within the château more lights appeared, and in the courtyard there rose the sound of hoofs striking the cobblestones and of orders being shouted back and forth in guttural German. Far away to the east a solitary cannon barked. The noise ripped the blue stillness with the sound of a tapestry being torn.

"You have forgotten," said Lily, "that I have a son and a lover in the war. You understand, they too are in the cavalry."

She had scarcely finished speaking when the air was shattered by the terrific rattle of a dozen rifles fired simultaneously below the terrace somewhere among the buildings of the farm. A faint glare trembled above the iron bridge and then a second volley, terrifying and abrupt, and a second brief glare.

The Uhlan did not move but Lily sat up suddenly. They remained thus for some time, the woman in an attitude of listening. It appeared that she was straining every nerve, every muscle, lest the faintest sound escape her. When the volley was not repeated she turned her head, slowly and scornfully, in the direction of her companion. In her eyes there was a look of terrible accusation, a look charged with contempt and hatred. The stranger watched her as if fascinated and unable to remove his eyes from her face. At last she spoke, slowly and distinctly, in an awed, breathless whisper.

"What was that?"

The face of the Uhlan remained smooth and empty of all expression, as clean of all emotion as a bit of smooth white paper. In the flickering light from the lanterns which moved among the trees, the countenance appeared vague and lineless, almost imbecile in its negation. Then slowly his lips moved.

"It is the curé, Madame. . . . They have shot the curé." The voice was as smooth as the face. It carried the hard, mocking cruelty of indifference. "They caught him signaling with his lantern from the steeple of the church."

Without a sound Lily lay back once more and buried her face in her cloak. Her body shook silently.

"I could do nothing else," continued the smooth voice. It came out from the thin lipped mouth as a serpent from a crevice in a rock. "It was not I who killed. I had nothing to say in the matter. I did what I could not help doing. Enfin, it was the monster!"

Across the fields of wheat from the direction of Meaux the faint crackling sound came nearer and nearer. It was as if the grain had caught fire and the flames were rushing toward them. Lily still lay with her eyes covered as if to shut out the picture which had risen in her imagination. M. Dupont . . . the friend of dying Madame Gigon, the priest to whom she had told her life . . . M. Dupont dead among the dungheaps of the farmyard!

Somewhere in the direction of the Trilport bridge, the solitary cannon fired again and as though it had summoned Madame Gigon back to life, they heard her speaking suddenly inside the lodge. She was talking rapidly in a low voice.

"You need not worry, Henri. To-morrow there will be fresh vegetables in from the barrier. At dark, a balloon with two passengers will be released at the Gare St. Lazare. Gabriel himself told me." And then for a time she muttered incoherently and when her speech became clear again, she was saying, "There is a notice on the Rue de Rivoli that they are selling animals in the Jardin de Plantes. For food you understand . . . I hear at ten sous the pound." Again more mumbling and then, "Ah, that one was close. Yesterday a shell exploded in the Boulevard Montparnasse. We must place our faith in God. . . . Yes, we must pray, Henri. There is not enough God in the world."

Then she became silent for a time and the Uhlan said, "Madame is delirious. She is living through 1870. . . . You see we have not progressed at all. It is merely turn about, first the French, and then we take a turn." He laughed a nervous laugh devoid of mirth. "Ah, it is a pretty business, Madame . . . a pretty business. The sooner we are all killed off the better. The animals could manage this world better than we have done."

He had not finished speaking when a sudden rattle of rifles sounded somewhere near at hand, a little to the east by the copse in the long meadow. At the same time the confusion in the stables and the little park redoubled. A horse whinneyed. Men shouted. Water pails were overturned. Out of the darkness a man in rough gray uniform appeared and addressed the Captain in excited, guttural German. The Uhlans had begun to leave the stable. They were making their way through the black trees over the neatly ordered flowers to the gate in the garden wall.

The stranger talked for a moment with the soldier and then rising, he said, "Good-by, Madame. It is not likely that we shall ever meet again. I thank you for the conversation. It saved the night for an insomniac. It is more stimulating to talk with a beautiful woman than with common soldiers."

Lily lay buried in her cloak. She did not even uncover her face, but the Uhlan bowed in a polite ironic fashion and slipped away through the trees, vanishing at once like a shadow. The uproar in the château gardens and in the stable increased. It swallowed the stranger.

As the sound of his footsteps died away, she raised herself cautiously and looked about her. The sound of firing continued. The air was full of an unearthly red glow. Supporting herself on one elbow she saw that the light came from the opposite side of the river. The farm had been fired by the departing troops. For a time she watched the flames, eating their way slowly at the windows and along the eaves, growing always in intensity. The iron bridge was filled with retreating Uhlans, all black against the red haze. The thunder of hoofs on the planks again filled the air.

LXXXIII

THUS she remained as if under a spell, ignoring the uproar that had arisen all about her, in the fields, in the château garden and along the tow-path. When at last she moved, it was to sit up and place her feet upon the ground where they struck some hard object that made a clicking, metallic sound as it grated against the stone. Reaching down, her fingers closed over the cold metal of a lugar pistol. In the confusion and the shouting it had slipped from its holster. The stranger had forgotten it. Slowly she raised the weapon and held it up in the glow of the burning farm. For a long time she regarded the pistol as if it held some sinister fascination and presently, leaning upon the back of her chair, she rose slowly and concealed it in the folds of her cloak. When she had gained a full sense of her balance, she moved off from the terrace through the black trees in the direction of the iron bridge.

The firing had increased. There were cries in French and in guttural German, and from the shrubbery along the garden wall the low moan of a wounded soldier. With the long cloak trailing across the dewy grass she continued to move in an unswerving line to the garden gate. As she passed through it a stray bullet, striking the wall beside her, chipped the ancient mortar into her face and her thick, disordered hair. Outside on the towpath she walked until she stood on the little knoll above the iron bridge.

In the center of the structure could be discerned the figures of three men silhouetted against the flames of the burning farm. Two were kneeling at work on some object which absorbed all their attention. The third stood upright shielding his eyes from the glow, keeping watch and urging them to hurry. He was slim and very neat, and carried himself with a singular air of scorn. Unmistakably he was the visitor, the stranger upon the

312

terrace. At the far end of the bridge, three horses, held in check by the rider of a fourth horse, curvetted and neighed in terror at the leaping flames.

All this Lily saw from the eminence of the low knoll. And when she had watched it for some time she raised her arm, holding the lugar pistol, and slowly took careful aim. The cloak slipped from her shoulders into the grass. Once she fired and then again and again. The slim, neat man stumbled suddenly, struck his head against an iron girder of the bridge and slipped struggling into the river. There was a faint splash and he disappeared. Of the other two men, one fell upon his face, struggled up again and, aided by his companion, crawled painfully toward the terrified horses. The flames roared wildly. The horses leapt and curvetted for a moment and then disappeared with their riders, followed by the horse whose rider lay at the bottom of the Marne.

On the low knoll the pistol dropped from Lily's hand and slipped quietly into the river. A party of three French infantrymen coming suddenly out of the sedges along the river discovered her lying in the thick wet grass. Bending over her they talked volubly for a time and at last carried her back through the gate into the lodge. They could wring from her no sort of rational speech. She kept talking in the strangest manner, repeating over and over again, "It is simply a matter of chance . . . like roulette . . . but one of a million chances . . . but one . . . but one. . . . Still one chance is too many."

Inside the lodge, one of the soldiers struck a sulphur match and discovered in the bed by the window the body of an old woman. He summoned his companions and they too leaned over the body. Beyond all doubt the old woman was dead.

LXXXIV

FROM that night on the sound of firing grew steadily more faint and the glow in the sky more dim. There were times when Lily, lying delirious in the lodge under the care of Madame Borgue, the farmer's wife, behaved in the wildest manner. When the wind blew from the north, it carried the sound of the guns across forests and wheatfields into the park at Germigny and the barrage, no longer confused and close at hand, took on a pulsing regular throb like the beating of surf upon a beach of hard shingle. At such times Lily would sit up and talk wildly in a mixture of French and English of Mills and monsters, of cauldrons, of white hot metal that absorbed the very bodies of men. The distant rumbling was for all the world like the pounding which had enveloped Cypress Hill in the days of Lily's youth. But Madame Borgue, knowing nothing of all this, could make no sense of the ravings of her patient.

She remained a long time ill. While she lay unconscious with the fever, Madame Gigon was buried among the beaded *couronnes* of the cemetery at Trilport between her obscure husband, the curator, and the father who had been ruined by his loyalty to Napoleon the Little.

It happened that on the very day of the lonely funeral, Madame de Cyon died in Paris of indigestion brought on by overeating and the loss of twenty francs at bridge, played secretly to be sure, for in those days no one played bridge in Paris. So Madame Gigon, by dying first, was cheated out of her triumphant, "I told you so!" Of course, it may have been that in another world she knew this satisfaction; for it was true that Nadine "went off just like that."

And in early October, on the first day that Lily ventured from the lodge out upon the green terrace, she read in the Figaro that she had been decorated with the Croix de Guerre. The citation appeared in the midst of the military news.

"Shane, Madame Lily. Widow. American by birth. Dec-orated for valor at Germigny l'Evec during the Battle of the Marne, when she prevented a detachment of Uhlans from de-stroying an iron bridge of the utmost importance to our troops."

This she read aloud to Madame Borgue. It was tiny para-graph, printed in very small black type, and it caused Lily to laugh, bitterly, mirthlessly. Letting fall the Figaro by the side of her chair, she lay back.

"As if," she said, "I had ever thought of the bridge! As if I even knew that they were trying to destroy it!"

And when Madame Borgue, alarmed by this outburst, sought to lead her back into the house, Lily said, "I am not delirious. . . . Truly . . . I am not. It is so absurdly funny!" And she laughed again and again.

She never knew that it was M. de Cyon who brought the af-fair to the attention of the Ministry of War and secured her the distinction.

Slowly it became clear that fate had not allotted to the dead Uhlan the chance of Césaire's death. She received no news of him. Even M. de Cyon, in the government at Paris, could dis-cover nothing. The hours grew into days and the days into months until, at last, she was able to leave the lodge and visit Jean in the hospital at Neuilly. There came at length a day when there was no longer any doubt. The Baron was simply among the missing . . . the great number concerning whom there was no news. It was as if he had bade her farewell at the vine-covered gate and galloped off on the black horse into a darkness which swallowed him forever.

In Paris, the house in the Rue Raynouard acquired an air of complete desolation. There was no one, not even Jean who lay at the hospital in Neuilly with his right leg amputated at the knee, to share it with Lily. The mirrors reflected nothing save the figures of the mistress, the servants and M. de Cyon who appeared to find consolation for his recent loss in visits to the big house at Numero Dix.

Ellen, escaped at last from Central Europe, had returned to America. Madame Gigon was dead. Of her friends none re-mained. Madame de Cyon was in her grave. Madame Blaise still lived in a polite madhouse, convinced that the war was only a revolution which would place her friend, the wine merchant, upon the throne of a glorified and triumphant France. The others? Some had gone into the provinces, and of those who remained, all were interested in their own families. They had sons, brothers, nephews, cousins, at the front. . . . There were no more *salons*. It was impossible to go alone to the theater. There remained nothing to do but visit Jean (a sad business though he seemed cheerful enough) and sit in the big empty house, so silent now, so empty of chatter, of music, of laughter. Even the great piano under the glowing Venice of Mr. Turner remained closed and silent save in the rare moments when Lily, as if unable any longer to endure the silence, opened it and played with only half a heart the tunes which once had filled the house and overflowed into the garden. It was clear that it required more than mirrors, jades, pictures and old carpets to make a dwelling endurable. As Lily remarked to M. de Cyon at tea one afternoon in early November, these things, each one the reminder of some precious association, only rendered Numero Dix the more unbearable.

"I can understand," she said, "that sometimes my mother must have died of loneliness in the house at Cypress Hill."

She told M. de Cyon the history of the burned house, bit by bit, from the day it was built until the day it was destroyed. Indeed she told him all the story of her father, of her own childhood, of the Mills and the Town. She even told him something of Irene's story, though not enough to be sure for him to evolve the whole truth, for there were certain barriers beyond which she allowed no one to penetrate; no one save an old village priest who was, after all, not a man but an agent of God himself. And he was dead now.

In those days the pair drew more closely to each other, as if they found in the friendship a consolation for the melancholy and overwhelming loneliness. And it is true that Lily had grown more sympathetic. The old carefree gaiety had given place to a new and more gentle understanding. The indolence, it seemed, had vanished before a new determination to dominate her own aimless existence. She had grown more calm. Indeed there were times now when she became wholly grave and serious, even pensive, as she sat quietly with the pleasant, white-haired Frenchman who found her company so agreeable that he seldom permitted a day to pass without calling at Numero Dix on his way from the Ministry of War. She became, as she had observed to Willie Harrison, more and more like her mother.

Each day was like the one before, and this monotony to Lily must have been a new and painful experience. The only variation occurred when Paul Schneidermann, returning from a hospital in Cannes, arrived in Paris and became a second visitor at the house in the Rue Raynouard. But even in this there was an inexpressible sadness, for the bullet which had wounded Schneidermann paralyzed forever his left arm. He was never again able to play the piano in the long drawing-room nor the cello he had brought to the house when Ellen was there.

With Ellen gone, the American newspapers no longer found their way into the house. Indeed it seemed impossible to obtain them anywhere in Paris, even if Lily had been capable of such an effort. So there were no more clippings for the enameled box. The last one bore the date of the first month of the war. Since then there had been nothing. It was as if Krylenko, too, —the Krylenko whose progress Lily watched from so great a distance—had died or gone away like all the others. There remained only the wreckage of a life which had once been complete, content, even magnificent in its quiet way.

When at last Jean was able to leave the hospital, he secured through M. de Cyon an appointment at the Ministry of War. As for Lily, she undertook presently the establishment of a soup kitchen for soldiers who passed through Paris on leave. But at this diversion she was no more successful than she had been at knitting socks for the strikers; and after a few months she abandoned it completely to the care of women less wealthy and more capable. She continued, however, until the end to supply it lavishly with money. In her enthusiasm for the charities of the war she succeeded in exhausting for the first time her annual income. She even dipped into her principal. The two hundred thousand dollars which the Town paid her for Cypress Hill she used to provide food and comfort for the soldiers of another nation.

LXXXV

IN the Town no new railway station raised its splendors because in those years the Town and the Mills were too busy making money. In all the haste even the new railway station was forgotten. The deserted park became a storing place for the shells which the Mills turned out in amazing numbers. Gas shells, high explosives, shrapnel cases . . . all these things were piled high along the brick paths where delphiniums and irises once flourished. Even the Venus of Cydnos and the Apollo Belvedere, cracked and smudged in the niches of the dead hedge, were completely buried beneath munitions. Because somewhere in the world men were being killed, the Mills did an enormous business. The Town grew as it had never before grown. Prices were tremendous. The place reeked with prosperity and progress. People even said that the war would finish Germany, that no longer would she be able to compete in the great steel markets of the world. And that, of course, meant more prosperity, more riches.

The flames leapt high above the furnaces. The great sheds echoed with such a pounding as had never before been heard upon this earth. Girls in gas masks worked long hours filling shells with corroding acids which turned their faces haggard, and yellow as the aprons they wore. Little clerks acquired automobiles. Men who dealt in real estate grew rich. Every one would have been content, save for an insatiable appetite for even greater wealth.

Once, to be sure, there occurred an explosion which was for all the world like the end of everything. Forty-seven blackened bodies were carried out under white sheets which clung to the scorched flesh. Of seventeen others nothing at all was found save a few bones, a hand or a foot, a bit of blackened skin; and from these it was impossible to construct any thing. So they **were** dumped into great trenches, and when the earth had

318

covered them, the world rushed merrily on. The flames leapt higher and redder than ever. The sheds fairly split with the sound of hammering. The little clerks dashed about madly in the sudden luxury of their motors. Every one had money. The Town was prosperous. It grew until it was the biggest in the state. Progress rattled on like everything, so nothing else mattered.

In Paris the war came to an end. One or two statesmen and a whole flock of politicians, after swooping about for a time, descended upon the peace.

In those days Paris acquired an insane and desperate gaiety such as it knew neither before nor since. The bright boulevards swarmed with the soldiers of fourteen nations clad in ten times as many gay uniforms. It became gay and frantic with the neurotic excitement of a madhouse. Street walkers from the provinces, even from Italy and England and Spain, rushed to Paris because business there was so good. In dives and cabarets a barbaric abandon reigned. Every one learned new vices and depravities. Brutes, vulgarians, savages stalked the avenues. Overnight boys became old men, burdened with a corroding wisdom which otherwise they might never have known.

And in the Town people shook their heads sagely and said that war was a great thing when it was fought in a just cause. "It purifies!" they said. "It brings out the finest side of men!"

What was prosperous was right. Wasn't success its own vindication? About this there could be no argument. Money talks, my boy! Money talks! What is successful is right. Germany, the bully among nations! Germany, the greedy materialistic Germany, was done in forever.

Of course it may have been that when they spoke of War as the Great Purifier, they were thinking of the vast army of the Dead.

LXXXVI

WHEN politicians gather it is necessary to have conventions, receptions, or some sort of a congregation where they may talk or at least make of themselves a spectacle. And so it happened that Paris, where most of the politicians in the world had congregated, began to break out as if suffering from a disease with receptions at this hotel, or that embassy or this palace. It was important that every one should see every one else. It was an opportunity not to be overlooked.

And so it happened that Lily Shane, one gray afternoon in the late winter, found herself for the first time in years surrounded by her countrymen. Rather weary, confused, and a little breathless, she discovered a refuge from the throng in a little alcove of the Hotel Crillon by a window which gave out upon the wide spaces of the Place de la Concorde. The white square was filled now with trophies. High on the terrace of the Tuileries gardens lay a row of shattered aeroplanes—hawklike Gothas, Fokkers like chimney swifts, all torn and battered now, their bright wings bedraggled by the mud and grease of victory. At intervals along the parapet rose great pyramids of German helmets, empty, ghastly, like the heaps of skulls strewn by Ghengis Khan to mark his triumphant progress across the face of Europe. Near the obelisk—so ancient, so withdrawn, so aloof, survivor of a dozen civilizations—the captured guns crouched together pointing their steel muzzles mutely toward the low gray sky. Some came from the great furnaces of the Krupps, some from the celebrated Skoda mills. In the circle marked by the seven proud cities of France, the statues of Lille and Strasbourg, no longer veiled in crêpe, stood impassive, buried beneath heaps of wreaths and flowers. The whole square appeared dimly through the mists that rose from the Seine. The fog hung low and gray, clinging in torn veils about the silent

guns, settling low upon the pyramids of empty, skull-like helmets, caressing the hard, smooth granite of the eternal obelisk
that stood aloof, mocking, ironic, silent.

Lily sat alone watching the spectacle of the square, as if conscious that in that moment she was at the very heart of the
world. Behind her at a little distance moved a procession of
figures, confused, grotesque, in the long crystal-hung corridors.
It circulated restlessly through the big rooms, moving about the
gilt furniture, past the gilt framed mirrors, brushing the heavy
curtains. There were British, French, Belgians, Italians, Portu-
guese, triumphant Japanese, smiling secretly perhaps at the spectacle in the misty Place de la Concorde. There was, of course.
a vast number of Americans, . . . politicians, senators, congress-
men, mere meddlers, some in neat cutaways, some in gray or
blue suits. There were women among them . . . a great many
women, brave in mannish clothes, dominating and active in
manner.

In all the crowd, so merry, so talkative over the victory, the
figure of Lily, withdrawn and silent, carried an inexpressible
air of loneliness. It was as if she imitated the obelisk and
turned a scornful back upon the restless, gaudy spectacle. She
was dressed all in black in a neat suit and a close fitting hat that
covered all but a narrow band of amber hair. About her full
white throat she wore a tight collar of big pearls. She was no
longer young. The voluptuous curves had vanished. She was
thinner and, despite the rouge on her lips and cheeks, appeared
old. The youthful sparkle of her dark eyes had given place to
a curious, hard brilliance. The old indolence appeared to have
vanished forever. She sat upright, and at the moment the poise
of her body carried a curious sense of likeness to the defiance
which had been her mother's. Yet despite all these things she
was beautiful. It was impossible to deny her beauty, even
though its quality of flamboyance was gone forever. The new
beauty was serene, distinguished, worldly—above all else calm.
Even the weariness of her face could not destroy a beauty
which had to do as much with spirit as with body. She was,
after all, no pretty blond thing of the sort which fades into a
haggard old age. She was a fine woman, a magnificent woman,
not to be overlooked even with youth gone forever.

After a time she turned away from the window and fell to watching the procession of figures. Her rouged lips were curved in the faintest of mocking smiles,—a smile which conveyed a hint of scoffing at some colossal futility, a smile above all else of sophistication and weariness, as if she were at once amused and saddened by the spectacle. Yet it was a kindly smile, tolerant, sympathetic, colored by a hint of some secret, profound, and instinctive wisdom. Motionless, she sat thus for a long time stirring only to fumble with the clasp of the silver bag that lay in her lap. No one noticed her, for she took no part in the spectacle. She sat apart, a little in the shadow, in a backwater, while the noisy tempestuous throng pushed its way through the long vista of gilded, rococo rooms.

LXXXVII

S HE must have been sitting there for half an hour when the smile vanished suddenly and the fingers fumbling with the silver bag grew still. Her face assumed an expression of rigidity, the look of one who has seen something in which he is not quite able to believe.

Moving toward her down the long vista of crystal and brocade curtains came a man. He was a big man, tall, massive, handsome in a florid way. He must have been in his middle fifties, although there was but little gray in the thick black hair which he wore rather long in a fashion calculated to attract the notice of passersby. He wore horn-rimmed spectacles and a flowing black tie in striking contrast to the gray neatness of his cutaway and checkered waistcoat. Unmistakably he was an American. His manner carried the same freedom, the identical naive simplicity which characterized the figure of the vigorous Ellen. He possessed the same overflowing vitality. Even as Lily stood, silently, with her back to the tragic spectacle of the square, the vitality overflowed suddenly in a great explosive laugh and a slap on the back of a friend he had encountered in the throng. Above the subdued murmur, the sound of his booming voice reached her.

"Well, well, well! . . . And what are you doing in wicked Paris? Come to fix up the peace, I suppose!"

The answer of the stranger was not audible. The pair withdrew from the path of the procession and talked for a moment. The conversation was punctuated from time to time by the sudden bursts of laughter from the man in the checkered waistcoat.

In her corner Lily leaned forward a little in order to see more clearly the figure which had fascinated her. Presently he turned, bade his friend good-by and moved away again, coming directly down the vista toward Lily. He walked with a swinging stride, and as he approached his large face beamed with satisfaction. He turned his head from side to side with a patronizing air, an air which to Lily must have been startlingly familiar. Even twenty years could not have dissipated the memory of it. It was this which identified him beyond all doubt. He beamed to right and to left. His whole figure betrayed an enormous self-satisfaction. It was impossible any longer to doubt. The man was the Governor. His success was written upon a face now grown heavy and dark.

When he had advanced to within a few paces of Lily's corner, she rose and moved toward him. Only once did she hesitate and then at the very moment he passed by her. Putting out her hand in a furtive movement, she withdrew it hastily. He passed and was on his way to disappearing once more in the throng. For a second she leaned against the wall and then, as if she could no longer resist the temptation, she moved quickly forward and touched his shoulder.

"Henry," she said softly and waited.

The Governor turned and for an instant his face was clouded by a look of bewilderment. Then slowly, almost breathlessly, he recovered himself. The beaming look vanished completely, replaced by an expression of the greatest gravity.

"Lily . . . !" he said. "Lily Shane. . . . For the love of God!"

She drew him aside out of the path of the procession.

"Then you remember me?" she said with a faint, amused smile. "Twenty years is not such a long time."

Again he looked at her. "Lily . . . Lily Shane!" he said. And he took her hand and pressed it with a savage, startled warmth.

"I knew you," she said. "I knew you at once. . . . There are some things about a person which never change . . . little things which *are* the person . . . not much . . . a gesture perhaps. . . . You were unmistakable."

And when he had recovered a little from his astonishment, he managed to say, "It's the last place I'd expect to see you."

Lily laughed at him, in a fashion which must have destroyed suddenly the wall of twenty years. It was a fashion of laughing which belonged to her alone. It was provocative, faintly mocking. Willie Harrison knew it well. "I've lived in Paris for the last twenty years," she retorted with an amused grimace, "and I'm still here. I will be until I die."

Spontaneity does not come easily to a conversation between persons reunited unexpectedly after twenty years; and it was plain that the circumstances surrounding the separation contributed nothing to the facility of the conversation. Lily appeared to have forgotten, or at least to have disregarded the night following the garden party at Cypress Hill. Her manner was that of an old friend, nothing more, nothing less. If she knew any shame, she concealed it admirably. Plainly it was not so easy for her companion. The sudden pallor which had attacked his florid face gave place to a blushing scarlet. He was like a little boy caught in a shameful act.

"You haven't changed much," she said as if to clear the way, "I mean you yourself have not changed . . . not your figure."

He laughed. "I'm fatter . . . much fatter."

It was true.

What had once been clearly a barrel-like chest was sunk to the low estate of a stomach. "But you," he continued, "You haven't changed at all. You're as young as ever."

"You still say the right thing, Henry. But it isn't the truth. I use rouge now. . . . I even dye my hair a little. We can't pretend we're not growing old. It's no use. It's written. . . . It's in our faces."

The Governor thrust a hand into his pocket and fell to jingling a few francs and a key ring. With the other hand he took out his watch. "Couldn't we find some place to sit?" he said. "We might talk for a little while." He coughed nervously. "I haven't much time."

At this she again laughed at him. Her laugh had not grown old. It remained unchanged, still ringing with the same good humor.

"I've no intention of keeping you," she said. "You may go whenever you like." For an instant she cast down her eyes. "When I saw you, I couldn't resist. . . . I had to speak to you. Nothing could have prevented it. I felt, you see, as if I were possessed."

And then she led him back to the corner by the tall window overlooking the misty square. It had grown darker and the cold fog now veiled completely the buildings on the far side of the river. There was only the great square filled with cannon and helmets and shattered planes and above the mass of trophies the rigid, eternal obelisk piercing the mist like a sword.

There they settled themselves to talk, lost in a throng which paid no heed to the middle-aged couple in the alcove. The Governor remained ill at ease, sitting forward upon the edge of his chair as if prepared to spring up and escape at the first opportunity. Lily, so calm, so placid, appeared only to inspire him with confusion. It may have been that she aroused a whole train of memories which he had succeeded in forgetting.

For a time, the conversation flowed along the most stiff and conventional of channels. There were polite inquiries after each other's health. Lily told him of her mother's death, of the fire at Cypress Hill, of the fact that she had severed the last tie with the Town and would never return to it.

"Never?" asked the Governor. "Never?"

"No. Why should I? It is not the same. I have nothing there to call me back. My life is here now. I shall probably die here. The Town is nothing to me."

The Governor's face lighted suddenly. He struck his thigh —a thigh which had once been so handsome and now was flabby with fat—a sharp blow.

"No, it is not the same. You've no idea how it has grown. I was there about six months ago. It's twice as big as in the old days. You know, it's now one of the greatest steel towns in the world. You've a right to be proud of it."

But Lily said nothing. She was looking out of the tall window into the white square.

"And Ellen," the Governor continued, "I hear she has become famous." He laughed. "Who would have thought it? I remember her as a bad-tempered little girl with pigtails. Of course I know nothing about music. It's not in my line. But they say she's great."

When she did not answer him, he regarded her silently for a time and presently he coughed as if to attract her attention.

At last he leaned forward a little and said, "What are you thinking?"

For an instant, an unexpected note of tenderness entered his voice. He peered at her closely, examining her soft white skin, the soft hair that escaped from beneath her toque, the exquisite poise of her throat and head. To this scrutiny Lily put an end by turning with a smile to say, "Thinking? I was thinking that there is something hopelessly sad about having no happy realities in the place where you spent your childhood. You see, if I were to go back, I should find nothing. Cypress Hill burned. . . . My Uncle Jacob's farm buried under new houses, each one like its neighbor, in ugly cheap rows . . . the brook ruined by oil and filth. Why, even the people aren't the same. There's no one I should like to see except perhaps Willie Harrison, and it's a long way to go just to see one person. I was thinking that if I'd been born in France, I would have had memories of a village and green country and pleasant stone houses. The people would be the same always. . . . I couldn't go back to the Town now. I couldn't. . . . I have memories of it. I wouldn't want them spoiled." For an instant the tears appeared in her eyes. She leaned toward him and touched his hand. "It's not that I'm disloyal, Henry. Don't think that. It's that I have nothing to be loyal to . . . nothing that I can cherish but memories. I couldn't be happy there because there's nothing but noise and ugliness. I suppose that somewhere in America there are towns full of realities that one could love, but they aren't in my part of the country. There's nothing there." There was a little pause and she added, "It's all happened so quickly. Think of it—it's all happened since I was a little girl."

All this the Governor, it seemed, failed to understand. He looked at her with a hopeless expression of bewilderment. But he said, "Yes, I understand." And again an awkward silence enveloped them.

At last Lily turned to him. "Tell me," she said, "you've been successful. Tell me about yourself."

The Governor leaned back a little in his chair. "But you must have heard all that," he said with astonishment. "It's been in the newspapers. If you're in politics you can't keep out of the press." The beaming look returned to his eyes and with it the old manner of condescension.

But you forget," replied Lily. "I haven't read American newspapers. I've been away from America for a long time."

"To be sure . . . to be sure." He coughed nervously. "There isn't much to tell. I've been elected senator now for five terms running. I guess I can go on being elected as long as I live. I've gotten what I've set out for. . . . I'm a success in my party. I helped to frame the tariff bill that protected American industry and gave the Town a bigger boom than it ever had before. Oh, I've done my share! . . . Perhaps more than my share! We have a good life in Washington, my wife and I. She's prominent, you know. She's chairman of the State Woman's Republican Committee. Oh, she's very prominent . . . a born leader and a splendid politician. You should hear her make a speech."

Lily listened with an air of profound interest. She was smiling again. As Willie Harrison said, "It was impossible to know what Lily thought. She was always smiling."

The Governor was over-zealous; somehow it seemed that he protested too much.

"Isn't that fine?" she said. "You see, Henry, it has worked out as I told you it would. I should have made you a wretched wife. I would have been no good in politics."

This. it seemed, made him nervous again. He sat forward on the edge of his chair. It was clear that he became terrified when the conversation turned too abruptly toward certain incidents of his youth. It was impossible for him to talk simply and easily. Something kept intruding. Lily may have guessed what it was, for she was a woman of experience in such things. Her companion was merely uncomfortable. He stood up and looked out into the misty square where the lights had begun to show through the fog in little globes of indefinite yellow.

"Extraordinary," he said, "the number of motors in the square." He turned toward her with a sudden enthusiasm. "There you have it! There's America for you . . . motor upon motor! There are more motors with the American High

Commission than with any other two combined. We're a rich country, Lily. The war has made us powerful. We can rule the world and do as we please. It's ours from now on. . . . The future is ours if these fools on the American commission don't spoil everything."

Lily smiled again. "Yes. It's quite wonderful. We ought to be proud."

"But you are, aren't you?" he asked severely.

"Yes."

"That's one reason I came over here . . . to put an end to this league of nations nonsense. We won the war and now they're trying to wriggle out. There's no reason we should be mixed up in their troubles. . . . There's no reason we should suffer for it. It's none of our affair."

He drew himself up until his stomach came near to regaining its old place as a chest. His manner became pompous. It was the identical manner Julia Shane had greeted with derision more than twenty years before in the paneled dining-room at Cypress Hill. It was astounding how little the years had softened him. They had, it seemed, brought him nothing of gentleness, nothing of humor, nothing of wisdom . . . only a certain vulgar shrewdness.

"No," he continued, shaking a finger at her, "I've no intention of letting this nonsense pass. There's no reason why we should help them out of what they themselves created."

Lily's eyes grew large and bright. The smile, mysterious, faintly mocking, persisted. "You're wonderful, Henry," she said. "I always knew what you would be like. Do you remember? I told you once. You are just like that . . . just like my prediction."

From her voice or her manner it was impossible to discover what she meant by this cryptic statement. The Governor interpreted it in his own fashion.

"Well," he said, "I have no intention of seeing the American nation being made a dupe just because we're rich and prosperous and the others have ruined themselves. My wife believes I am quite right. She too expects to make a speaking tour." He became enthusiastic again. "You should hear her speak. She has an excellent voice, and great power."

"Yes," said Lily softly. "I would never be able to do all that. I would have been such a failure. . . ."

"She's here with me now . . . in Paris," continued the Governor. "She'd never been abroad. I thought she would enjoy the sights, too, so I brought her along."

"Is she here to-day?" asked Lily. Again the Governor betrayed signs of an overwhelming confusion.

"Yes," he said, "Yes." And suddenly became silent.

For a moment Lily watched him as if the sight of his confusion provided her with some secret amusement. At length she said, "I'd like to see her. I don't ask to meet her, of course. That would be questionable taste. Besides, why should we meet? We could mean nothing to each other."

"No, perhaps not."

Again he began staring out of the window. Lily glanced at the watch on her wrist.

"I shall be forced to leave soon myself," she said. "My husband will be waiting for me."

With a start her companion turned from the window toward her.

"So you're married," he said. "And you never told me."

"You never asked me about myself. I didn't think you were interested in what my life had been."

He thrust out a great hand. "I must congratulate you!" he said with an overflowing enthusiasm. "I must congratulate you! I knew you'd marry some day. How long has it been?" The news appeared to furnish him with a genuine delight. Perhaps he felt more secure now, less frightened of Lily.

She shook hands with him quietly.

"Not for long. . . . Since three months."

"And what is his name?"

"De Cyon . . . René de Cyon. He is in the new ministry. . . . You see I married a politician after all."

She laughed again in that same mysterious, half-mocking, half-cynical fashion. It was impossible to penetrate the barrier of her composure. She was invulnerable. One could not hazard the faintest guess at what she was thinking.

"That is why I am here to-day." And then for the space of an instant she betrayed herself. "Think of it," she said.

"What a long way from Cypress Hill to being the wife of a French cabinet minister. We've both traveled a long way since we last met, Henry. A great deal has happened to both of us. On my side, I wouldn't change a thing. There are lives and lives, of course. Some like one sort and some another. I know you've been thinking what a lot I've missed by not marrying you." He moved as if to interrupt her. "Oh, I know you didn't say so openly. It's good of you to be so generous . . . to want me to have shared it." She cast down her eyes suddenly and her voice grew more gentle although it still carried that same devilish note of raillery. "I appreciate all that. . . . But I wouldn't have changed anything. I wouldn't have married you anyway."

Again the Governor coughed and looked out of the window. "We all come to it sooner or later," he said. "It's a good thing to be married."

"Yes . . . a lonely old age isn't pleasant."

And here a deadlock arose once more in the conversation. The crowd had begun to thin a little. Down the long vista of rooms it was possible now to distinguish a figure here and there in the throng. Outside the darkness had descended, veiling completely the white square. There was nothing now but the faint globes of light and the dim shooting rays of the passing motors.

The Governor turned suddenly and opened his mouth to speak. Then he closed it again sharply. It was clear that he had intended to say something and had lost his courage. He spoke at last, evading clearly what he had intended to say.

"Tell me . . . Where's Irene?"

"She's buried. . . . She's been buried these eleven years." The Governor frowned.

"I'd no idea," he stammered. "I wouldn't have asked if I had known." He was sinking deeper in his confusion. There was something almost pitiful in his manner, so empty now of pompousness, so devoid of complacency.

Lily smiled. "Oh, she's not dead. She's a nun. She's in the Carmelite convent at Lisieux . . . I meant that she was buried so far as life is concerned. She's lost to the world. She never leaves the convent, you know. It's part of her vow.

She's buried there . . . alive! It's a living death." All at once she cast down her eyes and shuddered. "Perhaps she is dead. . . . When one's faith is killed one is not alive any more. You see, I killed her faith in this world. That's all I meant. She's really buried, . . . alive, you understand."

The Governor made a low whistling sound. "I'm not surprised."

As if she did not hear him, Lily said, "I used to think that it was possible to live by one's self, alone . . . without touching the lives of others. It isn't possible, is it? Life is far too complicated."

The Governor flushed slowly. He turned the speech nervously once more to Irene. "You don't forget how she acted on the night . . ." Suddenly he choked. It was too late now and he finished the speech, inarticulately. "On the night of the garden party!"

LXXXVIII

IT was done now. He had betrayed himself. The wall was down, and before them both there must have arisen once more the painful scene in the library under the malignant portrait of John Shane. (Lily, a young girl, smiling and saying, "I love you, I suppose, but not better than myself. I might have married you once. I cannot now, because I know." Julia Shane, so long dead now, leaning on her ebony stick, hard, unflinching, in the face of everything. "You see, I can do nothing. There is too much of her father in her.")

It stood before them now, the crisis of two lives, naked, stripped of all forgetfulness. The Governor, his face scarlet and apoplectic, remained silent, unable to speak. Lily said softly, "I'm sorry . . . I'm sorry. I should never have mentioned it. I did not guess it would pain you so."

The new gentleness, the new sympathy revealed itself for the first time in all their talk together. It showed in her dark, lustrous eyes. There could be no doubt of it. She was no longer mocking. She was sorry for the lover, grown old, confused now by the memory of a youthful, overwhelming passion. She even touched his hand gently.

"It does not matter now," she said. "After all, it was simply a part of life. I'm not sorry, myself . . . and the world would say that it was I who suffered most. I didn't suffer . . . Believe me, I didn't suffer." She smiled. "Besides what could regrets possibly accomplish? It is the future in which one must live . . . not the past. The longer I live the more certain I am of that."

Still he remained silent. He had become humble, subdued, wilted before the memory of something which had happened more than twenty years before. She must have guessed then, for the first time, what in the unwitting cruelty of her youth

333

she had never known . . . that he had really suffered, far more deeply than she had ever imagined. It may have been hurt pride, for he was a proud man. It may have been that he had loved her passionately. He was, after all, a crude, unsubtle man who must have regarded the whole affair as dishonorable and wretched. It was clear that the wound had never healed, that it still had the power to cause him pain.

"I'm sorry," she repeated. "I'm sorry. . . . There was never any question of forgiveness. I was not injured. . . . Besides it was more my fault than yours."

And then the Governor did a fantastic thing. He bent over his own fat stomach and raised her hand gently to his lips. There was in the gesture a curious absence of sentimentality. It was not even theatrically self-conscious, as well might have been expected. It was the simple gesture of a man who made speeches before thousands and became helpless and mute before one woman. It was eloquent. It spoke more than whole volumes of words. And somehow it released his tongue.

"The boy?" he said, "What about the boy?"

For a moment Lily did not answer him. She turned away, looking out of the window. She trembled a little and when at last she spoke, it was with averted face, for she lied to him, coldly and with deliberation.

"He is dead," she said gently. "He was killed in the war . . . the very first year, at the beginning." And then she turned with a sudden air of domination over herself and her ravaged, saddened lover. "I must go now," she said. "Good-by, Henry. I wish you luck. I know now that what I respected in you is not dead. It has survived everything. It is not completely destroyed. Until just now, I was afraid."

"Good-by, Lily."

In a moment she was gone, down the long corridor to the spot where M. de Cyon awaited her. Halfway to her destination she turned and saw that the Governor was still watching her. She saw that he watched her despite the fact that he was talking now to a woman, a large woman who was unmistakably his wife. She was deep-bosomed, of the type which becomes masculine with the approach of middle age. She wore flat-heeled shoes and a picture hat with a series of flowing veils. Her gown was of dark blue foulard, figured with an enormous white pattern. Far out upon her massive bosom hung a gold pince-nez suspended from a little hook fashioned in the shape of an elaborate fleur-de-lis. Her manner was commanding, a manner appropriate to the chairman of the State Woman's Republican Committee. She could, no doubt, make wonderful speeches. Doubtless she had a powerful voice. Certainly her manner with the Governor was executive. It is easy to see that in the world of politics she had contributed much to the success of the husband she worshiped. What energy she had! What an appalling power!

As Lily turned away, she saw that he was still watching her, slyly, wistfully, with his head bent a little.

LXXXIX

IT was not until the spring of 1920 that work was at last begun on the new railway station in the Town. Months before the actual building was undertaken, the Town Council raised on each side of the triangular and barren park at Cypress Hill enormous signs with lettering three feet high. The signs faced the tracks of three great transcontinental railroads. Above the squalor and filth of the Flats they raised their explosive legends. Each read the same.

MAKE YOUR HOME HERE!!!!!
THE HIGHEST, HEALTHIEST, LIVEST, BIGGEST
CITY IN THE STATE
EIGHT STEEL MILLS
AND
SIXTY-SEVEN OTHER INDUSTRIES
WATCH US GROW!!!!

In the deserted park at Cypress Hill workmen appeared who cut down the remaining dead trees. The Venus of Cydnos and the Apollo Belvedere were pulled down from their pedestals in the dead hedge. One of the workmen, a Calabrian, carted them off, scrubbed them clean of the corroding soot and set them up in the back yard of his little house in the Flats. They came to a good end, for the workman cherished them earnestly. In the little garden behind his house, which by some miracle of devotion he managed to fill with green things, he placed the two statues on pedestals which he himself constructed of bricks and concrete. At the base he planted ivy which flourished and spread over the cracked marble and the adjoining fence. So in all the desert of the great mill town there was one corner at least where beauty was worshiped in a humble setting of cabbages and tomato vines. In the evening when the light was not too bright, the little corner looked for all the world like a bit of a Florentine garden.

The steam shovels set to work on a bright April morning with a terrific sound of hissing steam, of grinding cables and clattering chains. In great gulps they tore up the earth which had lain undisturbed since the passing of the second great glacier. For the Town was not satisfied with the destruction of the house at Cypress Hill; it was not content until the Hill itself was scooped up and carted away. It was a wonderful feat and brought the Town a vast amount of advertisement. Pictures of the hill's destruction found their way into the illustrated papers. They were shown in movie palaces in every part of the country.

It happened that on the very day the steam shovels set to work Eva Barr died in the boarding house where she had lived for more than a decade upon the pension provided by her cousin, Lily Shane. Of the family which had founded the Town, she was the last.

On the hill there remained a few people who remembered Cypress Hill in the days of its glory. But most persons had never heard of Shane's Castle and knew nothing of Lily and Irene Shane. When their names were mentioned, the old residents would say, "Yes . . . Lily and Irene. Of course, you never knew them. They belonged to the old Town. Lily was very beautiful and a little fast, so the stories ran, although no one ever knew for certain. Of course, they may be dead by now. I believe Lily was living in Paris the last that was heard of her."

That was all. Within a century Shane's Castle had risen and disappeared. Within a century the old life was gone, and with it the memory of a great, respectable family which had made the history of the county. It survived only in the name of the Town; and that it would have been unprofitable to change since the Town was known round the world as one of the greatest of industrial centers.

XC

WITH Lily's marriage and the end of the war, the house in Rue Raynouard regained something of its old life and gaiety. For M. de Cyon, the match was one surrounded by advantages. His wife was rich and beautiful. She had superb taste. She spoke excellent French and yet she was an American and thus provided a bond with the powerful nation whose favor was invaluable to every nation of Europe. His friends were charmed by her, for she had a way of listening to them, of drinking in their talk with a breathless air. Therefore they declared her not only beautiful but clever, a distinction which even Lily had never claimed. The world knew only that she was an American widow, wealthy, distinguished, beautiful, who had lived very quietly in Paris for more than twenty years. None knew anything against her. Indeed the only person who knew her story was dead, shot in the dungheaps of a French barnyard.

Yet there was, as people said, something about Lily de Cyon that aroused curiosity, even a tenuous suspicion. Somehow she did not fit the story of a quiet existence among the dowdy friends of Madame Gigon. She appeared to have mysterious resources, of instinct, of knowledge, of mystery. Enfin! She was a fascinating woman.

The strange gift of the crazy Madame Blaise appeared no longer to fill her with horror; for The Girl in the Hat and The Byzantine Empress were brought down from their hiding place in the dusty garret of Numero Dix and hung on either side of the flaming Venice of Mr. Turner. They were greatly admired by the painters whom Paul Schneidermann brought to the house. Some attributed them to Ingres, but none was certain. It was impossible to say who had painted them for they bore no signature. There were some who believed that they were the only great pictures of an obscure artist whose solitary rise from mediocrity came through the inspiration of a woman, a marvelously beautiful woman with dark amber hair and green white skin.

In the spring of 1920, the postman left with the concierge of Numero Dix a thin letter bordered in black bearing the postmark of Lisieux. It contained only a line or two, the mere mention of the death of Sister Monica. She was buried within the walls of the convent which she had not left in more than thirteen years.

XCI

THE pavilion in the garden Lily gave to M. de Cyon for a study. Here it was her habit to meet him daily on his return from the Ministry when his motor, a gift from her, left him at the gate on the Rue de Passy.

One bright October day of the same year, she went as usual to the pavilion to amuse herself until he arrived by reading the newspapers which were placed upon his table. They lay in a neat pile . . . Le Journal de Genève, Il Seccolo of Milan, La Tribuna of Roma, the London Post, the London Times, Le Figaro, L'Echo de Paris, Le Petit Parisien, Le Matin, L'Oeuvre.

She skimmed through them, reading snatches of news, of the opera, and the theater, of society, of politics, of races, the personals in the London Times . . . this or that, whatever caught her fancy.

In the drawing-room Ellen and Jean, with his crutches by his side, sat at the piano playing with four hands snatches of music from the operettas of the moment, from Phi-Phi and La Reine Joyeuse. They sang and laughed as they played. The sound of their gaiety drifted out across the garden.

Lily read the journals until she grew bored. Something had delayed M. de Cyon. Already he was late by half an hour. She came at last, languidly, to the bottom of the pile, to L'Oeuvre which lay buried beneath the more pompous and expensive papers. This she never read because it was a socialist daily and therefore dull. Doubtless she would have passed it by again for the hundredth time but a name, buried in one corner in the smallest of print, caught her attention. It must have struck her suddenly with all the force of a blow in the face, for she closed her eyes and leaned back in her chair. The paper slipped to the floor forgotten.

It was a brief paragraph, not more than three or four lines. It recounted the death of one Stepan Krylenko, a man well known as a leader in international labor circles. He died, according to the despatch, of typhus in Moscow whither he had been deported by the American government.

(Perhaps, after all, the Uhlan was right. The Monster would devour them all in the end.)

After a time Lily rose and went out of the pavilion into the garden where she walked slowly up and down for a long time, seating herself at last on the bench under the laburnum tree.

Inside the house the wild merriment persisted. Ellen was singing now in a rich contralto voice a valse which she played with an exaggerated sweep of sentimentality. From the peak of her hard and cynical intelligence, she mocked the song. She sang,

> "O, la troublante volupté
> de la première etreinte
> qu'on risque avec timidité
> et presque avec contrainte
> Le contact vous fait frisonner. . . ."

In a wild burst of mocking laughter, the song came abruptly to an end. The shattered chords floated out into the garden where Lily sat leaning against the laburnum tree, silent and thoughtful, her eyes filled with sorrow and wonder. She was in that moment more beautiful than she had ever been before . . . a symbol of that which is above all else eternal, which knows no bonds, which survives cities and mills and even nations, which is in itself the beginning and end of all things, without which the world itself must fail.

And presently, far down among the plane trees, the gate in the high wall swung gently open and, against the distant lights of the Rue de Passy, the figure of the white haired M. de Cyon came into the garden.

THE END